HOUSEKEEPING MANAGEMENT

HOUSEKEEPING MANAGEMENT

Edited by

Amrik Singh Sudan

ANMOL PUBLICATIONS PVT. LTD

NEW DELHI-110 002 (INDIA)

ANMOL PUBLICATIONS PVT. LTD.
Regd. Office: 4360/4, Ansari Road, Daryaganj,
New Delhi-110002 (India)
Tel.: 23278000, 23261597, 23286875, 23255577
Fax: 91-11-23280289
Email: anmolpub@gmail.com
Visit us at: www.anmolpublications.com

Branch Office: No. 1015, Ist Main Road, BSK IIIrd Stage
IIIrd Phase, IIIrd Block, Bangalore-560 085 (India)
Tel.: 080-41723429 • Fax: 080-26723604
Email: anmolpublicationsbangalore@gmail.com

Housekeeping Management

First Edition, 2001
Reprint, 2010
ISBN 81-261-1067-8

PRINTED IN INDIA

Printed at Mehra Offset Press, Delhi.

Contents

Preface

Hotel industry has close relation with tourism industry. With the flourishing of international tourism, Hotel industry has also gone drastic changes and has grown leaps and bound. In the current age of globalisation and liberalisation it is growing rapidly—having cosmopolitan touch. In true sense, hotel, hospitality and catering are enthusing the feeling of international integration, thus the world as a global village.

The present work is intended to bring together authentic information on diverse aspects of hotel, hospitality, and catering management such as—hotel management, restaurant management, housekeeping management, hospitality marketing, food and beverage management, and foodservice operations. The entire information is logically organised under above titles. The concepts and developments are supported by facts and figures.

To make the work comprehensive we have gathered the information from various sources. We are grateful to all the scholars whose writings are cited or substantially made use of in the present venture. I am also thankful to my colleagues and friends who have assisted me in one way or other while preparing the manuscript. Last but not the least, I am indebted to Mr. J.L. Kumar, Managing Director, Anmol Publications Pvt. Ltd., New Delhi for his constant moral support and also for bringing out this work within a short span of time.

—Editor

1

Introduction

Hospitality is the cordial and generous reception and entertainment of guests or strangers, either socially or commercially. From this definition we get the feeling of the open house and the host with open arms, of a place in which people can be cared for. Regardless of the reasons people go to a home away from home, they will need care. They will need a clean and comfortable place to rest or sleep, food service, an area for socializing and meeting other people, access to stores and shops, and secure surroundings.

Facilities in all parts of young America were commensurate with the demand of the travelling public, and early records indicate that a choice was usually available at many trading centers and crossroads. The decision as to where to stay was as it is today, based on where you might find a location providing the best food, overnight protection, and clean facilities. Even though the inns were crude, they were gathering places where you could learn the news of the day, socialize, find out the business of the community, and rest. With the growth of transportation-roadways, river travel, railroads, and air travel-Americans became even more mobile. Inns, hotels, motor hotels, resorts, and the like have kept pace, fallen by the wayside, overbuilt, or refurbished to meet quality demands. Just as the traveller of earlier times had a choice, there is a wide choice for travellers today. We therefore have to consider seriously why one specific hotel or inn might be selected over another. In each of the areas we mentioned-food, clean room, sociable atmosphere, meeting space, and security-there has been a need to remain competitive. Priorities in regard to these need areas, however, have remained in the sphere of an individual property's management philosophy.

In addition to the areas of hospitality we discussed, professional housekeeping requires a staff with a sense of pride. Housekeeping staffs must show concern for guests, which will make the guests want to return-the basic ingredient for growth in occupancy and success in the hotel business. Such pride is best measured by the degree to which the individual maids (guestroom attendants or section housekeepers) say to guests through their attitude, concern, and demeanour, "Welcome, we are glad you chose to stay with us. We care about you and want your visit to be a memorable occasion. If anything is not quite right, please let us know in order that we might take care of the problem immediately." A prime responsibility of the executive housekeeper is to develop this concern in the staff; it is just as important as the other functions of cleaning bathrooms, making beds, and making rooms ready for occupancy. Throughout this text, we will present techniques for developing such attitudes in housekeeping staffs.

Origins of management

While the evolution of the housekeeping profession was taking place, professional management was also being developed. In fact, there is evidence that over 6000 years ago in Egypt and Greece complex social groups required management and administration. It is even possible to derive evidence of the study and formulation of the management process as early as the time of Moses. Henry Sisk reminds us that in the Bible (Exod. 18:13-26)

Jethro, Moses' father-in-law, observed Moses spending too much time listening to the complaints of his people. Jethro therefore organized a plan to handle these problems that would in turn relieve Moses of the tedium of this type of administration. A system of delegation to lieutenants thus emerged. We can therefore assign some of the credit to Jethro for establishing several of the principles of management that we recognize today: the principles of line organization, span of control, and delegation.

Schools of management theory

The classical school of management theory can be divided into two distinct concerns: administrative theory and scientific management. Administrative theory is principally concerned with management of the total organization, whereas scientific management is concerned with the individual worker and the improvement of production efficiency by means of an analysis of work using the scientific these two branches of the classical school should be viewed as being complementary rather than competitive.

Considered by many to be the father of administrative theory, Henri Fayol was a French engineer who became the managing director of a mining company. Fayol sought to apply scientific principles to the management of the entire organization. His most famous work, *Administratim Industrielle et General (General and Industrial Management), first* published in 1916 and later in English in 1929, is considered by many to be a classic in management theory. Fayol asserted that the process of management was characterized by the following five functions:

1. Planning-the specification of goals and the means to accomplish those goals by the company

2. Organizing-the way in which organizational structure is established and how authority and responsibility are given to managers, a task known as delegation
3. Commanding—how managers direct their employees
4. Co-ordinating—activities designed to create a relationship among all of the organization's efforts to accomplish a common goal
5. Controlling—how managers evaluate performance within the organization in relationship to the plans and goals of that organizations

Fayol is also famous for his Fourteen Principles of Management and his belief that administrative skills could be taught in a classroom setting.

Fayol's counterpart in the management of work was Frederick W. Taylor (1856-1915), the father of scientific management. Taylor was an intense (some would say obsessive) individual who was committed to applying the scientific method to the work setting. In 1912 Taylor gave his own definition of scientific management to a committee in the U.S. House of Representatives by stating what scientific management was not. Scientific Management is not any efficiency device, nor a device of any kind for securing efficiency; nor is it any branch or group of efficiency devices. It is not a new system of figuring cost; it is not a new scheme of paying men; it is not a piece-work system; it is not a bonus system, nor is it holding a stop watch on a man and writing down things about him. It is not time study, it is not motion study nor an analysis of the movements of men.

Although Taylor's definition of scientific management continued at length in a similar vein, he did not argue against using the aforementioned tools. His point was that scientific management was truly a *mental revolution,* whereby the scientific method was the sole basis for obtaining information from which to derive facts, form conclusions, make recommendations, and take action. Taylor's contribution was a basis for understanding how to administer a project and the people involved.

In his *Principles of Scientific Management* published in 1911, he outlined four principles that constitute scientific management:

1. Develop a science for each element of a man's work, which replaces the old rule-of-thumb method.
2. Scientifically select and then train, teach, and develop the workman, whereas in the past he chose his own work and trained himself as best he could.
3. Heartily cooperate with the men so as to ensure all of the work being done is in accordance with the principles of the science which has been developed.
4. There is an almost equal division of the work and the responsibilities between the management and the workmen, while in the past almost all of the work and the greater part of the responsibility were thrown upon the men.

Taylor also pointed out that the mental revolution had to take place in the workers' as well as the managers' minds.

An outgrowth of "Taylorism" is the school of management science, or, as it is alternatively known, operations research. Management science is defined as the application of the scientific method to the analysis and solution of managerial decision problems. The application of mathematical models to executive decision making grew out of the joint U.S. and British efforts during World War II to use such models in military decision making at both the strategic and the tactical level.

A predecessor to the human relations school of management was the nineteenth-century Scottish textile mill operator, Robert Owen. He believed that workers needed to be "kept in a good state of repair." Owen urged other manufacturers to adopt his concern over improving the human resources they employed. He claimed that returns from investment in human resources would far exceed a similar investment in machinery and equipment. Unfortunately, it was not until the second decade of the twentieth century that the results of Elton Mayo's Hawthorne Studies affirmed Owen's position and caught the imagination of American management.

Mayo was a faculty member of the Harvard University School of Business Administration when he began to study workers at the Hawthorne Works of the Western Electric Company in Chicago in 1927. From this study Mayo and his colleagues concluded that there were factors other than the physical aspect of work that had an effect on productivity. These factors included the social and psychological aspects of workers and their relationships with managers and other workers.

Mayo's work effectively demonstrated to managers that in order for them to increase productivity in the work setting they must develop human relations skills as well as the scientific management methods of Taylor and the other classical theorists.

Managerial temperament

The behavioural school does not end with Mayo. Douglas McGregor summarized certain assumptions about traditional or work-centered theory of management under the heading Theory X McGregor's Theory X assumption is summarized in the following four statements:

1. Work, if not downright distasteful, is an onerous task that must be performed in order to survive.

2. The average human being has an inherent dislike of work and will avoid it if he can.
3. Because of the human characteristic to dislike work, most people must be coerced, directed, controlled, or threatened with punishment to get them to put forth adequate effort toward the achievement of organizational objectives.
4. The average human being prefers to be directed, wishes to avoid responsibility, and has relatively little ambition, and wants security above all.

Simply stated, Theory X indicates that there is no intrinsic satisfaction in work, that human beings avoid it as much as possible, that positive direction is needed to achieve organizational goals, and that workers possess little ambition or originality.

Another leading theorist in the behavioural school was Frederick Herzberg. Herzberg and his associates at the Psychological Service of Pittsburgh found that experiences that create positive attitudes toward work come from the job itself and function as satisfiers: or motivators. In other words, satisfiers are created by the challenge and intrigue of the job itself.

A second set of factors related to productivity on the job are conditions outside of the job itself. Things such as pay, working conditions, company policy, and the quality of supervision are all a part of the working environment but are outside of the task of the job itself. When this second set of factors is inadequate, that is, when you believe that these conditions are not up to par, they function as dissatisfiers, or demotivators. When these factors are adequate, however, the), do not necessarily motivate employees for a lasting period of time but may do so only for a short time. Stated another way, Herzberg argued that the presence of satisfiers tends to motivate people toward greater effort and improved performance.

The absence of dissatisfiers; has no long-lasting effect on positive motivation; however, the presence of dissatisfiers has a tendency to demotivate employees.

Participation occurs when management allows hourly workers to discuss their own observances and ideas with department managers. (Such techniques have been seen as being one of the greatest motivators toward quality performance in a housekeeping operation.) More about this technique will be said when we discuss employee morale and motivation. Theory Z, the highly vaunted Japanese management model, is heavily based on this participative management model.

Blake et al. presented a revolutionary idea concerning the methods that underlie the thinking process involved in decision making. They found that a managerial-grid could be established whereby a maximum or minimum concern for production could be equated with a maximum or minimum concern for people. The managerial grid attempts to define the various ways in which people think through decisions. Knowing why people think or feel the way they do can have a great influence on the quality of commitment from a group decision, especially when it comes to resolving conflicts. Blake and Mouton held that the best managers have both a high concern for production and a high concern for people in the organization.

One of the most recent attempts at group involvement in decision making has come out of a major concern for the loss of U.S. prestige in its own automobile market. Specifically, Japanese managers and workers have coined the term "quality circle," which is a way of explaining total worker involvement in the processes as well as in the management decisions about production and quality that will ultimately affect worker welfare. Quality circles are now undergoing heavy scrutiny in the

United States and are being used to help rekindle automobile production.

Situational leadership or the contingency approach's to management asserts that there is no one universally accepted approach to a management problem. It maintains that different problems require different solutions. This approach perhaps best reflects the complex nature of management in the organizational setting. Adherents to this approach agree that there is no "one best" way to manage; flexibility is the key to successful management. The works of Fred Fiedler, Victor Vroom, and Ken Blanchard and Paul Hersey have contributed to this model.

So, what do managers do?

Ask a manager that question and you will probably receive a hesitant reply, leading to answers such as, "What do I do?" or "That's hard to say," or "I'm responsible for a lot of things," or "I see that things run smoothly," none of which are responsive to the question asked. After many years of researching the diaries of senior and middle managers in business, extended observation of street gang leaders, U.S. presidents, hospital administrators, forepersons and chief executives, Mintzberg, was able to codify managerial behaviour as follows:

1. Managers' jobs are remarkably alike. The work of foremen, presidents, government administrators, and other managers can be described in terms of ten basic roles and six sets of working characteristics.
2. The differences that do exist in managers' work can be descried largely in terms of the common roles and characteristics-such as muted or highlighted characteristics and special attention to certain roles.
3. As commonly thought, much of the manager's work

is challenging and nonprogrammed. But every manager has his or her share of regular, ordinary duties to perform, particularly in moving information and maintaining a status system. Furthermore, the common practice of categorizing as nonmanagerial some of the specific tasks many managers perform (like dealing with customers, negotiating contracts) appears to be arbitrary. Almost all of the activities managers engage in-even when ostensibly part of the regular operations of their organization-ultimately relate to back to their role as manager.

4 Managers are both generalists and specialists. In their own organizations they are generalists-the focal point in the general flow of information and in the handling of general disturbances. But as managers, they are specialists. The job of managing involves specific roles and skills. Unfortunately, we know little about these skills and as a result, our management schools have so far done little to teach them systematically.

5. Much of the manager's power derives from his or her information. With access to many sources of information, some of them open to no one else in the organizational unit, the manager develops a database that enables him or her to make more effective decisions than the employees. Unfortunately, the manager receives much information verbally, and lacking effective means to disseminate it to others, has difficulty delegating tasks for decision making. Hence the manager must take full charge of the organization's strategy-making system.

6. The prime occupational hazard of the manager is superficiality. Because of the open-ended nature of this job and because of the responsibility for information processing and strategy making, the manager is induced to take on a heavy workload and

to do much of it superficially. Hence, the manager's work pace is unrelenting and the work activities are characterized by brevity, variety, and fragmentation. The job of managing does not develop reflective planners; rather, it breeds adaptive information manipulators who prefer a stimulus-response milieu.

7. There is no science in managerial work. Managers work essentially as they always have-with verbal information and intuitive (nonexplicit) processes. The management scientist has had almost no influence on how the manager works.
8. The manager is in kind of a loop. The pressures of the job force the manager to adopt work characteristics (fragmentation of activity, emphasis on verbal communication, among others) that make it difficult to receive help from the management scientist and that lead to superficiality in his or her work. This in effect leads to more pronounced work characteristics and increased work pressures. As the problems facing large organizations become more complex, senior managers will face even greater work pressures.
9. The management scientist can help to break this loop by providing significant help for the manager in information processing and strategy making, provided he or she can better understand the manager's work and can gain access to the manager's verbal database.
10. Managerial work is enormously complex, far more so than a reading of the traditional literature would suggest. There is a need to study it systematically and to avoid the temptation to seek simple prescriptions for its difficulties.

Perhaps managers are not readily adept at answering the question about what they do because they are too mindful of what they are doing when they are actually performing their jobs. This writer also recalls once being asked the question, "What did I do?" I was stumped by the same question until many years later, when I discovered that a manager performs more than just the *sequential* functions. There are also those *continuous* functions—analysing *problems, making decisions,* and communicating—as noted in the next paragraph.

Principles of management

Executive housekeepers today recognize the need for a clear understanding and successful application of management principles. They may, however, feel overwhelmed by the many terms in the field of scientific management, both from the past and in the present. It is important for executive housekeepers to be familiar and comfortable with these terms and principles, since there is no department within the hospitality industry in general and hotels in particular that will provide a greater opportunity for applying management skills.

In order to help you understand the concept of management, we will present an ordering of the management process as developed by R. Alec Mackenzie. Building on the works of Fayol, he has created a three-dimensional illustration relating the elements, continuous and sequential functions, and activities of managers.

According to Mackenzie, the elements that today's managers work with are ideas, things, and people. These are the main components of an organization and are in the center of the figure. The manager's task that is related to ideas is to think conceptually about matters that need to be resolved. The task related to things is to administer or manage the details of executive affairs. The task related to people is to exercise leadership and influence people so that they accomplish desired goals

The functions of a manager can be thought of as continuous functions and sequential functions. Many times a question may be asked: "But what does the manager do?" The manager should be seen to do several continuous functions, as well as several sequential functions. The continuous functions relating to ideas and conceptual thinking are to *analyse problems.* Those related to things and administration are to *make decisions,* and those related to people and leadership are to *communicate* successfully. Problems are analysed, facts gathered, causes learned, alternative solutions developed, decisions made, conclusions drawn, communications generated, and understanding assured.

The sequential functions of management are more recognizable as a part of the classical definition of management. They involve the planning, organizing, staffing, directing, and controlling of ideas, things, and people. Mackenzie sets forth various activities in each of these sequential functions that should be studied and recalled whenever necessary.

Activities of sequential functions

According to Mackenzie, a manager's sequential functions are divided into five areas-planning, organizing, staffing, directing, and controlling.

The management plan involves seven basic activities:

I. *Forecasting.* Establishing where present courses will lead
2. *Setting objectives:* Determining desired results
3. *Developing strategies.* Deciding how and when to achieve goals
4. *Programming:* Establishing priorities, sequence, and timing of steps

5. *Budgeting:* Allocating resources
6. *Setting procedures:* Standardizing methods
7. *Developing policies.-* Making standing decisions on important recurring matters

Getting organized involves arranging and relating work for the effective accomplishment of an objective. Managers organize by making administrative or operational decisions. The four activities involved in getting organized are as follows:

1. *Establishing an organizational structure:* Drawing up an organizational chart
2. *Delineating relationships.-* Defining liaison lines to facilitate coordination
3. *Creating position descriptions:* Defining the scope, relationship, responsibilities, and authority of each member of the organization
4. *Establishing position qualifications:* Defining the qualifications for people in each position

The third sequential function, staffing, involves people. Leadership now comes into play and communication is established to ensure that understanding takes place. There are four activities:

1. *Selecting employees:* Recruiting qualified people for each position
2. *Orienting employees:* Familiarizing new people with their environment
3. *Training:* Making people proficient by instruction and practice
4. *Developing.* Improving knowledge, attitude, and skills

The first three sequential functions of management-planning, organizing, and staffing-might be performed before an operation gets under way. The last two sequential functions-directing and controlling-are carried out after the operation has begun or is in process. As with other managerial relationships involving people, leadership is accomplished through communication. In the directing of operations, there are five basic activities:

1. *Delegating:* Assigning responsibility and exacting accountability for results
2. *Motivating:* Persuading and inspiring people to take a desired action
3. *Coordinating:* Relating efforts in the most efficient combination
4. *Managing differences:* Encouraging independent thought and resolving conflict
5. *Managing change:* Stimulating creativity and innovation in achieving goals

The final sequential function of management is to control organizations and activities to ensure the desired progress toward objectives. There are five basic activities in the controlling of operations:

1. *Establishing a reporting system:* Determining what critical data arc needed
2. *Developing performance standards:* Setting conditions that will exist when key duties are well done
3. *Measuring results:* Ascertaining the extent of deviation from goals and standards
4. *Taking corrective action:* Adjusting plans, counselling to attain standards, replanning and repeating the several sequential functions as necessary
5. *Rewarding:* Praising, remunerating, or administering discipline

Management theory and the executive housekeeper

The question now is, "How can the executive house keeper apply these diverse management theories to the job at hand, that being the management of a housekeeping department?" Before we attempt to answer that rather encyclopedic question, perhaps we should first turn our attention to some of the inherent organizational and employee-related problems facing man), housekeeping departments.

To begin, housekeeping is not a "glamorous" occupation. Cleaning toilets for a living is not, nor has it ever been, the American dream. No one wishes for his or her child to become a guestroom attendant or a housekeeping aid. Housekeeping is viewed by a majority of the American public as being at the bottom of the occupational hierarchy in terms of status, pay, benefits, and intrinsic worth.

Even in the hotel industry, housekeeping employees are among the lowest-paid of all workers in the hotel. Thus, the housekeeping department has traditionally attracted individuals who possess minimal levels of education, skills, and self-esteem. Even the management positions in the house keeping department have an image problem. In hospitality education, students normally tend to gravitate to the front office, marketing, food and beverage, and even human resource areas before they will consider housekeeping.

Normative characteristics by housekeeping employees

In order to more effectively manage housekeeping employees, we must attempt to understand their cultural, psychological, and social make-up. The following employee characteristics are commonly found in man), housekeeping departments.

— Cultural diversity abounds in most housekeeping departments. Racial minorities, particularly black and Hispanic employees, are to be found in numbers that are disproportionate to their representation in the general population.

— The reason for this situation is obvious; the doors of opportunity have been closed to these Americans for generations (many of these doors are not yet fully open). Consequently, these Americans have gravitated to those few areas of employment left open to them.

— In many parts of the country, particularly the Southwest, Florida, New York, and many major urban centers, English is not the predominant language spoken in the housekeeping department. In fact, in many housekeeping departments many workers can neither speak nor write in English.

— Housekeeping often attracts individuals with little formal education. Many workers are functionally illiterate, and others can be classified as being "math illiterate." This can have a particularly telling effect upon departmental efficiency and communications.

— Many of the employees come from lower socioeconomic backgrounds. These environments can often be a major factor in the formation of employee attitudes and behaviours that are not compatible with traditional corporate values. For instance, these individuals tend to have a work ethic that is far different from that of middle America. These employees often need to be taught such fundamentals as the need for punctuality, personal hygiene, and how to communicate with the guest.

— A worker may often have emotional or economic problems, or may even have a dependency problem. It is not suggested that the executive housekeeper is the only manager within the hotel who faces these problems, but many would argue that the frequency of these problems is higher in housekeeping than in other areas. Housekeeping often attracts displaced housewives, single parents, and former welfare recipients who have a higher incidence of these problems.

Although there may be numerous properties throughout the United States where these traits and characteristics are not found in the employees of the housekeeping department, they do appear frequently enough to require the astute housekeeping manager to prepare for such eventualities.

Motivation and productivity

Motive is defined by Webster's as "something (as a need or desire) that leads or influences a person to do something." The motivation of employees is accomplished by the manager having created an environment in which employees can motivate themselves.

Managers cannot hope to directly motivate other human beings; however, they can provide a climate where self-motivation will take place. What we as managers want our employees to do is to become more productive. We want them to accomplish their duties in a more effective and efficient manner. We want to substantially reduce turnover, absenteeism, and insubordination in the organization. We want our organization to be populated with happy, competent people who believe, as Douglas McGregor postulated, that "work is as natural as play or rest."

To do that we must empower our employees with the abilities and inspiration to accomplish the mutually held objectives of the organization and the individual. There is no magic formula to achieve this goal. It takes dedication, perseverance, a plan, and plain hard work. What follows is not a fail-safe prescription for leadership success, but a series of approaches, methods, procedures, and programs that incorporates the best that the previously discussed schools of management theory have to offer the housekeeping department. Although not all of these applications may work in every setting, they have been shown to positively affect the productivity of a number of housekeeping departments.

First, find out what motivates your best long-term employees to perform as well a's they do. Find out why they stay with you. This can be best done by interviewing these people one-on-one (this is also a great opportunity to personally thank your best employees) in a distraction-free setting.

Second, find out why others leave. Conduct exit interviews with all persons being separated, but do not do it yourself and do not do it at the time of separation. Employees will be less than honest with you about the real reason for their resignation if you are part of the problem. Interviewing at the time of separation may also provoke the employee to be less than honest. They may give an "acceptable" reason for separation, such as more money, so they do not jeopardize a potential reference source. The best approach is to have a third person call oil the former employee a month after the separation. Make sure that the interviewer is able to convey an image of trust to the former employee.

Third, find out what current employees really want regarding wages, benefits, and working conditions. Administer a survey that assures the anonymity of the respondent. If English is not the predominant language of the employees in your department, take the extra time to have a bilingual survey prepared. Also, form a committee of employees to assist you in designing the survey. This will help to lessen the effects of management bias and ensure that the survey reflects the attitudes of your department.

Have the employees mail the survey back to the company (be sure that the form has a stamp and return address), or have a ballot box for the forms. You may even want a third party, such as an outside consulting firm, to administer the survey. Finally, administer this survey on a periodic basis-for example, twice a year-in order to remain current with the prevailing employee attitudes. Use the information you have collected to assist you in strategic policy-making decisions and in the day-to-day operation of your department.

Far too often in housekeeping we take the first warm body that applies for the job. Recruiting is often viewed as a costly and time-consuming process for the management and the property. It is an endeavour fraught with failure; prospective employees don't show for interviews, newly hired workers quit during their first week on the job, and so on.

There is one method that can help to substantially reduce the cost and time involved in recruiting prospective employees. It can also help to reduce employee turnover and its associated costs. This method is employee referral; that is, asking your employees (your best employees in particular) to refer people whom they know (friends, family, and acquaintances) for entry-level position openings. In order for this procedure to work, the employer must be ready to pay a significant reward when a suitable candidate is presented.

Typically, the reward is paid in instalments over a time span of several months to a year or more to ensure the continued presence of both the employee who recommended the candidate and, of course, the candidate. One benefit to this system is that most conscientious employees will only recommend candidates whom they honestly feel will be good employees and will not reflect negatively on their recommendation.

However, safeguards must also be established to prevent unscrupulous employees from taking advantage of the system. Other nontraditional sources of applicants for the housekeeping department include tapping into the disabled worker pool. Most communities have rehabilitation agencies where contacts can be established and cooperative programs initiated. Senior citizens, young mothers, and legal immigrants are other potential sources of nontraditional labour.

As most housekeeping administrators know, a formal training program is an indispensable element in achieving productivity goals. There are, however, certain training approaches and concerns that are not being addressed by all housekeeping administrators. These concerns include the educational background of the staff. As was mentioned earlier, many housekeeping workers may be illiterate or may not be able to communicate in English. Written training materials, such as manuals, posters, and written tests, are quite useless when the staff cannot read, write, or speak the English language.

Special audio/visual training materials are often required in housekeeping departments, and the written training materials must often be made available to the workers in Spanish or other languages. The introduction of these materials does not rectify the problem, however. Consequently, many housekeeping departments have initiated remedial educational programs so that employees can not only learn to read and write in English; but can also earn their high school diplomas.

The executive housekeeper does not have to implement these remedial programs from scratch; he or she can turn to a number of sources of assistance found in most communities, such as the public school or the community college system. These sources can often provide qualified bilingual adult instruction at little or -no cost to the company. Another tactic is to reimburse employee tuition if remedial classes are completed at the local community college. The payoff to the housekeeping department is twofold. First, productivity benefits because the level of communication has increased. Second, the esteem level of the employees should certainly increase when they begin to achieve their personal educational goals, and a self-assured workforce will ultimately become a more competent and productive workforce.

Delegation

According to Mackenzie, delegation is one of five activities of direction. Others view delegation as the most valuable activity. The other activities-motivation, coordination, managing differences, and managing change-can be seen as stemming from a manager's ability to delegate properly. Too often we hear the phrase, "delegation of responsibilities and authority." In fact, it is impossible to delegate a responsibility. To delegate actually means to pass authority to someone who will act in behalf of the delegator. The passing of such authority does not relieve the delegator of the responsibility for action or results, although there is an implied accountability of the person to whom power has been delegated to the person having that power.

The responsibility of a manager for the acts or actions of his or her subordinates is therefore absolute and may not be passed to anyone else. When an executive housekeeper is assigned overall responsibility for directing the activities of a housekeeping department, carrying out this responsibility may require the completion of thousands of tasks, very few of which may actually be performed by the executive housekeeper. It is therefore a responsibility of management to identify these tasks and create responsibilities for subordinates to carry them out.

A good operational definition of delegation is the creation of a responsibility for, or the assignment of a task to, a subordinate, providing that person with the necessary authority (power) to carry out the task and exacting an accountability for the results of the subordinate's efforts. The lack of any one of the three elements of this definition creates a situation whereby the manager abdicates the responsibility to manage. Thorough and complete delegation, where possible, will free the manager from tasks that can be performed by subordinates, allowing the manager time to manage the operation. The manager is then left free to (1) coordinate the activities of subordinates, (2) manage change (implies that the manager now has time to be creative and search for changes that will improve operations), and (3) manage differences (a form of problem solving).

Methods of delegation

1. *By results expected:* The manager can make a simple statement of the results that are to be obtained when the task has been completed properly.
2. *By setting performance standards.* The manager can create conditions that will exist when a task has been performed satisfactorily. An example of this type of delegation is found in inspection forms, which specify conditions that exist when the tasks are adequately performed.

In hospitals and health care institutions, standards may become more strict and even require that the instituтions meet agency assigned to other people as soon as they have been properly trained. Group 3 contains tasks that must be done *only* by the manager. People are assigned group 1 tasks as soon as staff is available. Training is started for people to undertake group 2 tasks. As soon as training is complete and competence is shown, the tasks in group 2 are assigned. Group 3 tasks remain with the manager. The number of tasks remaining in group 3 is usually a measure of the manager's confidence to train people and let them become involved.

Often managers do not delegate tasks properly. The reasons can be summed up as follows:

1. *Some managers do not understand their roles as managers.* This happens most often with newly appointed managers who have been promoted from within as a reward for outstanding service.

   For example, the section housekeeper who has been doing an outstanding job as a room attendant is rewarded by being promoted to the position of supervisor, although he or she is given no supervisory training. Having been physically very bus), in the act of cleaning guest rooms, the person is now in charge and as such feels out of place. The new supervisor (manager) has been moved from a realm in which he or she was very competent to a position in which he or she has little or no expertise.

   A manager should be continually analysing problems, making decisions, and communicating. Failing to understand this new role, the new supervisor does someone else's work. For this reason supervisory training is an absolute must when promoting first-line workers into positions requiring managerial performance such as supervising.

2. *Managers who enjoy physically doing work arc sometimes reluctant to let go of such tasks.* Again, this is a matter of training. The new manager needs to be reminded that doing the task is not what he or she is being paid to do. A new manager may need to be reminded that, by doing physical work that should be delegated, situations requiring management decisions may go unnoticed because the manager is too busy to observe, evaluate, and direct operations.

3. *Less competent people fear the consequences of being outperformed.* There are managers who refuse to delegate routine tasks for fear that their own

incompetence will be magnified. Surprisingly enough, their incompetence will be in managing the activities of others, not in their ability to perform the task that they do not delegate. These people are uneasy because they fear that a stronger person will eventually be able to perform their jobs. What some managers forget is that they cannot be promoted themselves until someone is available and competent enough to replace them.

4. *Some managers feel that delegation is an all or nothing situation.* This may occur in spite of the fact that there are several degrees of delegation. Imagine the situation in which a manager needs to investigate a situation, decide if action is needed, and, if so, take the appropriate action. This task, or portions of it, may be delegated to another person, depending upon the degree of training and demonstrated ability of the person. Here are several degrees of delegation, any one of which might be used, depending upon the skill level and reliability of the subordinate.
   a. Investigate and report back
   b. Investigate and recommend a course of action
   c. Investigate and advise of intended action
   d. Investigate, take action, and keep manager informed
   e. Investigate and take action
5. *Some managers feel that if they do not do the task themselves, it will not be done properly.* This is synonymous with the often heard phrase, "If you want something done right, - do it yourself." Sometimes it is ego that prompts this type of thinking, but more often it is the mark of a Theory X thinker. This type of attitude encourages inaction on the part of the employees and a feeling that they are not trusted with important matters. More

importantly, it is counter-productive to the creation of good morale-building environments. Many managers fear the possibility that some subordinate will rise to the occasion of being able to replace the manager. Said another way some managers keep themselves in the position of being indispensable. Other managers recognize that until someone is capable of replacing them, they themselves are not promotable. What is important to remember is that until the manager trains people to act in his or her behalf and delegates as much as possible to subordinates, the manager need not think of promotion, vacation, or even becoming ill, lest the operation crumble.

Thus far, primary considerations have been those seen in the management sphere. Although *exercising leadership* has been shown only as a task associated with the peopling of an enterprise, it now becomes necessary to raise the banner of *leadership* as it relates to *management.* Thomas Atchison identified a significant difference between the tangibles and the intangibles associated with management and leadership. He consulted with many organizations regarding the industrial downsizing which took place in the early 1980s, and he noted the tremendous pressures which befell many organizations beleaguered with the necessity of either downsizing or declaring bankruptcy. As a result of his investigations as a consultant, he was instrumental in helping several companies *prepare for change* as they moved toward new life in the twenty-first century. Atchison was able to identify the significant difference between the *tangible* and *intangible* inputs and outputs that occurred in the business world.

Atchison was able to recognize that it was the *tangible* inputs and outputs that produced easily *predictable and measurable results* (money, inventory, sales, productivity, quality—the goals we recognize as management goals), but it was the *intangible* inputs and outputs of business that produced inspired followers (those things that defy measurement—culture, commitment, satisfaction, pride, morale, trust, team spirit. These are the things that should be our goals in leadership).

Essential leadership activities must include:

1. Challenging the process by seeking out opportunities, without being afraid to take risks.
2. Inspiring a shared vision by seeing the future and communicating to others; making it their vision also.
3. Enabling employees to act by fostering teams and empowering others.
4. Modelling the way by setting an example, and remembering that success is gradual.

Atchison concluded that when you lead well, others become willing followers in a new direction of *managed change.* He also concluded that management, in a sense, might be nothing more than a title. You are a manager until you get promoted, become retired, or are fired. Leadership, however, is earned, by having followers, and it is re-earned every day. There is no accrual, no equity, no transfer in leadership. Every day, one must inspire followers.

The significance of these thoughts is that, as time goes on, you have only one choice. Are you going to *react* to change, or are you going to *manage* it, because change is going to happen at a continually accelerating rate. Autocratic change always produces passive aggressive behaviour, and this will destroy an organization. To the contrary, *managed change is* inspiring and what most employees actually hope for. Managed change has five ingredients.

1. Change-for something. Be specific in what change is desired.
2. Think small. Break the project into small increments.
3. Move quickly from one small increment to the next.
4. Evaluate whether or not progress is being made. 5. Celebrate the completion of each small segment.

It is important to put *fun* into work. Good work can be made enjoyable by remembering to provide *ownership* to the person who is responsible for the work being done. When the manager recognizes and passes credit to the person who performed well, and to that person's assistant, self-motivation emerges.

Consensus is the glue that seems to hold us back in America, but trust is the glue that binds leaders to followers. One has to work hard and steady to earn trust, but trust not cherished and protected can be easily destroyed.

Rewards and motivation

Recognizing and rewarding proper employee performance is essential. Virtually all employees want to know if their performance meets management expectations, and most want to see a linkage between that performance and rewards. The question often asked by managers is, "What form should these rewards take?"

Some experts believe that although certain intangible rewards, such as recognition for achievement, may be nice, they are not as crucial to raising productivity as are the more tangible rewards (that is, money). This theory seems to be borne out by some recent experiments linking pay to productivity levels. The Country Lodging by Carlson chain, a subsidiary of the Carlson Hospitality Group, pays their housekeepers by the rooms they clean rather than by the hour. This approach has reduced their need for full-time housekeepers and it has reduced the turnover and hiring costs in the housekeeping department. Housekeepers earn more and they earn it, on average, in a shorter workday.

Three cautions regarding the implementation of a pay-per-room program should be addressed. First, management must not take advantage of the employee by raising the benchmark standards of how many rooms ought to be cleaned in an hour. As Country Lodging's Vice President Kirwin says, "The goal is to get your rooms cleaned, not to take advantage of people." They have set the productivity standard at 2.25 rooms per hour at Country Lodging. Second, an incentive room inspection program should be part of the program so that the hotel's room cleanliness standards do not erode because of the pay-per-room program. Third, it is doubtful that this program could be adopted in most union environments at this time.

We stated in the beginning of this section that intangible rewards, such as recognition, may not be as crucial to the improvement of productivity as the more tangible effects of money. While we believe this to be true, we certainly hold that recognition for employee achievement is an essential management technique.

One outstanding example of employee recognition in housekeeping is the annual Hotel Association of New York City Bed Making Contest. Forty-five New York hotels participated in this event in 1989. The final contest was held in the Grand Ballroom of the New York Hilton with representatives of the broadcast and print media from the United States and Europe in attendance. The 1989 winner, Ms. Hazel Maye, won an all-expense-paid trip to the Fontainebleau Resort Hotel and Spa in Miami Beach and a brass bed trophy. Ms. Maye's picture appeared in hundreds of newspapers and on dozens of television stations. Here is an excellent example of a promotional vehicle that engenders a sense of pride and accomplishment in a hotel's housekeeping staff.

We have looked at the roles of employee participation, management delegation, training, and rewards in influencing productivity in housekeeping. Each of these practices evolved from management theories. The answer, then, to the question of which theory should be applied in the housekeeping department is none of them, and at the same time, all of them. Each of them is appropriate at different times and under different circumstances (situational leadership).

Current research also seems to favour the situational leadership or contingency approach. Studies have indicated that different circumstances demand different management approaches; the same leadership style does not work as effectively as a flexible style. The key variable that influences a manager's style, according to the situational leadership theorists, is the ability and attitude of the follower. Although a manager's behaviour may change, or an approach to a problem' may be dictated by the ability and attitude of the follower, we believe that a manager should always maintain a high level of concern for both the organization and the employee; this concern should be reflected in everything that is said and done by management.

New horizons in management

Recent attempts to gain better guest acceptance of the service product being presented have yielded reports that the root problem noted by the guests was usually centered around the employee failing to perform adequately. Employee attitudes and motivations were also highly suspect; this was noticed when guests were asked to rank their most common complaints when visiting a hotel. Appearing at the top of most lists were the guests' concerns about employee attitudes. More detailed studies, however, have indicated that a clear 85 percent of all guest and service quality problems were the result of systems, policies, and procedures that were either outdated, inappropriate, or restrictive to the need to take care of the guest. Only 15 percent of quality problems were associated directly with the employee's failure to perform properly in the employee's relationship with the guest. Basically, in our industry, employees have been "you will have to talk to the manager."

By placing the guest's problem in front of those employees (focus group) who had the greatest knowledge about how to solve a problem (because they did the work in the area of the problem), quality standards would be raised. Having been involved in creating the new and better-quality standard, the employees would be more inclined to personally commit themselves to meeting the new standards. These new standards then became the benchmarks for training or retraining of all employees: standards set by employees and agreed to by management. The results of the changes developed through this sponsored study, as reported by Sheraton Scottsdale general manager Ken MacKenzie, included "growth in revenue of twenty-eight percent in the first year of the program, twenty-five percent in the second year, and a group of supportive employees. You don't buy them or hire them, you develop them."

2

Housekeeping Operations

The chronology of the housekeeping day may be divided into several distinct parts. This chronology differs depending on the type of property to which it is related and whether or not a computer application is in effect. For the purpose of illustration, the model hotel (commercial transient type; uncomputerized in housekeeping communication to the front desk) will continue to be the basis for system development. You should recognize, however, that destination resorts and resorts that are located in the center of activities may present different chronologies due to different types of markets.

Daily routine

Opening the house is the first step in the chronology of the housekeeping department day. Information communicated from the front desk to housekeeping via the Night Clerk's Report to Housekeeping is transcribed onto working forms for the housekeeping department. Adequate staffing is assured, and preparation is made for the arrival of workers. The conveyance of direction and delegation to other segments of the housekeeping staff (yellow, brown, and green teams) occur in a similar manner.

Most housekeeping departments start their daily routine at about 8:00 A.m. The time for the start of morning activities may vary based on the ability of guestroom attendants (GRAs) to gain access to guestrooms. In commercial transient properties in which weekend packages might be offered to families, the start of work may be delayed until 9:00 A.M. or even 10:00 A.m., depending on how late guests are known to sleep in.

In hotels in which business people are the major occupants, however, there are sufficient numbers of early risers to allow GRAs to start work at about 8:00 A.M. Such will be assumed for the morning activities in the model hotel, which commence at 8:00 A.M. In small properties, employees simply clock in for work and proceed directly to their central housekeeping area to pick up their assignments. Frequently employees come to work in their uniforms and are essentially ready to pick up their assignments and proceed directly to their floors.

Some hotels, however, do not allow their employees to take uniforms off the property. Others do not even have locker rooms where street clothing can be stored during working hours. In these latter cases, changing rooms are provided adjacent to wardrobe departments, which help facilitate large numbers of employees reporting to work at the same time. For example, at the Mirage Resort in Las Vegas, Nevada, employees clock in at a time clock area as they enter the building. The employees then proceed some distance to a wardrobe department where they pick up preassigned plastic hang-up bags.

The hang-up bag has one of four or five (costumes) that have been purchased for each employee. The suit bags with the fresh uniforms are then checked out by the employees who proceed to the changing room. Upon changing into the costume the employees then place their street clothing into the hang-up bag, then return the bag to the wardrobe department for storage while the employees are at work. At the end of the workday the procedure is reversed and the soiled costumes are returned to the wardrobe department. The employees will be resupplied with fresh costumes for the next workday.

As workers arrive, GRAs and senior GRAs pick up work assignments and sign for keys on the Passkey/ Beeper Control Sheet. The Supervisor's Daily Work Report had notations of rooms expected to be checked out of that day. The question how is this: Have any of these or other rooms actually been vacated as of 8:00 A.M.? If checkouts have actually occurred, the front desk would have conveyed this information as soon as possible to housekeeping central. This type of information (rooms actually vacated) will flow all during the day from the front desk, through housekeeping central, to the satellite linen rooms where it will be picked up by the floor supervisors. They in turn will pass this information to the GRAs in order that the latter may clean the rooms as soon as it can be done. Early in the shift, the executive housekeeper might choose to communicate with housekeeping central to ensure that the day's work is well under way.

Some rooms that had been expected to remain occupied (such as Rooms 1228 and 1096) are now showing checkout status. These guests were early and unexpected departures, resulting in additional checkout rooms. In either event, the actual checkout is recorded by circles around the C/O notation. This information is passed to the GRA in order that she or he might immediately enter the rooms to service them for reoccupancy. Upon arriving at the satellite linen room, the supervisor ensures that members of the team are properly prepared and move toward their assigned work stations as soon as possible.

GRA's carts should have been properly loaded the day before and should require only slight attention before being completely in order for work. Each GRA now moves toward the assigned area of room cleaning responsibility. The section housekeeping aide begins a routine inspection of corridors, elevators, stairwells, and other public areas to determine if any place needs emergency attention as a result of some accident during the night (spills, cigarette urns turned over, and so on). The section housekeeping aide records notes any project work that will become a part of the regular day's cleaning assignment or of a future plan.

Daily A.M. room checks are performed to determine whether the status of rooms reported by the front desk is in fact the correct status from the preceding night. For example, if the front desk reports certain rooms as occupied (with guest or with luggage) and in need of service, the A.M. room check determines if these rooms are actually occupied or the status is incorrect. The report verifies rooms reported as ready to rent or on change (in the process of being serviced for reoccupancy; sometimes called checkouts or simply C/O) are as reported. Are these rooms in fact ready to rent and vacant? Or has a discrepancy been uncovered in the status held by the front desk? Since this information is needed and must be accurate, room checks are conducted in the early morning in most hotels. GRAs knock on doors and, where necessary, enter rooms. Some hotels do not even use an opening-the-house routine. Daily routine simply starts with someone in the housekeeping department entering every room to determine if service is needed.

In some cases an A.M room check is conducted, and the results are assembled into an A.M. Housekeeper's Report. The report is submitted to the accounting department as a cross-reference and audit check on the revenues reported by the front desk from occupied rooms. The primary function of an *A.M.* Housekeeper's Report, then, is to ascertain that revenue is reported for every room that was occupied last night.

There is a simpler way to ascertain the status of rooms for which revenue Should be reported than to disturb every guest in the hotel every morning. Rooms that are thought to be occupied have been scheduled for service. Rooms that are thought to be vacant and ready to rent have not been scheduled for service and their boxes are blank on the Supervisor's Daily Work Report.

Since the primary concern is whether or not there are rooms occupied for which no revenue is being received, there is no need to check rooms known to be occupied; senior housekeepers need to inspect only those rooms thought to be vacant and/or ready to rent. Such rooms in this category that are found occupied (or obviously not ready) need to be investigated immediately to determine why their statuses are incorrectly held by the front desk. A discrepancy report may therefore be generated from the inspection of ready rooms only. There are several reasons why discrepancies occur:

1. A guest was to have been in room 2204 but was inadvertently handed the key to room 2206. A simple error in key selection went unnoticed by the clerk and the guest went to the address (2206) found on the key. At this point the front desk thought that room 2204 was to have been occupied when it will actually be discovered at morning room check that 2206, thought to be vacant, is the one that is occupied. This type of error is of no major consequence involving revenue; however, the possibility of inadvertently double rooming another person into room 2206 call occur, which may prove embarrassing to both hotel and guest.
2. Another and more- major concern is the possibility

that the room may have been given away by someone who did not have the authority to do so. (No records kept, therefore no questions asked!)

3. Finally, there is the possibility that some member of the hotel staff (bellperson, night security watch, desk clerk) who had access to guestrooms keys did, without proper authority, use a guestroom for an unauthorized night's rest—or whatever.

Regardless of the reasons for rooms that have been used and not recorded for revenue, they must be uncovered and corrective measures taken to prevent such happenings in the future.

A matter of quality service. It is indeed unfortunate that many hotels cling to the notion that it is necessary to knock on every guestroom door at 8:00 *A.M.* in order to conduct an accurate room check. Other hotels recognize that it is not necessary to disturb a guest in a room thought to be occupied in order to determine whether a room thought to be vacant is in fact vacant. It is not necessary to disturb a guest only to conduct a room check; A.M. room checks should be confined to rooms thought to be vacant and read), or vacant and on change (checked out 00. If this procedure is followed, GkAs need not approach any room in the morning until they are ready to clean that room. A.M. room checks may then be left to the senior GRA, who will open every door of guestrooms thought to be vacant to assure their status.

Communication and supervision. The supervisor circulates throughout the assigned division, communicating with GRAs and section housekeeping aides and progressing work during the day. The supervisor is constantly receiving information and conveying it to GRAs. The supervisor receives information about rooms having been vacated by communicating with the status board operators. This information is passed on to GRAs so that these rooms may be cleaned as soon as possible. Information—about rooms that are cleaned and ready for reoccupancy—that is received from GRAs is conveyed back to the status board operators, who in turn passes it on to front desk personnel.

Communication symbols. The following list is a summary of the communication symbols regarding the progress of work for each room on the supervisor's Daily Work Report.

1. A check mark indicates a room requires service.
2. The symbol CO indicates that the room is expected to be vacated at some time today.
3. A circle around the CO indicates that the room has actually been vacated (GRA notified).
4. The symbol R indicates that the room has been reported serviced by the GRA to the supervisor.
5. A line drawn through the entire entry indicates that the room has been reported to the status board operator as a ready room (no further routine action required in that particular room that day).

The supervisor is capable of progressing a large number of rooms each day and can keep up with this progress by a simple system of symbols used to indicate varying degrees of status change. When every room has a line drawn through its entry, all routine services have been concluded. Progressing work in the status system. A duplicate copy of each of the four divisions' Supervisor's Daily Work Reports has been displayed in the main linen room on the counter (or may be viewed on video monitors, where computer status boards are in operation).

Therefore, the status operator, who is in contact with the front desk can forward relayed information concerning recently cleaned ready rooms. If the hotel has an electrowriter, which was mentioned previously, it transmits a facsimile of the sender's handwriting. The numerous communications sent in both directions by housekeeping and the front desk are thereby preserved. This may also be done in a computer system.

Priority for cleaning rooms

It would seem that nothing could be more convenient for each GRA than to begin cleaning rooms at one end of an assigned section and proceed from room to room down the corridor until reaching the other end, at which time all rooms in the assigned section are completed.

Although this may seem to be the most efficient way of proceeding through the work day, it does not take into consideration concern for guests who do not want to be disturbed or who may want their rooms cleaned first or last. As the GRAs first move into their work areas each day, they should survey each room assigned for cleaning (both regular and pickup rooms) to determine rooms in which the guest has indicated "Do Not Disturb," and rooms in which the guest has indicated "Please make up ASAP."

Rooms in which the guest has put the night latch on the door will normally be in evidence by a small pin that will protrude through the doorknob. This small pin is easily discerned by feeling the Center of the doorknob. When the pin is out, the GRA should consider the room occupied and not to be disturbed until the night latch is taken off or until a later time of the day. A priority for cleaning rooms can be established as follows:

1. Rooms in which the guest has requested early service
2. Early morning checkouts that are specially requested by the front desk (usually required for preblocking of preregistered guests expected to arrive)

3. Other checkouts
4. The balance of occupied rooms requiring service
5. Requests for late service

A proper priority for cleaning rooms provides the greatest concern for the guest's needs and desires. While it is true that some occupied rooms (stay overs) will be the last to be cleaned each day (about 4:00 Pm.), the guests who wonder why their rooms are not serviced until the afternoon need only be reminded that a phone call to housekeeping or a sign on the door requesting earlly service will be accommodated as soon as possible. Otherwise, a room occupied by a stay-over guest might indeed be the last room cleaned that day in a particular section.

Especially on weekends and holidays, many guests will-indicate that they do not wish to be disturbed until late in the morning. A large number of such rooms could interfere with a particular GRA being able to enter any of the assigned rooms. If such is the case, a notification to the supervisor may warrant the GRA helping another housekeeper in a different part of the division until such time as rooms begin to open up. At the later time the "favour" can be returned. This is another example of the significance of teamwork and team operation within the division. Many times during the morning the GRA may visibly notice rooms being vacated. When such is the case, that room immediately becomes a checkout and can be entered next; provided there are no rooms of a higher priority (guest requests or front desk requests) that have yet to be serviced.

Cleaning the guestroom

At this point the "Housekeeping Day" scenario will be suspended temporarily and the specific techniques and systems on how to clean a guestroom will be addressed.

We will first look at the large hotel where all guestrooms are quite similar in size and furnishings. Then we will investigate the "suite type" hotel, where more than one room may be involved in an individual unit.

The national standard for numbers of rooms cleaned in one eight-hour shift by one person can vary from 13 to 20 rooms per day. This is usually dependent on the type of market being served, the type of furniture and bathroom that is involved, and the facility itself. The numbers of rooms cleaned each day will not, therefore, be at issue in this section. Most hotels have set routines for guestroom cleaning based on their own objectives and experiences.

There are many hotel corporations that have had years of experience to build upon in their procedures. Through experience they have developed and honed their procedures until they become quite unique. Other hotels take a different approach by letting their executive housekeepers start from scratch and develop new room cleaning procedures based on their own individual experience. What follows, then, is not necessarily unique or generic, but an example of the systematizing of routines that must take place in any individual hotel if the operations are to become systematic, effective, and efficient. Although the following procedural examples are specific, they do not rule out the possibility that other examples can be made as to the best way to clean a guestroom.

Entering the guestroom

The GRA should knock softly with the knuckles, not with a key (Over a period of time a key can damage the door finish.) The attendants should announce themselves either as "Housekeeper," "Room Attendant," or simply "Housekeeping." After waiting about fifteen seconds, if there is no response, they should repeat the procedure and insert their key or card entering device into the door lock. If there is still no answer; after another five seconds, she should open the door announcing once again "Housekeeper, may I come in please"' If there is a guest in the room who failed to answer the door previously, then the guest should be addressed as follows: "I am sorry I disturbed you. When would it be convenient for me to service your room) I will be glad to come back at a later time if you wish."

The guest's answer should prevail as to whether the room is to be cleaned now or the attendant should come back at a later time. If the- guest indicates it is all right to service the room now (while the guest remains in the room), the attendant might start a conversation by asking, "Did you have a nice sleep last evening?" or offer any remark which will allow pleasant conversation to develop. The GRA might also ask, "Will you be staying another night with us, or will you be leaving later today?" The answer to this question will determine 'whether only the bed should be made and the room tidied with the intent of returning later to finish the work for a new guest.

The GRA might also conclude this remark by saying (if the guest is leaving later today), "All right, I will Just make the beds and tidy the room and bathroom for you now and I'll return later to finish after you have departed." If the guest is staying another night, simply continue with a complete servicing of the room. If there is no guest in the room at the time of entry, continue with the cleaning procedure. The attendant should pull the housekeeping cart across the doorway, positioning the linen side towards the room and as close to the wall as possible.

The vacuum cleaner should be taken into the room, not left in the hallway. As the GRA enters the room, he or she should turn on all lights and open all drapes for proper light. If the TV was left on, it should be turned off. The GRA should check around the room for items missing, damaged, or broken. If noticed, they should call the room status operator and notify a supervisor in order that an engineer or security person can be dispatched immediately.

The GRA should be sure to inspect the following items in every room, regardless of whether or not the room is a check-out or a stay-over. They should report immediately & room status operator any discrepancies found with the following items that cannot be immediately attended to:

1. Check all lights in the room, replace burned-out bulbs in the swag lamp, dresser lamp, or night-stand lamp. Report any other burned-out lamps to the room status operator.
2. Check drapes, cords, and pulleys.
3. Check shower doors or shower curtains for serviceability.
4. Check shower, toilet, and sink for leakage or other problems.
5. Check TV for proper sound and picture.

If any room service or bar items need to be returned, remove them to an assigned location or to the hallway and notify a housekeeping aide so that they can be further positioned for retrieval by the appropriate department.

The supervisor should see to their quick removal from the hallway since they are unsightly and can begin to smell. If these items are not removed in a reasonable period of time, notify housekeeping central by phone. If the room is an occupied room, pick up magazines and newspapers, fold neatly and place on the table or dresser.

Never throw away these items unless they are in the wastebasket.

Suggested cleaning methods

Before actually entering into the servicing of a guestroom, a list of cleaning methods should be reviewed. All dusting should be done with a damp washcloth or a cloth treated with an en-dust type chemical. Here are several suggested methods of cleaning specific items:

1. Mirror—Rinse with hot water and finish with a dry cloth.
2. Lampshades—Brush lightly with a dry cloth or feather duster.
3. Shower stalls—Use an all-purpose cleaner and dry with a towel.
4. Bath Floor—Scrub wet floor with all-purpose cleaner and dry with a towel.
5. Shower Doors—Scrub with all-purpose cleaner, rinse, and dry with a towel.
6. Sinks—Use all-purpose cleaner, rinse, and dry with a towel.
7. Tubs—Scrub with all-purpose cleaner or scouring powder, rinse, and dry with a towel.
8. Chrome—Use all-purpose cleaner, rinse, and dry 9. with a towel; make sure there are no water spots.
10. Toilet Bowl-Wash the toilet inside and out. Use a germicidal cleaner and dry with a towel.

The following items should be dusted with a damp, or treated, washcloth: luggage rack, drawers and shelves, wastebaskets, lamp bulbs, air conditioner, thermostat, pipes under sink, tables and chairs, TV and stand, headboards, nightstands, picture frames, and window sills. Special considerations in cleaning may require special products. When this happens, the supervisor should closely control the use of special cleaning compounds. All employees should be cautioned against "becoming chemists" and mixing chemicals, thinking a better solution can be attained if a few products are mixed together. For example, acid bowl cleaner used to remove spots and build-ups in toilet bowls, when mixed with Clorox, can create deadly chlorine gas.

In addition, some people may be allergic to certain kinds of products in concentrated form. All-purpose cleaners are supposed to be used at specified dilution ratios for specific cleaning jobs. Employees should be trained in this area and should be required to comply with the manufacturer's specifications for dilution. For protection, it is advised that rubber gloves be worn for all cleaning duties to guard against germs, infection, and possible chemical reaction. Although few products are used which can cause harm in cleaning, as mentioned elsewhere in the text, HAZCOMM requirements direct that the dangers of each product used should be clearly labelled on each container. This information must be made available to the users of such products.

The bedroom

The GRA should collect all waste and trash, remove it, and empty it into the trash receptacle bag on the cart. Take trash receptacles into the bathroom for cleaning. Collect all ashtrays in smoking rooms and empty into the toilet. Flush, then wash all ashtrays and wipe dry. Damp wipe all trash receptacles, then replace ashtrays and trash receptacles. Bring clean linen and any other supplies needed to service the room into the room. Do not place clean linen on the floor while preparing to make the bed.

Shake all bed linen carefully when stripping the bed. Guests tend to leave articles and valuables in and under the bed and in pillow cases. Notify the floor supervisor and follow lost-and-found procedures for any item left behind by the guest.

Check mattresses and box springs for soiled or torn spots. Also check for wires that may be sticking outside of the box springs. The mattress and box spring should be straight on top of each other and should be placed firmly against the headboard. Check bed-frames where used (a dangerous item if out of place). If adjustment is needed, notify the floor supervisor.

Any bedding in need of replacement (wet mattresses, soiled bed pads, torn or soiled bedspreads, damaged or soiled pillows, soiled, damaged, or torn blankets) should be reported to the floor supervisor and replacement items secured immediately in order that work can continue efficiently. Fresh linen should be placed on every bed that was used or turned down the night before. Do not use torn or spotted linens. Place any rejected linen in the reject linen bag in the linen locker (satellite linen room).

The bottom sheet should now be placed on the mattress so as to facilitate tucking in the top at the head of bed with a mitered corner. The bottom sheet should also be tucked in on both sides of the bed, but not necessarily at the foot. The second sheet should be placed on the bottom sheet with the smooth fabric finish down (so as to be next to the body), with the major hem (if any) placed "jam-up" against the head board. This should leave plenty of top sheet at the foot of the bed to perform another mitered fold after the blanket is placed in the proper position.

The blanket should now be placed on top of the second sheet, nine inches from the head of the bed. When the blanket is properly squared on the bed, the top sheet should be folded back across the top of the blanket. The top sheet and the blanket should now be tucked in together at the foot of the bed, and a mitered fold made on both sides of the foot of the bed.

Some hotels employ a snooze sheet (a third sheet placed precisely on top of the blanket). This step also gives a quality application to the appearance of the bed if the spread is turned back or removed, but it is primarily done to protect the blanket from spills and spots. If a snooze sheet is employed, it will be tucked in at the foot of the bed simultaneously with both the blanket and the second sheet before the mitered corner is made. Some hotels now tuck in the second sheet, blanket, and snooze sheet on both sides of the bed. Other hotels leave both sides untucked.

When sides are tucked in, the guests will more than likely "unmake" the bed when they try to get into it. As top sheet and blanket are pulled back, the bottom sheet becomes untucked also. This writer suggests the best of both methods. Tuck in the top sheet and blanket on the side of the bed opposite to the side the guest is more likely to use when entering the bed. Leave the side that the guest will most likely use to enter the bed untucked.

Because the bed is most often the major focal point of the guestroom, the bedspread must be properly positioned, smoothed, and without lumps upon completion of the make-up. Assuming the spread is properly fitted, it should just miss touching the floor on three sides and be properly tucked in at the head of the bed. The corners of the spread at the foot of the bed should either be tucked or pleated.

The spread at the head of the bed is easily dressed by first turning the spread back about 12 inches from the headboard. The pillows should be placed about 15 inches from the headboard on top of the turned back spread. Once done, the front edge of the spread can be carried back over the pillows on both sides of the bed, and then the entire unit can be rolled together toward the headboard. GRA turning back the spread about 10 inches from the head of the bed. The spread should then be smoothed as necessary for a complete and dressed look. This technique of making the head of the bed is easily mastered with practice and is especially useful when one person is making up a king bed with three pillows.

Portable beds are to be made with clean linen and, unless otherwise instructed, no bedspread is used. Most are made with a snooze sheet, which will act as a bedspread. If the room is a "check-out" the bed is to be made up, pillow strapped vertically under the retaining strap and stood up on its rollers. Once standing upright, the bed can be replenished under the retaining strap with one bath towel, one hand towel, one washcloth and two fresh bars of soap neatly tucked in with the pillow.

A housekeeping aide can now be called to remove the bed from the room and have it properly stored. Remember, portable beds are to be made up before being moved into the hallway. Clean (damp-wipe) chairs, tables, dresser tops, window sills and tracks, head boards, air conditioner, thermostats, hanging swag lamps, pictures, luggage racks, and closet shelves. GRA using a Solution diluted and prepared especially for damp-wiping furniture. Also dust all light bulbs and lamp shades. Properly adjust lamp shades and move the shade so that the shade seam is located in the rear of the light as would be seen by the guest. Dust bar areas (if applicable) and clean all mirrors in the bedroom.

Replace and/or reposition all literature, ash trays, and hotel guest service directories or PR items. Matches should be carefully placed in ashtrays (not thrown into them) striker side up with advertisement facing the front of the table or desk where they are supposed to be located according to hotel specifications.

Drawers should be opened in "checkout" rooms and damp-wiped. Check carefully for any items the previous guest may have left behind. Do not go into drawers of stay-over rooms.

Dust the desk area, including lamp and chairs. Check the phone directory. If the cover is torn or is marked or bent, replace it. All literature on and in the desk drawer should be checked for completeness, and writing items should be clean and Unmarked. Damp-wipe the phone and use a disinfectant to wipe the mouthpiece.

Check all drawers and closet shelves. Check safes (if provided) and check underneath beds for items left behind. If any item is found, complete a lost-and-found slip, place the item and the slip into a plastic bag, and turn into the lost-and-found at the end of the shift. Remove any clothes hangers not belonging to the hotel; replace hotel clothes hangers as necessary.

For the *final dusting* step, if the room is a connecting room, open the connecting door and damp-wipe inside of the door and wipe the door sill. Damp-wipe inside the entrance door around the lock area. Damp-wipe the door sill. Clean the entire area and damp-wipe plastic covers (if applicable) on any signs on the back of the room door. Some hotels require that every room be vacuumed every day. Others call upon the judgment of the GRA to make this decision based on a standard set of appearance criteria and a critical look at the floor by the GRA.

Most times the GRA's Judgment is well founded and time can be saved in the room cleaning routine. If the GRA's judgment is not good, the supervisor must work with him or her regarding their power of observation.

Cleaning the bathroom

Clean the inside and the outside of the toilet with the designated cleaner and a johnny mop. Make sure to clean under the rim where the flushing water emerges. To clean the Tub/Shower area, first place a dry towel inside the tub/shower. Then, with the designated cleaner, clean the shower walls, soap dish, and shower doors inside and out.

Clean the sink with the designated product and a soft scrub applicator. Pull the sink stopper and clean thoroughly. Wipe clean and dry all faucets. Check other chrome fixtures, including the toilet tissue, facial tissue holders, and chrome towel rods. Damp-wipe and ensure they are free from water spots. "Re-point" the toilet tissue and facial tissue (the first extended sheet of paper from each fixture should be folded so as to present a neat triangle-pointed tip for the next user of the bathroom).

Clean the mirror, and damp-wipe the sides of the mirror frame (if applicable). The mirror should be spotless. A damp cloth with no cleaner will usually give the best results. Wipe all chrome plumbing fixtures underneath the sink and behind the toilet. The toilet should be cleaned with a germicide cleaner. Clean the outside of the toilet tank, the toilet, lid, seat, and base. With a johnny mop, clean the inside of the bowl. Flush; rinse the johnny mop carefully so as not to drip on the floor and return it to the housekeeper's cart.

The floor should first be wiped with a damp cloth to remove any hair and dirt. Wipe the floor (using the germicidal cleaner), including all corners, behind the toilet and the door. Damp-wipe the waste basket and reposition.

Most guestrooms should be equipped with one bath towel, one hand towel, and one washcloth for every pillow in the guestroom. Also include at least one bar of bath soap and one bar of facial soap. Some hotels use two bars of each kind of soap in every guestroom. Still others are using the amenity package for soaps, shampoos, softeners, and powders. Additional rolls of toilet paper and boxes of facial tissue are also included. Do not replace the toilet tissue in the fixture until the roll is less than one fourth full. Fold towels properly and set up the bath room as instructed. For the Final bathroom check, recheck all lights in the bathroom. Check room once more before leaving and lightly spray with air freshener. Turn off all lights in the bathroom.

For the Final inspection of the bedroom, the guestroom attendant should move to the front of the room next to the entrance door and observe the entire room. Remember, what is now seen is what the guests will see as they enter the room. The attendants should also be prideful about, their work. They should leave behind what they would be willing to enter upon if they were paying what the guest is going to be paying.

In general, the GRA will come into more contact with the guest than will the department head or even the general manager. For this reason, the GRA should remember to wish the guest a happy visit with us, and invite them back again. After all, the guest pays everyone's salary. Should the guest be present when the room is being serviced, the GRA should act the way a hostess would in her own home. After all, it is the first-line employee (in this case, the GRA) who delivers hospitality in our industry. At the request of the guest, the GRA locates a magazine suitable for relaxing entertainment. (Employees must remember that the guest is the reason for our work, not an interruption to it.)

The GRA should now back out of the room, ensuring that the door is completely locked, and either move to the next room to be cleaned or, when finished with the shift, move to the satellite linen room and restock the housekeeper's cart for the next day.

If this had been a *room made ready* (after the prior guest had checked out), the supervisor would have been notified that the room is properly serviced. In this case, she may choose to inspect the work for completeness and standardization of setup. A Housekeeping Manager stops by to add his input. After praise, he indicates that price information on bathrobes (available for guests to buy should they choose to do so) should be visible.

Suite hotels

There are many different types of hotel offerings that involve standard but, in their own way, unique routines. A good example of this type of hotel would be a suite hotel where more than the standard bedroom and bath are offered. Such facilities might include a formal sitting room or parlour, bedroom, kitchen and dining area, fireplace, and formal patio. A good example of such a facility would be the chain of hotels known as Marriott's Residence Inns.

The Marriott Corporation reaches into several market areas of the hotel industry; the Marquis and Full Service Hotels arc at the top of the line, Marriott Courtyards and Fairfield Inns are upper-scale apartment type accommodations to guests expecting to stay anywhere from one night to six months. This type of operation is designed to reach the guest who might be moving into a community or someone working in a community for a limited period of time. Because this operation caters more to the-individual who is having to maintain a home away from home, it is not unreasonable to find that linen would not be changed as often as in a full-scale hotel, where guests are expected to come and go almost daily.

What follows is the daily routine of the guestroom attendant (GRA) for this unique type of hotel. The reader should assume that the GRA is equipped as before with the necessary cleaning equipment and supplies. Specific details on how to clean or make beds will not be, repeated. Grateful appreciation is extended to Marriott's Residence Inn, Las Vegas, Nevada, for allowing part of their systems to appear in this text.

Cleaning the suite areas

Daily Cleaning (Vacant and Ready Rooms) is accomplished as before, by observing the proper protocol for entering the room. The suite attendant will then turn on all lights to check for burned-out bulbs; replace as necessary, then clean all light switches, lamps, and lampshades. Any carpet stains present will be treated.

Wastebaskets, trash containers, and ashtrays will be emptied. After emptying, clean and damp-wipe all wastebaskets as necessary, wipe and dry ashtrays. Replace liners in wastebaskets, if applicable, and reposition.

Furniture and shelves will be damp-wiped and the carpet vacuumed as necessary. Make sure that all furniture out of place is restored to its proper position. Check patio doors and the outside door. Make sure they are locked and the security bar is set and in place with security chain ii; place. Check for finger smears or dirt on the sliding glass doors or windows; clean as needed. Clean all window sills, windows, curtain rods, and doors, including the door tracks. Ensure that the telephone is restored to its proper place and that the phone cord is not tangled. All pretreated spots on carpets should now be scrubbed, rinsed, and dried as necessary.

Entrance area and closets

Using a damp cloth, wipe the inside and outside of the entrance door, door facing, the threshold plate, door knob, and all door hardware. (Abrasive cleanser is not to be used on hardware.) Clean and vacuum the entrance mat. Ensure that a flyswatter is positioned on the closet shelf. Check also that the proper type and amount of clothes hangers are in the closet. Foyer closet has four hangers, main closet has four to six regular/skirt hangers. Vacuum interior of closet. Ensure that the room rate card is properly in place.

Living area

If the fireplace has been used, notify a houseman to come and clean the residue. Clean all fireplace the, the black face plate, flue handle, screen, and poker. Close the flue and clean the picture above the fireplace. Such routines become instinctive after repeatedly following the prescribed procedures. Ensure that all reading and PR materials are in place. The radio should be tuned to an "easy listening" channel.

Dry-wipe the TV screen. Damp-wipe the TV stand and face plate. All cords to standing lamps should be dust-free and placed safely out of the way. Ensure that the candy jar is clean and has the required candy pieces. Make sure that the live plant is in its proper place.

Beds

Empty and clean the bed bench and nightstand drawers., Return all phone books to their proper place. Check the spread for stains, topside and underside. Replace with a clean spread if necessary. Check blankets for holes, stains, and tears. If a hole is smaller than two fingers, triple sheet the bed. Mattress pads should be stain free. Make the bed. Sheets should be changed at least twice a week in stay-over rooms. M checkout rooms must have linen changed. Check the alarm clock and ensure that the time is accurately set.

Bathroom

Wipe and dry the shower curtain and rod with a cloth dampened with all-purpose cleaner. Clean the tub enclosure with the assigned product. Clean all mirrors and polish chrome with glass cleaner. Clean the toilet bowl. Check holes under the rim. Disinfect weekly or upon checkout. Clean the toilet seat/lid hinges, base, and caps with all-purpose cleaner. Clean sinks with all-purpose cleaner. Remove any burn marks.

Reset the shower area with clean bathmat and fresh soap. Replace other soaps and tissues as necessary. If facial tissues are low, leave extra supplies on the vanity. Always leave an extra roll of toilet tissue. Place clean bath towels, hand towels, and washcloths in the bathrooms according to Placement Standards.

Kitchen

Wipe clean the front, controls, and crevices of the dishwasher. Check inside the dishwasher for objects left behind by the guest, or for any small items that may have fallen into the bottom. If dirty dishes have been left by the guest, load them in the dishwasher and turn on or, if the dishes do not make a full load, wash them by hand. Place any clean dishes and utensils in their proper place according to the Quest for Quality Standards Placement Guide. (This is a small publication of photographs indicating the proper setup of every item in the kitchen and other parts of the suite. Every dish, pot, pan, knife, fork, and spoon has its place.) Pots and pans should be cleaned daily; make sure that any black marks or stains are removed.

Check the inside of the refrigerator and freezer:

— Wipe up any spills.

— Remove any items left behind.

Clean the outside, top, hinges and the door gaskets of the refrigerator door. Clean and leave dry. Check oven burners for operation; check inside the oven for spills; clean as necessary. Damp-wipe the oven front and control panel as necessary. Clean the oven hood and air cleaner.

Cupboards. Wipe all shelves. Ensure that all dishes and glasses are clean and free of water spots. Wipe the fire extinguisher and store properly. If small appliances have been used (toaster, coffee maker, popcorn popper), clean and/or polish the exteriors or wash as needed. Replace in appropriate positions. Wipe any crumbs off the bottom of the toaster tray.

Wash down counter tops and behind sinks and ledge. Clean sink and polish chrome.

Check dishwasher soap supply. Replenish as needed; no less than one third of a small box is to be left.

Replace the first-nighter kit.

Gather dirty napkins and replenish the clean napkin supply as necessary.

Place a clean kitchen towel and dish cloth by the sink according to standards.

Replace all ashtrays in their proper position.

Before leaving the room

On checkouts, set the thermostat; air conditioning at 75 degrees, heat at 65 degrees. Ensure that the fan is left on "auto." Turn off all lights except over the kitchen sink.

When completed, stand back and observe your work. Complete any maintenance request forms and turn in to the supervisor. When servicing suites where guests are present, experience has shown that guests will more than likely remain out of your way, allowing you to get on with the work. This does not rule out the opportunity to be pleasant and extend hospitality to the guest. All suite attendants are encouraged to participate in friendly conversation when the opportunity presents itself.

Daily Cleaning Guide for Stay-Overs is essentially the same except that in the kitchen, soiled dishes are placed in the dishwasher and the machine started. Check the refrigerator and freezer for any spills. Clean as necessary.

The H.O.M.E.S. manual

The above steps involving suite hotels are contained in one of the Residence Inns' Hospitality Operations Manual For Excellent Service (H. 0 M. E. S.). There are other H.O.M.E. S. manuals for procedures involving the Front Office, Maintenance Department, Hotel and Housekeeping Management, Uniform and Grooming, and Commitment to Quality.

There is also a "Quest for Quality Placement Standard Guide" for every item in a suite. Additional guidance is offered when working in guest contact areas, As should now be evident in the scenarios just presented, there is great detail in the step-by-step procedures involved in cleaning the guestroom. At first glance, what has been shown might seem almost insurmountable. What appears to be overwhelming becomes quite instinctive, however, with training and practice. At the Residence Inn, the experienced GRA cleans over 16 rooms a day.

As the GRAs complete each room, they should make a written record of each room cleaned in order to know when the daily work assignments have been completed. In addition, the GRAs should reevaluate the priority of cleaning rooms after each room is finished. A new request for early service may have appeared or checkouts may have been noticed while cleaning a particular room; these situations can cause a small change in the order in which the work schedule should be progressed.

During "opening of the house" the supervisor was notified on the Daily Work Report which rooms were expected to check out that date. However, the GRA was not so notified.

When the GRA is told about expected checkouts, it is important to know whether to wait for those rooms to be vacated before rendering service. What if a room is scheduled to be vacated and the outgoing guest requests early service? The room might have to be serviced twice in the same day; once by special request of the guest for early service and then again after the guest departs. A reasonable compromise can exist provided the early service request is honoured.

The GRA asks all guests requesting early service, "Will you be staying another night with us?" Then expected departures will be noted and the GRA may say, "Very well then, I will just spread up your bed and tidy the bathroom until after you have left, then I will come back and completely service the room. In this way, your room will be straight and I need not disturb you for any great length at this time." Such an answer is usually well received by any guests expecting to have visitors in their rooms and are departing later.

The GRA continues throughout the day cleaning each room assigned in a priority order as described above until the last room on the schedule has been serviced. Likewise, the section housekeeping aide and the supervisor continue with their functions as described above and as further set forth in their job descriptions.

The working team takes a 15-minute break from work in the morning, a 30-minute lunch break, and a 15-minute break in the afternoon. Most housekeeping departments operate in such a way that lunch breaks are on employee time—that is, employees punch out for lunch and are on their own time—and the 15-minute morning and afternoon breaks are on company time.

During the rest breaks and lunch periods it is advisable that some member of the team stay behind in the general work area until the main portion of the work team returns. This staggering of break time allows for someone always to be present in the event of some emergency or priority of work requirement. The priority of work and chronology of the day continue very much as described until 1:00 P.M., at which time those rooms heretofore noted as "do-not-disturb" must be resolved.

Let us assume that no prior specific notification has been received by the housekeeping department regarding a known late sleeper and that no specific request for late service has been received. (If such had been the case, a specific time would have been arrived at for the receipt of daily room cleaning service.)

It then becomes necessary to resolve the status of those rooms which have heretofore been noted as do not disturb (DND). This also involves determining the status of rooms in which pins have been out on doors. It would not be uncommon for GRAs to have several such rooms in their sections each day.

Since 1:00 P.M. is checkout time, this is a reasonable time to resolve the DND status of such rooms. Room doors with pins out are simply knocked on. Since it is difficult to knock on a door in the face of a sign indicating do not disturb, a more practical method of resolving this dilemma is to call the room. This call may be made from a vacant room possibly as close as across the hall. Before actually making the call, it is appropriate to consider all of the possibilities you could face by making such a call:

Case 1: The answering guest either

(a) was awakened, or

(b) was not awakened but was not aware that the DND sign was on the door

Case 2: The guest does not answer

In case 1 it would be appropriate to open the conversation as follows: "Good afternoon, this is Mary from the housekeeping department. I am calling to find out at what time you would like to have your room serviced today." Most answers to such a question asked over the telephone fully resolve what is to be accomplished in the DND rooms. Such answers as, "You may conic now" or "Come in about one hour" or "Do not come until 6:00 P.M." or even "I do not want service today" resolve the problem. However, any guest not desiring service today should prompt the following type of reply: "Very well; however, I have an attendant on her way up to your room with some fresh towels. She will be there in just a moment."

What has been accomplished with such a scenario is that even though the guest has paid for a room that comes with daily service, including a change of bed linen, you cannot force service on a guest. It is imperative, however, that someone get a peek into the room in question to verify that nothing illegal is happening in the room. (Most illegal acts being performed in hotel rooms are covered by a DND sign and a statement that no service is desired that day.) The peck will be obtained under the guise of delivering the fresh towels into the room. In every case in which service is being refused, the supervisor and a housekeeping manager should be notified.

The supervisor or manager might deliver the towels to verify that service was in fact being refused, as well as to engage the guest in conversation to ensure that no illegal activity is taking place within the room. In case 2, in which there is no answer to the phone call, the GRA should go immediately to the room, knock on the door, and enter the room. In most cases in which a phone call has received no answer, entering the room will reveal only that the guest is out of the room or has checked out. In either case, the guest has usually left the room forgetting to remove the DND sign from the door. If the door pin is out and the guest has failed to answer a knock on the door or a phone call, immediate management attention is warranted.

The main concern in this case is that someone in the room has locked him or herself in and is now incapacitated to the extent that he or she cannot answer the door. Without delay, this room requires a manager with an emergency key that will allow immediate entry. A similar situation exists if the GRA attempts to enter a room with the floor master key after a phone call to a room arid, as the door is opened slightly, the chain lock is found to be on the door. Concern in this situation is great enough to warrant calling a manager and an engineer with a bolt cutter in preparation for cutting the chain on the door.

There are two specific exceptions to the concerns stated, both of which should be considered before using the emergency master key or the bolt cutters. The room may have been sold as a part of a suite that adjoins the adjacent room. Quite often when guests have two rooms, they will chain lock and/or bolt latch one room and enter the locked room through the internal door of the adjacent room.

A quick check at the front desk will reveal whether or not this has happened. The other exception occurs when the room is on the first floor arid is capable of being vacated through a sliding glass door. It is not unusual to find that guests have chain locked arid placed the latch bolt on the hall door, left a DND sign on the door, and checked out, departing through the sliding glass door to the street. This possibility should always be investigated before cutting chains arid using emergency keys on first-floor room doors. Although the possibility might seem remote, guests have been found dead in the hotel guestrooms, and this possibility will always confront the GRA when access to guestrooms cannot be immediately gained.

The fact that a deceased person could be discovered in a guestroom should be covered well in training sessions. Having resolved all rooms previously seen as DNDs, the GRA continues cleaning guestrooms, following the same priority as in the morning. The first part of afternoon cleaning of guestrooms will find heavier involvement with checkout rooms, since most checkouts would have departed by 1:00 P.M. The overload of vacant arid checkout rooms will be eliminated within about two hours, leaving mostly occupied stay-over rooms to be finished in late afternoon. Afternoon rooms cleaning will be interrupted only by the necessity to make a P.M. room check.

Unlike the A.M. room check during the morning activities, there is now a need to obtain a factual "look" at the status of *every* room in the hotel and report this status in order that the front desk may purify the room rack in preparation of selling out the house each night. The Pm. room check is carried out by each GRA, at a specific time and as quickly as possible, checking every room in the normally assigned section. There are exceptions to the need to knock on every door. Should the GRA see a guest vacate a room a short time before the room check, there is no need to open that door since the room is known to be vacant.

Likewise, should the GRA see a guest check in just a short time before room check, the room will obviously be occupied. Sometimes stayover guests make themselves known to their GRAs. Again, known occupancies do not require the guest to be unnecessarily disturbed. However, accuracy must take precedence over bypassing a room at the P.M. status inspection.

The GRAs were given a blank copy of their section reports and that the supervisors were given a blank cop), of the open section reports. Thus, in the model hotel there are 20 section P.M. Report sheets available in the house each day upon which to record the results of the Pm. Report. At approximately 3:00 P.M., most expected checkouts have departed (there could be exceptions) and a majority of today's arrivals have not yet arrived. Therefore, 3:00 P.M. is an appropriate time to conduct the P.M. room check and prepare the report.

The P.M. inspection is conducted in such a way as to ensure accuracy. Except for the Situations mentioned earlier, every door in each section will be opened between 3:00 P.M. and 3:10 P.M. There are many different ways of knocking on room doors and announcing the GRA's presence. The worst possible situation Occurs when the GRA knocks on the door with the key (thus damaging the woodwork finish on the door) and yells "Maid," thereby disturbing everyone within hearing distance. There is a much more professional manner in which to proceed:

It should be standard practice that the GRAer knock on guestroom doors 'only with the knuckles, never with an object of any kind that could damage the door with repeated abuse. The term "housekeeper" should be used in place of "Maid." The following is a professional procedure that may be followed:

1. Knock on the door with the knuckles.
2. Announce yourself as "Housekeeper." If there is an

answer, say; "Please excuse the knock, I am conducting a room status check. Thank you, have a nice stay with us." Then go to the next room. If there is no answer, continue the procedure.

3. Knock on the door again.
4. Insert the key in the door.
5. Announce again "Housekeeper."
6. Open the door and, as the room is entered, say "May I come in, please?"

Someone who may not have heard the first knock usually hears the key enter the door. At any time there is a reply, simply apologize and indicate that a room status check is being conducted. When no one answers, enter the room to determine the room status.

The person conducting the room check observes the room to determine the following:

— *Ready Rooms (R):* Rooms that are clean and read), to rent.

— *Occupied (OCC):* Rooms that have a guest on residence (rooms that contain luggage are also considered to be occupied).

— *Chcckout (C/O) or on change:* Rooms that have been vacated and have not yet been made ready for a new occupant.

One of the three defined statuses—C/O, OCC, R—will be indicated for each room by placing a check mark in the appropriate column. Any special remarks that need to be forwarded will be noted. Those rooms provided to Julia in the morning as pickup rooms are not checked by Julia since they will appear on another section sheet. It is therefore only the printed room numbers (left column) that need to be checked. Each room should always have one of the three statuses marked next to it--never more than one.

After each GRA has completed a room check for the section and filled in the P.M. Report, the report is placed on the GRA's cart to await pickup. After the supervisors have completed checking all open sections within the division, they circulate among their teams and pick up the completed room reports. In the four divisions in the model hotel there will be 20 reports, all of which should be brought to the main linen room by about 3:30 pm. It is at about this time that the second, or evening, shift will be reporting for work; there will be a shift overlap of about one hour.

Other activities during the shift

There are many other activities associated with cleaning guestrooms that are not as obvious as those done by the room attendant. The GRA is assisted by someone keeping soiled linen and trash off the housekeeper's cart. That person is a section housekeeping aide and is usually a member of the team working in the area.

Other matters of resupply are also significant. Having the necessary linen to resupply the housekeeper's cart along with the other supplies needed to service the guestroom requires a whole new army of support personnel involved in total linen handling, especially when linen must be sent out from large hotels to commercial laundries. There is the resupply of major cleaning chemicals, most of which must be diluted to specified dilution ratios. To maintain control of dilution, it is usually accomplished in a separate place by one person qualified to do so.

Shift overlap: first and second shift coordination

When the night Supervisor and night housekeeper report to work at about 3:30 P.M., their first task will be to accept the 20 GRAs Daily reports. They will then transcribe the information from each of these 20 reports onto the Housekeeper's Report for later forwarding to the front desk and the controller's office. This report is somewhat tedious to transcribe because of the different order in which rooms will be arranged on the Housekeeper's Report (which follows a pattern laid Out on the front desk room rack).

The form on which the Housekeeper's Report is prepared is identical to the form on which the night clerk prepared the report early in the morning that was used to open the house. However, on the Housekeeper's Report, every room will have an indication next to the printed room number of the status in which it was seen over a time span of about 10 minutes (between 3:00 and about 3:10). The report will normally take about 30 minutes to transcribe. No sooner will the transcription be completed than the report will need to be updated before forwarding. Between 3:00 and 4:00 P.M. many things happen to cause the status reported at 3:00 P.M. to change. Guests are checking into ready rooms; a few guests will be departing after 3:00 Pm.; but most significant is that the rooms reported as checkout rooms will now have been made ready. (It is quite possible that a GRA who had reported three rooms as checkouts would have been able to service all of them between 3:00 and 4:00 Pm.)

As each GRA leaves the floor at 4:00 P.M., fie or she notifies the supervisor of the rooms previously reported as checkouts that are now ready. As the GRA moves to the satellite linen room to resupply the cart with linen for tomorrow's work effort, each senior housekeeper carries the updated information to the main linen room. The night supervisor uses this information to update the Housekeeper's Report.

There is also an update recap at the top of the page. What had been originally noted as 45 checkout rooms has now been reduced to 13. Also, the vacant and ready rooms have been increased from 158 to 190. It is not uncommon to erase the original indications and replace them with the correct indication. However, passing the updated information on to the front desk in both its original and corrected forms may help front desk personnel resolve discrepancies, since they will know which rooms were rented or vacated between 3:00 and 4:00 P.M.

In the meantime, GRAs should have finished loading carts for tomorrow's work- schedule. There is a fresh supply of linen that the section housekeeping aide brought from the laundry and placed in the satellite linen room before 4:00 P.M. The section housekeeping aide collects all soiled glasses in cases, places them on rolling dollies, and moves them to the main linen room for washing and rebagging by the night crew. The supervisor returns to the satellite linen room to see that all carts are properly loaded and stowed for the night.

Finally, all linen rooms are checked to ensure that trash has been removed and the linen room has been left in an orderly and locked condition. If top caddies are used on carts, they are returned to the main linen room for restocking. All workers who started work at 8:00 A.M. clock out at 4:30 Pm., having concluded an eight-hour workday in 81/2 hours lapsed time. (Recall that each employee was not on the clock during a 30-minute lunch break.) Before leaving the facility, each employee checks the Tight Schedule to see if he or she is scheduled to work on the next day.

Discrepancies and rechecks generated

After the A.M. shift has departed, some member of department management or one of the day supervisors inspects all corridors and service areas to ensure that no piece of equipment, soiled linen, trash, or debris of any kind has been left in any hallway. Satellite linen rooms are spot checked to ensure that no trash cans (fire hazard) have been left unemptied and that all service doors are properly locked. Before the departure of the last department manager, the lost-and-found is chain locked. Barring any late administrative work or the need to remain behind to visit and/or work with the night crew, management's day can now be considered at an end. Evening operation of the department is now left in the control of the night supervisor, who will direct the activities of the night GRA, night section housekeeping aide, and night public area housekeepers.

A short time after the Housekeeper's Report is delivered to the front desk, the night supervisor would have transcribed all checkouts remaining on the Housekeeper's Report to the Night Supervisor's Report of Evening Activities form. Turn-down service is usually begun when guests are out of their rooms during the evening dinner hour and continues until all rooms are completed. It is a service once reserved for V.I.P. guests but is now provided in many higher-priced hotels as a routine function in all guest rooms.

The last column of the Night Supervisor's Report, Guest Requests, indicates services specifically requested by guests during the evening hours; room numbers and the services needed are recorded. If a guest loan item is needed, a receipt should be made out for the guest to sign and the item-logged out of the linen room in the Guest Log Book to ensure proper return of the item. By 6:00 P.M. the front desk would have had the opportunity to use the Housekeeper's Report to purify the room rack. This is a procedure in which the status of each room as reported on the Housekeeper's Report is compared to the status of each room as indicated on the room rack. There will be numerous discrepancies, primarily because of the changing of room status that has been occurring between 3:00 and 6:00 P.M.

Discrepancies may show the opposite condition. The front desk can show a checkout, whereas the Housekeeper's Report shows an occupied room. This type of discrepancy may have occurred as a result of a late checkout or of a departure after the room had been cleaned. Such discrepancies must be rechecked. All discrepancies that cannot be reconciled by the front desk and all rooms that the front desk indicates are checkouts must be physically rechecked. The room numbers of guestrooms to be rechecked are sent to housekeeping via the electrowriter or in writing. Each recheck is listed on the Night Supervisor's Report of Evening Activities in the first half of column three.

The evening supervisor or night GRA should immediately recheck the status (take another look) of each of the rooms so listed and record the results of the recheck in the second half of the column. As an example, refer to the Housekeeper's Report to note the first status listed for each room in which there is a discrepancy. Rooms 1007, 2083, 3055, and 4105 were first listed as OCC but upon recheck were found to be CO/T; the T refers to a condition requiring a tidying. A tidy is a room that had been serviced earlier in the day when it was occupied but has now been vacated.

Tidies require only a very light service; removal of small amounts of litter, replacing a glass, cleaning an ashtray, or perhaps smoothing a bed. A change of linen is required if a bed has been turned back and slept in or on. Night GRAs must check to make sure that the departing guest did not remake the bed after sleeping on what had been clean linen, leaving an unwelcomed surprise for the next guest. The bathroom might also require a light touch-up. A tidy requires two to five minutes of service, provided the guest did not get back into bed before departing.

The front desk must continue to research two rooms to determine why the front desk status remains in error, since on two occasions both rooms were viewed by housekeeping as ready rooms. Possibly a room found vacant (RFV) has occurred, which happens when a Customer intends to pay the account with a credit card and expects the hotel to find the room vacant, total the bill, and send through a voucher for what is owed. The other possibility is that someone has skipped without paying the account.

All rechecks will have their status determined for the day. Most rechecks will need a light tidy. On many occasions, these tidies can be completed as they are discovered and the room reported as a ready room immediately by phone to the front desk. The final status of all rechecks is recorded and sent back to the front desk in writing or on the electrowriter.

Evening activities

The workload of the evening crew can be summarized as follows:

1. To transcribe the Housekeeper's Report and then update the report,
2. To transcribe the remaining checkouts to the Night Supervisor's Report of Evening Activities and the night GRA to begin cleaning these checkouts.
3. Public area housekeepers to assume responsibility for public area cleaning and servicing.
4. Evening crew to begin providing special services as requested by the guests and to note each service on the report.

5. At about 6:00 P.M. to receive rechecks and to check the statuses of rooms listed for recheck to determine what, if anything, must be done by the housekeeping department to service these rooms. Many rechecks will require a light tidy; some rooms will require a complete make-up; others require only the verification of correct status. Rooms tidied and any other special projects required of the night crew are noted on the report.
6. Turn-downs are begun at about 7:00 Pm, and are continued until completed.
7. The night housekeeping aide usually washes all guestroom drinking glasses and helps repackage them in sanitary containers for use during the next day. These glasses are delivered to satellite linen rooms at night.
8. The night supervisor, assisted by other members of the night crew, may restock cart-top baskets with the proper par of guest supplies; these baskets will be picked up the next day by GRAs as they proceed to work.

Of greatest significance is the fact that the night supervisor is in *charge* and must *take charge* of the evening activities of the housekeeping department. She or be must therefore wear a beeper and not be confined to an office. Electrowriter messages are reviewed upon return to the office, and telephone messages are intercepted and relayed by the PBX operator.

The supervisor works closely with the night supervisor at the front desk to ensure that all rechecks are properly resolved and that every room is left clean and salable. The hotel should *never* lose room revenue because the housekeeping department failed to clean a room. The night supervisor must also make inspections of public rest rooms to ensure that they are being properly maintained. A night guestroom attendant may service ten or fifteen rooms each night to ensure their availability for guests who arrive late. The night supervisor should see to it that the main linen room is cleaned and properly prepared for the oncoming supervisor who will be opening the house the next morning. Of greatest importance is that the night supervisor keep an eye out for the unexpected. A change in the weather at 10:00 P.M. can have a surprising effect on tomorrow's schedule.

Any unusual change in expected occupancy may warrant notification to the executive housekeeper in order that special direction may be forthcoming for the unusual occasion. When all vacant rooms are clean and ready to rent, turn-downs are completed, linen room is clean and ready for the oncoming shift, glasses washed and packaged for use the following-day, and cart-top caddies replenished for GRAs to pick up in the morning, the evening activities are essentially finished. The final step in each evening's activity is for the supervisor to assemble all reports, records, forms, and paperwork associated with the day's activities for filing chronologically according to date. The following is a list of documents that should be filed:

1. Night Clerk's Report to Housekeeping (used to open the house that day)
2. Original and copies of all Senior Housekeeper's Daily Work Reports (original was given to each senior housekeeper; copy was used on the linen room counter to progress work by each division)
3. All Section Housekeeper's Pm. Reports
4. Copy of the Housekeeper's Report
5. Completed passkey/beeper control sheet
6. Night Supervisor's Report of Evening Activities

There will be numerous occasions when the above

information will need to be researched. It is therefore imperative that it be retained for at least one year.

Computers come of age in the world of housekeeping

The subject of computers and their application to the techniques of rooms management in hotel operations has at last come of age. Once confined to the realm of top management, statistical analysis, corporate planning payroll, and the like, state-of-the-art development of computer application to property management systems is now commonplace.

The race to devise and provide economical information-handling and reporting systems has been nothing short of spectacular. Although the race goes on, hardware (input terminals, microprocessors, disk drive components, and printers) and hotel software packages (programs by which computers assimilate information) once thought to be out of reach of housekeeping personnel have become part of the daily routine of housekeeping operations. Computers are now just another tool to help housekeeping departments become more efficient in handling management information. The development of computers is currently seen to be in its fifth generation. With each step into the future, computers have become less expensive, allowing even the smallest hotel the opportunity to modernize the efficient handling of information.

Although the hotel industry seems as ageless as history, the 1980s introduced not only the computer into housekeeping information-handling, but also the telephone switch (system) as the vehicle by which computer technology is applied. Since every guestroom has one, the telephone has become the chief instrument for housekeeping to use in accessing the computer. This technique greatly reduces the cost of updating existing facilities since major expenses can be avoided in adding wiring to each individual room. For example, an interface is created between the telephone system and the central processing unit (CPU) of the computer network. This is accomplished by the guestroom attendant dialling a specific sequence of numbers on the phone from a specific guestroom. Once connected, the computer immediately recognizes the room number to which it is being connected. After the connection, a specific list of dial-up codes becomes available to the GRA by which he or she can now transmit information.

The GRA is not the only person who can make a status change entry for a guestroom. When the front desk clerk rents a room, a selection is made from the inventory of rooms identified as being READY FOR SALE. In the process of inputting check-in information for a guest, the desk clerk, through a computer terminal, changes the status of the room to OCCUPIED NOT (no longer) AVAILABLE FOR SALE. The front desk clerk can also put rooms into a special status, such as RUSH. Rooms in this status are rooms which have been preassigned and have guests waiting for them. These rooms are given priority attention by housekeeping from among other ONCHANGE Rooms.

Housekeeping central operations can also make inputs into the system. Many times a status change needs to be reported that cannot be directly inputted from a guestroom (guest might be using the telephone, or is a Do Not Disturb). Status changes can be phoned into the status board operator in housekeeping. This information can then be inputted by the status board operator.

At different times during the day, or on call, the status board operator can print out the status of all guestrooms at a given instant and provide floor supervisors information regarding their particular sections. Also, management can review total rooms status at an), time by calling for a printout. This is an example of only one of many ways a computer can be employed in the management of guestroom information. New hotels can be wired for different types of systems that can give housekeeping information, and also can turn on air conditioning systems and lights when a room becomes rented, tell whether or not the GRA is currently in a specific room, and, through the door-locking system, tell who were the last 24 persons to enter the room.

The Night Clerk's Report, opening the house, and, the scheduling of work for supervisors and GRAs are now available through computers. Information about rooms not to be disturbed, rooms out of order, and late check-outs are updated and available, and P.M. Reports and information about rooms requiring immediate service or about turn-down requirements on specific rooms are created instantly. Room status discrepancies are handled efficiently, allowing for the cleaning of questionable rooms for reoccupancy earlier in the day.

As for spectacular advancement in the realm of computers for housekeeping, consider the following scenario:

> A supervisor or manager inspects a guestroom and records the findings vocally into a handheld tape recorder. Upon completion of the inspection, the recorder is *pluggcd into* a receptacle located in the guestroom. The inspection information is immediately transmitted to a microprocessor where it is voice read into a data memory bank. At any time from that moment on, a printout of inspection results for all rooms inspected is immediately available to the manager. Microprocessors have the capability to sort, codify, and classify information in such a fashion that inspection comments requiring maintenance work requests to engineering would be immediately transmitted. As work is completed, additional input from the guestroom would cause reports to be updated. Should

> rooms be necessarily held in out-of-order status, information would be available indicating the nature of the problem, corrective action being taken, and expected time the room will be back in service.

This is only one of many possible uses of computer applications in the housekeeping department. However, that before computer application becomes a reality, a thorough understanding of systems as they might be conducted by hand is most important; otherwise extraneous capability might be purchased when what might have been needed can only be found installed in the hotel across the street.

Hotel housekeeping subroutines

Subroutines can be presented through standard operating procedures (SOPs), key control, and procedures for changing door locks). It may appear that much of what will be described in this chapter cannot be delegated without abdication of responsibilities. This is not a correct assumption, as the astute professional manager will realize. Budgeting, for example, occurs so seldom (once a year) that junior managers may never have an opportunity to become involved before they are transferred and/or promoted. Every manager within the department therefore must become involved at every opportunity if professional development is to take place.

As with the daily routine, subroutines lend themselves to control by forms. Some require only limited planning and policy formulation regarding their substance, whereas others need detailed planning and careful implementation. We will now look at each of these subroutines, keeping in mind the importance of proper delegation on overall department morale, effectiveness, and efficiency of operation.

Cleaning and maintenance

GRAs are efficiently used when their efforts are confined

to the guestroom areas of the hotel. The section housekeeping aide provides support to the housekeeping team and performs certain duties related to the maintenance of guestroom corridors stairwells, elevators, vending areas, and satellite linen room stocking and maintenance.

There are, however, other areas that require cleaning and maintenance throughout a facility and for which the executive housekeeper is responsible. There may be many public areas under the executive housekeeper's umbrella of responsibility that require daily if not hourly attention. Hotel lobbies, public restrooms, lobby thoroughfares, offices, banquet area restrooms, employee locker rooms, and assorted service areas require scheduled cleaning and maintenance. Such functions normally fall under the supervisor), responsibility of the *senior housekeeping* aide, who should be a specialist in unique cleaning and maintenance tasks. Recalling the established organization for the model hotel, the lobby housekeepers, housekeeping aides, and utility housekeeping personnel normally report to the senior housekeeping aide and are available for the large number of specialized tasks that must be performed. Such personnel should be uniquely uniformed and temperamentally suited for work among the general public.

Cleaning and maintenance circuits (rounds) need to be established in order that all areas of concern are kept under control. The straightening and repositioning of furniture, the employing of ash urns and ashtrays, the cleaning of smudges from glass doors and mirrors, and the servicing of public restrooms can require attention as little as once every eight hours and as often as once every 15 minutes, depending upon the circumstances. Employees functioning under the senior housekeeping aide must be trained to respond to these needs without immediate and direct supervision.

Special initiative might be expected of the lobby housekeeper to modify the cleaning circuit based on observations of crowds as the), migrate through the hotel. For example, lack of activity in the lobby during certain hours of the day would indicate that less attention is required once an area has been properly serviced. Times of heavy check-in may warrant the prolonged and continued attention of the lobby housekeeper to the point that this person cannot leave the specific lobby area until the crowd subsides. Supplies and equipment must be Suitable and, where necessary, specialized for the tasks. Standard equipment for lobby personnel is a specially designed cart that is stocked with necessary supplies. Kex floor mops (special hard floor mops treated with a dust-attracting chemical), vacuum cleaners, and dusting materials are carried on carts with good trash-handling capability and paper supply transport.

The lobby housekeeper and aide should be equipped to handle not only routine tasks, but they should have specialized equipment on hand, such as paint scrapers to keep ahead of (or behind) those who deposit chewing gum on concrete walks, hard floors, or even carpets. Indoor hard surfaces such as decorative Mexican clay tile or terrazzo floors require specialized equipment for cleaning and maintenance. In most cases, carpet shampooing requires the use of special equipment and skills in equipment maintenance.

Normally, specially trained employees who perform work such as carpet shampooing will be under the direction of the senior housekeeping aide. After the day shift has been relieved by the second shift, the night supervisor is responsible for public area cleaning and maintenance as well as guestroom cleaning. The senior housekeeping aide and the night supervisor are therefore vital to the success of the overall housekeeping operation.

The executive housekeeper should work to establish, then strengthen, the technical and supervisory skills of these two employees. Most of all, the executive housekeeper should delegate properly and then allow these Supervisors the opportunity to do their jobs and not interfere other than to coach and counsel in the performance of assigned tasks.

Both the senior housekeeping aide and night supervisor should be involved in establishing the standard operating procedures for performance of public area housekeeping and in developing job descriptions for employees under their control, Although actual employment is a management decision, these two supervisors Should be allowed to question and give indication of their approval of any employee considered for assignment to areas under their supervisory control.

General cleaning of guestrooms

The routine servicing of guestrooms normally Includes removing rubbish, changing linens, thoroughly cleaning bathrooms, vacuuming floors (when necessary), lightly dusting or damp-wiping flat surfaces, and setting up and supplying the room for the next stay-over guest. Guestrooms also need a periodic general or deep cleaning.

Tasks such as high dusting, vacuuming drapes and casements, wiping clown walls, cleaning carpet edges and vent filters, moving beds and furniture, and turning mattresses must be performed on a regular but not daily basis. The frequency of such general cleanings depends on heaviness of use, weather conditions, and quality of routine maintenance. General cleaning can be performed by the GRA or by a special team of employees who do nothing other than general cleaning of rooms.

A good general cleaning-should take approximately

twice as long as a routine room servicing. For example, consider a typical day of 8½ hours. Remember that each employee has 30 minutes for lunch and two 15-minute breaks, leaving 7½ hours for work. Let us assume that a GRA can service three rooms routinely in one hour and needs ½ hour to service the housekeeping cart at the end of the day. Depending on the nature of the hotel and its clientele, each GRA can service from 14 to 20 rooms per day. This leaves 15 minutes to add to one room for deep cleaning. If each GRA general cleans one assigned room each day, each room will receive a deep cleaning once every 15-20 days,

The section housekeeping aide also becomes involved in general cleaning because of the need to move furniture and perform high dusting of several rooms. A section housekeeping aide may be required to help more than one GRA. If the section housekeeping aide becomes overloaded, a utility housekeeping aide might be employed to assist in the general cleaning of guestrooms. Supervisors should keep records of rooms that have received general cleaning in order that each room receive such cleaning on a regular basis.

Projects

The management of every housekeeping department requires the performance of occasional special projects, Periodic shampooing of a specific carpeted area, stripping and refinishing a hard surfaced floor, removing scuff marks on a seldom-used but accountable space and sanitizing rubbish-handling equipments are projects that must be scheduled from time to time based on someone's observation during an inspection. These projects are usually the purview of the senior housekeeping aide.

The results of an early morning inspection conducted by the senior housekeeping aide may lead to such projects. Special projects are performed by utility personnel under supervision. Records of projects should be maintained and reviewed periodically to determine the extent of man-hours being expended on this type of work. Many projects can be eliminated in the future by making them part of routine work. Additionally, projects justify the maintenance of man-hour expenditure records that can later be used to substantiate the need for additional budgeted hours in the staffing of the department.

Maintenance work-request programs

Many times the quality and condition of a facility can be assessed by investigating the relationship that exists between the executive housekeeper and the chief engineer. When this relationship is positive and the people are mutually respectful of each other's responsibilities and workload, the physical appearance of a hotel will be excellent. When such positive relationships do not exist, property inspections will reveal little in addition to what might be expected—a substandard facility.

Specifically, the chief engineer is charged with the repair and physical maintenance of a hotel facility (maintenance not referring to guestroom servicing). The executive housekeeper is responsible for cleanliness and maintenance (servicing) of specific areas, The housekeeping department staff is much larger than the engineering department and is therefore in a better position to look for and find areas in need of repair and maintenance.

The major concern is to have a reporting and follow-up system between the two departments that allows for the orderly flow of information. The Maintenance Work-Request Form is composed of two soft copies and one hard copy and is serialized for easy reference when communicating about a reported discrepancy. The top copy (usually soft white) is filled out and kept by the department initiating the report; the other two copies are forwarded to engineering, where the request is logged in so that materials can be ordered and work scheduled.

When work is completed, the balance of the form is filled in and the second (soft blue) copy is returned to the initiating department for comparison and progressing of the original request. Work is then inspected, and, if completed satisfactorily, the soft (white and blue) Work Request Forms may be destroyed. The hard (bottom) copy remains with the engineering department as a record of time and materials expended. The system is simple, but in many cases it is not used in a manner that will ensure that repair and maintenance are property accomplished. The secret to a successful maintenance and repair program stems from understanding two important precepts: (1) the executive housekeeper will not be allowed to dictate the priorities of the chief engineer's workload, and (2) paper is cheap.

If the discrepancy is not corrected in a reasonable period of time, write it out again and mark it second request. Should there be a parts or material problem, the chief engineer may communicate this fact to the executive housekeeper and indicate that further Maintenance Work Request forms will be unnecessary.

Additionally, second requests might indicate that the priority of the engineer's workload precludes the immediate response to certain types of requests, or that the engineering department will schedule certain service requests with others of a similar nature (such as vinyl repairs, furniture repairs, and painting). Items that will cause a guestroom to be out of order should be given the highest priority by the chief engineer. If a property is to be kept in a proper state of repair, there will be an~

abundance of Maintenance Work Requests, many of which will be repeated. The age of a property will determine how many requests from the housekeeping department might be in the pipeline at any given time.

The prime consideration is remembering that personnel in the housekeeping department are the "eyes" of the engineering department in areas under the responsibility of the executive housekeeper and that everything nor in order and not cleanable must be repaired if the property is to be maintained in a like-new condition. The executive housekeeper must develop a system that fosters the writing of Maintenance Work Requests. It is best to require that a certain number of Maintenance Work Requests be written by the department each week. Such specific requirements help ensure that every defect has a chance of being reported. Examples of what should be reported are minor tears in hallway and room vinyl, chips and scratches in furniture, leaky faucets, broken lamp switches, and burned-out light bulbs (not under the purview of housekeeping). Areas in need of paint, noisy air conditioner, bad TV reception, minor carpet repair problems (seams coming unglued), doors that rattle when closed, and unsightly the caulking in bathtubs are also subject to Maintenance Work Requests.

Another system whereby 'the executive housekeeper and chief engineer would cooperate is combining the general cleaning program with the maintenance program. Clarence R. Johnson suggests that each month 25 percent of the rooms receiving a general deep cleaning should also receive a thorough maintenance inspection. Every room would therefore be completely checked three times a year and maintained in a near-perfect condition. Proper relationships inspiring mutual cooperation between the executive housekeeper and the chief engineer may at times be difficult to maintain. This usually stems from differences in background. This fact, however, should in no way detract from the *professional effort* necessary to make a relationship work for the good of the property. Gentle persistence and persuasion are usually the key and can cause strong relationships to grow.

Operational controls

Methods of conducting room inspections of guestrooms may take many forms. Additionally, room inspections may be given great, varied, or no emphasis, depending on the management style of the hotel's department heads and general managers. Some hotels employ inspectors and inspectresses—people whose only operational function is to inspect guest rooms and report their findings. Other hotels never inspect guestrooms, and still others have sophisticated inspection procedures. A project for students in a senior housekeeping management class in the Las Vegas area was for them to survey inspection techniques of several hotels. Students had to describe the results and effectiveness of the inspection programs they surveyed.

Certain hotels employed inspectors and inspectresses, others used floor supervisors to inspect every room before its being reported ready for occupancy, others had periodic room inspections by a general manager, and some had no inspection programs at all. Results were measured by the appearance and cleanliness of guestrooms inspected. Surprisingly, those hotels employing inspectresses did not fare well in the surveys; nor did hotels with elaborate inspection forms used regularly by supervisors. Hotels with well-maintained and very clean rooms were those that were intermittently inspected, or spot-checked, by people in the operational supervisory chain (floor supervisors, section managers, the executive housekeeper, sometimes GRAs, occasionally someone out side the department, and especially the hotel general manager). Inspection forms that stated simple and reasonable standards of performance were also in evidence in these hotels.

Inspectresses outside of the operational framework for cleaning guestrooms (floor supervisors and GRA's) risk nothing if they complain heavily about substandard items or conditions, since they would not be held accountable for correcting them. These inspectresses are therefore resented by those having to do the work. Human dynamics dictates that the inspectresses would be better liked if they did not complain heavily about discrepancies.

Floor supervisors who spot-check employees assigned to operational control are much more likely to find Solutions to substandard performance and, as a result, improve the performance of employees. Spot-checking two or three rooms each day from each section seems to give all the indication needed to bring about top-quality performance from each employee. Such action also allows each GRA to report her or his own rooms read), for reoccupancy, thus enriching the job and improving efficiency of communication between housekeeping and the front desk. There is also much to be said about displaying trust and confidence in employees, which is a great motivator for proper performance.

Additionally, most section housekeepers are proud of their work and look forward to exposing the results of their efforts to those in authority. It is for this reason that the executive housekeeper and the resident and/or general manager Should regularly inspect guestrooms. The importance of managers inspecting guestrooms regularly cannot be overemphasized. Not only is the inspection of the room paramount, but the opportunity for the manager to associate with his or her employees on the job is or great importance. There are over 600 employees in the housekeeping organization at the Excalibur Hotel in Las Vegas. Such a large number of employees can present a layering problem within the organization that might be hard to overcome.

There will always be a few problem employees, but those who are outstanding need the "positive stroke" of the manager who cares about his or her employees as individuals. When the work is well done, some well-placed humour helps to express warmth and acknowledge the value of a good employee. Such expectation of inspections by higher authority usually brings about an added emphasis on total work quality on inspection day and, as a result, tends to improve the appearance of each room cleaned.

A technique of inspection that has merit in areas in which specific employees are not performing up to standard is to let the GRA conduct the inspection in the presence of the designated inspector and supervisor. Specifically, the person inspecting invites the person who cleaned the room to inspect and report while the manager or Supervisor writes notes on the inspection form. This technique has proved enlightening to many GRAs who must, in the presence of their supervisor and manager, expose not only their questionable work but also their quality work. Inspection programs for guestrooms should be Conducted in such a way that quality performance is amply noted and publicized.

Programs involving "the housekeeper of the week" who earns points toward a meaningful prize over some given time period is effective in motivating employees to excel. GRAs must understand that their reputation as a GRA will never be better than the weakest of all GRAs in the department. This information reminds each of them that they need and must support each other to accomplish quality work and fosters commitment to standards. Another technique whereby room appearance and cleanliness can be made to flourish is with a team system of reward.

Performance systems were designed whereby each GRA was expected to clean 18 guestrooms in each eight-hour shift. There are programs whereby each team that properly finishes its work has rooms spot-checked by an outside supervisor or manager and, given proper results, is provided with an added incentive of leaving early and receiving credit for the full eight-hour shift. (This would only be allowed on a team basis, never on an individual basis; otherwise the team aspect of performance could be destroyed.)

Room inspections are essential to quality guestroom cleanliness and servicing and should be conducted regularly. The more efficient systems do not involve the total inspection of every guestroom cleaned. Spot inspections, properly recorded by floor supervisors, department managers, and the general manager have proven to be the most effective form of room inspection program. Recognition should be given for quality work, and work incentives should be created to encourage high-quality performances, especially team performance.

Total property inspections

If hotels are to be maintained as top quality facilities, it is not enough that the executive housekeeper inspect only guestrooms or, for that matter, be the only one who does inspect rooms. Not only does the entire property require a thorough, regular, and carefully orchestrated property inspection program, but guestrooms need to be looked at by more than one management person. A fresh look is needed to ensure that items viewed but not seen are eventually picked up for correction. Managers above the executive housekeeper in the table of organization may delegate the task of rooms maintenance to the executive housekeeper but may not abdicate their own responsibility of ensuring that the hotel is properly maintained. Other departments also have cleaning responsibilities.

The restaurant manager, bar manager, chef, and catering manager have large areas for which they are held accountable for proper cleaning, maintenance, and safe operation. The chief engineer may be held accountable for the entire outside area of the facility, including shrubs, grounds, and parking areas. There should be a manager responsible for every square foot, corner, and crack of the hotel. The Division of Work Document should in fact be used to establish a zone inspection program whereby every part of the property is identified and periodically looked at to ensure that proper maintenance, cleanliness, and safety of both space and operation are being maintained.

Finally the fresh look we mentioned not only brings another pair of eyes into an area, it also allows for orientation and development of management personnel in areas in which they may not normally be operationally involved. A property inspection that uses the front office manager to inspect housekeeping and the executive housekeeper to inspect kitchens is good training for future growth and development of managers for promotion and greater responsibilities.

Zone inspection

There are many inspections that might be conducted on a subroutine basis, but none should be more thorough and, as a result, more beneficial to total property maintenance than the zone inspection program. Zones are usually created by dividing the entire facility into equal parts, whereby each inspector is responsible for an equal workload in a given period of time. Zone inspections should be conducted in not more than three hours, otherwise they lose effectiveness. The inspection should be documented, and a technique must be developed whereby the person or persons responsible for each zone of the inspection may react to items found deficient and corrective measures taken before the next inspection. Documentation about unsafe conditions is also important.

Liability in claims regarding negligence may be greatly reduced if it can be shown through documentation that regular, thorough, and controlled inspections of an entire property are conducted and that there is adequate follow-up on significant items.

Weekly maintenance inspections

Although zone inspections are all encompassing for the entire property, there may be times when a particular zone is not inspected because of prior superior condition. This does not preclude public area portions of the rooms department from receiving a regular weekly maintenance inspection that is conducted by the senior housekeeping aide or a department manager.

Inventories

There are some subroutines related to ordering and keeping track of these inventories. Items of furniture, fixtures, and equipment (identified as FFE) along with software items (bedspreads and so on) form the basis of capital expenditures. These items have limited useful lives and are depreciated over several years. Other material items are operational in nature and are expended over much shorter business cycles (usually a four-week or monthly period); they are part of the cost of doing business in the production of revenue over the same period of time. Items such as cleaning supplies, guest supplies, and the amortized cost of basic bed and bath linens are among costs that occur monthly. Not only must the expenditure of such supplies and linens be expensed against revenue produced, such items that are on hand form the basis of balance sheet assets and must be periodically accounted for. Thus, use, balances on hand, and supply levels are critical control information that must be routinely maintained to ensure availability of materials when needed.

The cost of operations should include only that portion of inventory that has been used up during the period. Such costs should not include the value of amounts purchased but still on hand. Most hotel controllers agree that unopened cases of supplies on hand will be valued at full price in inventor),. Once a case is opened, however, items are considered expended. There may be exceptions to this rule, allowing departments to account for individual items remaining in storage in opened cases at full price. Individual items out of the main storeroom that can be sighted in satellite linen rooms may also be considered in inventory. Once established, whatever accounting systems are specified by the controller must be followed.

Storage

Operational supply storage rooms must be closely controlled and access to storerooms limited only to personnel in charge. Certain items of high unit cost or high usage such as speciality soaps might even warrant cage storage to prevent pilferage. Operations in which storage rooms are thrown open for the day usually have inordinate supply costs, and profits are proportionally affected. Tight storeroom controls are usually evidenced by cleaning supply costs that do not exceed three-tenths of 1 percent of revenues and guestroom supply costs that are within six-tenths of 1 percent.

Personnel utilization

Another important subroutine is the weekly (or

sometimes daily) forecasting of man-hour requirements-the most expensive operational cost in the entire rooms department. Executive housekeepers should be involved in the annual budgeting process (discussed later) whereby they help determine man-hour requirements based on budgeted occupancies. Once the budget has been established, it is imperative that a weekly forecast of expected man-hour utilization be developed and substantiated based on the weekly forecast of occupancy. Forecasts must be in line with expected occupancies and workload, or higher management must be notified.

The man-hours for supervisors in the model hotel are the total hours of the four team leaders, the linen room supervisor, the night supervisor, and the senior housekeeping aide (minus hours of those scheduled off). Planned number of hours for each day is listed. Hours are totalled both for the seven-day week for each wage department and for the four wage departments for each day. Forecast statistics are then compared with those budgeted to determine whether man-hour forecasts are in control. Once the forecast is prepared, it is submitted to top management, who evaluates whether planned operations for the upcoming week appear to be in control.

Weekly wage analysis

Not only should wages be forecast, but actual expenditures of man-hours should be analysed after the week has been completed. The information reflects actual expenditures, which should now be compared with the same week's forecast to evaluate forecast accuracy and to determine where variances may be occurring that may need adjusting.

In situations in which occupancies were not as predicted, the executive housekeeper would have made the necessary adjustments during the week through the Tight Schedule, which would compensate for actual occupancies being less than or more than expected. Note that Wednesday had been expected to be a 100 percent day but was not by a considerable amount. Adjustments were made to accommodate the lower occupancy, and GRA man-hours were adjusted to keep labour utilization in line, thereby keeping statistical targets in line. Executive housekeepers who do not forecast and analyse man-hour utilization run the risk of having uncontrollable wage costs telegraph the department into an favourable labour-cost situation for the year that cannot be recuperated.

Statement critiques

Period statements provide results of period operations, especially results in attempts to control costs during these operating periods. Efficient hotel organizations require that costs be kept in line with revenues and that statements be analysed to determine where unacceptable variations may be occurring.

Many hotel organizations require that statements be critiqued to determine where revenues and cost are out of prescribed tolerances. Critiques are usually required by top management within five days after statements are received. Typical standards for cost control may require that a critique be made at any time a cost variance is greater than one-tenth of 1 percent of revenue. Such critiques must explain why costs are out of tolerance and what will be done to bring them back into tolerance.

Purchasing

Purchasing is a subrouting that can take up a part of each day for the executive housekeeper. Even though some hotel chains have centralized national purchasing of items that bring quantity discounts, for the most part cleaning and guest supplies will be purchased either by the purchasing agent in the hotel (if there is one) or by the department heads for their respective departments. Considering the size and variability of the housekeeping cleaning, and guest supply inventory, there will be many suppliers and purveyors who will do their best to obtain the business from the executive housekeeper.

Suppliers can be outstanding allies in the conduct of services within the housekeeping department, or they can be outstanding nuisances. Competitively shopping for suppliers or vendors will simplify the question as to who will be used and for what products. A separate shopping form should be maintained for each and every product that is used in the cleaning and guest supply inventory. Product prices should be reviewed at least once every six months. Comments such as how well the vendor or purveyor services the account and how well products are understood and demonstrated by the vendor are significant when selecting vendors.

Price, although important, should not be the only criterion for selecting a product. Quality, suitability, storage requirements, and lot sizes each play an important part in making the right selection. It is not unusual to find that one vendor will be selected for all paper products, another vendor for cleaning chemicals, and another for mops, brooms, and the various and sundry items used in day-to-day cleaning. If the number of salespeople being dealt with can be limited, more efficient use of time is possible. Some suppliers call on the executive housekeeper on a weekly basis; others will call less often. Orders might be placed by phone, whereby suppliers will visit only occasionally to ensure that the account is being properly maintained. Periodic or drop shipments might be arranged, whereby the supplier rather than the hotel retains the storage problem.

There are two major areas of caution that need be mentioned at this point. Most suppliers budget funds to service the customer. Some will offer prizes and personal discounts to executive housekeepers for allowing them to have the hotel's account. Great caution is necessary to ensure that it is the hotel that is receiving the discount, not the executive housekeeper. Said more simply, watch out for offers of kickback. Every executive housekeeper should know and thoroughly understand company policy about accepting gifts before Christmas time or other periods of benevolence when suppliers are generous with their clients. Usually, hotel organizations have set guidelines about what should or should not be accepted.

Linens

In housekeeping operations the term "linens" normally refers to items associated with guestroom beds and bathrooms—sheets, pillowcases, bath towels, hand towels, washcloths, and fabric bathmats. Several subroutines concerning linens might be developed. Some might warrant simple policies and standard operating policies describing the movement of linens to and from the laundry and floor areas each day, whereas others might relate to routines involving condemnation, storage, repair, and normal care of linens. Linens rank second, next to wages, in departmental costs, For this reason, particular interest must be taken in the subroutines associated with the inventory and ordering of linens.

Linen inventories

The initial supply of house linens might be a part of preopening expenses, whereby initial requirements would be placed in position for operational use and amortized over an extended period. Replacement of this initial supply, however, is an operational expense. Because of relative costs (labour versus linens) the total supply of linens should never be so small as to cause employees to have to wait for linens to service rooms. Overall linen supplies therefore should be in amounts several times that required to cover all rooms one time (one par).

If the hotel has an on-premise laundry, an initial supply of linens includes the following:

1 par	*To cover all beds* and baths (after daily service is complete)
1 par	*Soiled* or just removed from beds and baths after daily service (tomorrow's workload for the laundry)
1 par	*Clean* and ready to use in servicing guestrooms the next day
1/2 par	*New*, in storage to be used as replacements when necessary
31/2 par	Total

If the property does not have an on-premise laundry, add one par for linen in transit to and from a commercial laundry. Because an unnoticed reduction in the supply of linens can cause a reduction in efficient service to guestrooms, physical linen inventories should be conducted regularly and accurate records should be maintained to ensure forewarning of additional needs.

Many hotels inventory linens monthly. In situations in which inventories are under good control and count systems are accurate, inventories may be conducted on a quarterly basis. Let us assume that a 3.5 par is to be maintained for the model hotel and that linen usage and control are stabilized, allowing for a quarterly inventory.

On days when inventories are conducted, special care must be taken to ensure that every piece of linen can be located for counting. Inventories should be conducted at the end of the normal work when linen movement is at a minimum. (After laundry has completed work, usually all guestroom regular servicing has been completed and each section housekeeper's linen cart has been loaded for the next day's routine.) The more employees involved in counting linens, the faster the inventory process can be completed. Additionally, when employees are involved in the actual count, they become more aware of the significance, importance, and value of the linen.

Each GRA counts linens loaded on his or her cart; supervisors count linens found on mobile linen trucks and shelves in satellite linen rooms. The linen room supervisor and assistant count all items found in the main linen room. Section housekeeping aides count linens on made-up roll-away beds. Laundry workers count soiled linen in the laundry, which will comprise the next day's laundry workload, as well as any clean linen that might be lingering after the day's workload has been completed. The senior housekeeping aide and assistants count new linen in storage.

When counting bed sheets, differentiation must be made in sizes of sheets. For convenience, other items not necessarily a part of linens, such as pillows, blankets, bedpads and bedspreads, might also be counted at this time. Where items were located when counted and who counted them at that location should be noted on the Count Sheet so that managers might audit certain counts. (It would not be unusual for the hotel controller to participate in the inventory by auditing certain count sheets.)

When counts have been completed, Count Sheets are collected and recorded in a Period Linen Inventory Count Record. The Count Record is used to compile all count sheets and record total linen in use and total new linen on hand. Once total counts have been determined, they are compared with the prior inventory to determine usages. The separation of linen in use and new linen is done to assign a proper value to the inventory. Most hotel operations will value new linen (linen in unopened boxes) at full price and linen in use at half price. Total linen valuation is thus determined as follows:

$$\left(\frac{\text{Linen in use} \times \text{Price}}{2}\right) + (\text{New linen x Price})$$

$$= \text{Linen valuation}$$

Care should be taken in counting linen to ensure that unexplained growths do not occur in specific items. For example, a prior inventory indicates 1000 double sheets on hand. Between inventory periods there were 500 double sheets purchased. Total availability of double sheets thus should not exceed 1500. A current inventory, however, reveals that 1724 double sheets are now on hand, giving an unexplained growth of 224 sheets. When such growth occurs, either the prior inventory or the current inventory is suspect, requiring that a recount be made. When such unexplained growths occur, inventories need to be conducted more frequently until inventory subsystems are under control.

Linen purchases

Linen inventories reveal the need for purchases, and there are many linen brokers who gladly service this type of need. When linen must be purchased from a linen broker, however, it should be expected that a premium will be paid. Savings of up to one-third may be available when the services of a linen broker are not used and linens are purchased directly from linen mills. Direct purchases from mills require long-range planning and purchase arrangements contracted up to 1½ years in advance, allowing the mill to produce ordered linens at their convenience.

A linen order for double sheets (DS) is to be

developed on 30 June and will be initiated on 1 January for the upcoming year, said order to be drop shipped on a quarterly basis during the year the order is in effect. The 3.5 par value of DS is given at 2000. On 30 June, inventory counts reveal 1750 DS on hand (250 short of 3.5 par). Shortly after the 30 June inventory, a drop shipment (prior order) of 500 DS is expected to arrive that will raise the count of DS to 2250.

Prior quarterly shortages indicate that a forecast shortage in September may be expected, but a second drop shipment of 250 DS (already ordered) will again arrive that will return the inventor), count on I October to a value of about 1950 DS. A similar quarterly usage is then forecast for the final quarter of the year, creating a forecast shortage on 31 December of 225 sheets. An order may now be created on 30 June, which will include annual usage (four prior quarterly shortages) plus the shortage forecast to exist on 31 December. This annual order may then be divided into four quarterly drop shipments and the order placed directly with a mill a full six months before the effective commencement of the order. Hence the formula

Linen on hand (today) + Linen expected to arrive (prior orders) - Shortage (-expected at the end of the current order) - Annual usage - 3.5 par = future order (a negative number)

Order/4 × case lot size = expected quarterly drop shipments to commence six months hence

The preplanned purchase of linens for future use can produce great economics of operation. Whereas linen brokers are available and willing to fill linen needs, the profits made by Such brokers represent true cost savings for housekeeping departments who order linens directly from mills. Linen brokers should therefore be used only in an emergency.

Personnel administration

Another subroutine requiring the daily attention of management is time card control. Employees should be counselled at the time of employment as to how many hours Constitute the work shift each day. Some organizations specify an eight-hour Shift, including time off for work breaks and lunch. Others require that employees clock out for lunch, thus leaving them on their own time for lunch.

A housekeeping operation may be arranged in such a way as to have employees on the property for 8½ hours, including two work breaks of 15 minutes each on company time, but require the employee to clock out for lunch, creating a net eight-hour workday. The above arrangement is specified; however, employees are still required to punch a time clock at the beginning and end of each shift, as well as clock out for lunch and back in after lunch. Federal regulations require that time card records be maintained on each employee to guarantee fair wage administration.

Some employees, although understanding that their shifts begin at 8:00 A.M., may clock in early (7:45) and then expect to be paid for all time worked as indicated on the time card. Employees must not be allowed to enter times on a time card indiscriminately and expect to be paid for these times. It therefore behooves department managers to set specific ground rules about overtime and the time spread in which employees may punch in and out each day.

Then, should employees be available and needed before the normal working day, they may be asked to clock in earl), and can expect to be paid for this early time; otherwise, clock-ins between 7:55 and 8:05 A.M. will be considered 8:00 A.M. clock-ins. Similar policies apply to clock-out times. Many hotels have two time card racks for each employee; one is for time cards when employees are off the property, and the other is for time cards when employees are on the clock. In large operations, quick note of where the time card is located can determine whether or not ail employee is actually at work. While the employee is on the property, there should be a record of a clock-in with no clock-out yet showing. During this time, managers can audit clock times on cards from the previous day and indicate the number of hours that are to be paid based on the punched indications. This allows employees to note exactly how many hours they may expect to be paid for the previous day. Any questions that arise may then be immediately resolved. Also, indications of overtime authorization can be noted.

Note the pencilled indications wherein the manager has audited the card and indicated the amount of time for which the employee will be paid. On Wednesday the early punch, and hence overtime, was authorized. On Tuesday, overtime was not authorized and the employee may need to be reminded of rules and procedures for clocking in and out. This type of audit of time worked by employees is a subroutine that should be done on a daily basis. It is easy to audit time cards using a 24-hour time clock that records hours and hundredths of hours.

Payroll administration

The proper payment of wages due an employee is a matter requiring great attention to detail by the department manager. Employees have a right and do expect to be paid for work performed. It is therefore vital that department managers ensure that hours worked during a given workweek be properly recorded on time sheets from which actual pay will be calculated.

Time sheets are normally given to department managers by the payroll department before the end of each workweek. Time sheets contain an alphabetical listing of all employees on the payroll. Employees hired after time sheets are originated may be added.

Assuming there has been a daily audit of time cards at the conclusion of the workweek, the time cards must be totalled and their values entered on time sheets, which will be submitted to the personnel department timekeeper or paymaster. Weekly time sheets indicate the number of hours for which employees will be paid. Days off are also indicated so that no blanks are noted for any day; special forms of pay are entered where appropriate. Items such as sick pay, vacation pay, total regular time, overtime, and wage rates are entered, as are the wage department classification under which the employee is to be paid.

Some employees may have a secondary job code for which they may be paid at a secondary rate. For example, the section housekeeper in wage department (07) may work one day during the week as a relief for a senior housekeeper in wage department (02). The employee should then be paid at the higher wage rate for that particular day. After all time has been correctly recorded, summaries of information are included on Weekly Wage Analysis reports.

Proper wage administration includes orientation of the employee in understanding when wages will be paid. Given a workweek that runs from Saturday through Friday, time sheets would normally be prepared at the end of work on Friday. Lapse time, which ranges from 5 to 10 days, is required to prepare checks. Depending on methods of payroll preparation, pay due an employee for the week ending Friday, June 5, for example, may not be presented until Wednesday, June IS, creating what is known as time in the hole.

The employee must be counselled at the onset of employment that pay for work completed on the upcoming Friday of the first week worked will not be received until Wednesday, 10 days hence. Even though this procedure may be burdensome for some employees, it is better to have a payday far enough delayed to guarantee that paychecks will be available on the stated payday than have earlier stated paydays that are not met due to late arrival of paychecks. Late paychecks tend to produce major uproars and should be avoided.

Employees need to understand that upon termination of employment, pay owed will be received and termination will not affect amounts owed. Employees who quit their jobs should expect to wait for scheduled paydays to receive their pay. It is best if employees who are terminated by the company be paid off immediately with a special paycheck in order that they need not return to the property after termination. Since the department manager is controlling the employee's working time and pay, the passing out of paychecks is the department manager's responsibility, which should not be passed on to any other department (such as the personnel department).

Employees whose names appear on time sheets for which no pay is entered constitute two categories of personnel; those on legal and granted leaves of absence (LOA) and those who have been terminated but for which no terminating paperwork has been received by the payroll division. This latter category requires the immediate attention of the department manager to ensure that time sheets do not contain the names of employees who no longer work for the company. The subroutine of time sheet preparation is a tedious and time-consuming one requiring great attention to detail.

With proper training, however, the task can be delegated on a rotating basis to all department supervisory personnel. An authenticating signature of the department manager (or acting manager) should be required on all time sheets.

Performance appraisals

One Subroutine that must never be neglected is performance appraisals of all employees within the department. Every employee has a right to know management's expectations and to receive appraisals of how well responsibilities and tasks are being carried out. Performance appraisals should be conducted at stated intervals and at other times when appropriate. The first regular appraisal occurs at the end of a probationary period of employment. Employees are usually hired for probationary periods, which may last from there to six months.

An employee should be notified at the end of probationary periods that his or her performance has been satisfactory and that he or she is now considered a full-time permanent, temporary, or pool employee in good standing. Or the employee should have been advised well in advance of the end of the probationary period that the performance was lacking. Managers who wait until the end of a probationary period to inform an employee that performance has been unacceptable are being insensitive to the human dynamics of supervisory responsibilities.

Routine performance appraisals should occur at stated intervals. After successfully completing periods of probationary performance, the time of the next performance appraisal should be made known to the employee (usually one year hence). When probationary periods are successfully concluded it should be presumed that the employee is capable of performing the task assigned properly. Failure to continue to perform in a like manner is an indication of unsatisfactory performance and becomes worthy of a special performance evaluation.

When performance is noted as being routinely outstanding, it should also be made the subject of a special performance evaluation. Satisfactory and outstanding performance evaluations should offer consideration of pay increases in accordance with company policy.

Assuming that an employee has successfully passed from a probationary status, a raise in pay is appropriate. One year later, given satisfactory performance, another pay increase might be expected. Many companies have pay scales that allow for a start rate, base rate, one-year rate, and maximum rate for each job classification. For example, for the GRA the following rates might apply:

Start rate	$9.50/hour
Base rate	$10.00/hour
One-year rate	$10.50/hour
Maximum rate	$12.50/hour

The start rate is applied when the person begins employment. Given satisfactory performance at the end of a three-month probationary period, pay will be increased to the base rate. Satisfactory performance throughout the year warrants an additional pay increase at the end of the year if for no other reason than inflation. The same might occur for the next three years.

Upon reaching the maximum rate, no further increases may be obtained, other than for changes in wage scales due to cost-of-living increases or promotion increases. Essentially satisfactory performances warrant standard increases to the limit specified by the type of work performed, not years in service in a specific job category. The wage scale might be expected to increase each year due to cost-of-living increases, not seniority. To achieve better-than-standard wage increases, the worker must be above average or be promoted to the next higher classification.

Technique of performance appraisal

Performance appraisals should be personal between the manager and the employee. The manager may consult with other supervisors, but the actual appraisal should come only from one of the department managers.

The human resources department helps the executive housekeeper recall when performance appraisals are due on each employee by pulling the most recent PAF and sending it to the housekeeping department. The subroutine of performance appraisal requires action when such appraisals are sent to the department (usually within one week). A set time each week might be scheduled for writing and presenting these appraisals to employees.

The appraisal form requires the following:

1. A statement of observed strengths
2. An indication of whether objectives assigned have been met
3. A statement of observed weaknesses. (It is highly doubtful that an employee's performance will be perfect. Weaknesses therefore should be noted in order that the employees know where they need improvement. A performance appraisal indicating no weaknesses is an implied statement that improvement cannot be made in any aspect of performance.)
4. A statement of counselled action-what the employee should do to improve performance and what the employer will do to assist
5. An estimate of when the employee should be ready for promotion (does not guarantee that promotion will be gained)

Once the appraisal has been prepared, a conference with the employee should be scheduled. The written appraisal is used to discuss the employee's performance. After discussion and assured understanding, the employee should sign the appraisal as an acknowledgment that he or she has in fact received the appraisal and is aware of the meaning of its contents. The signature is not an acknowledgment of the accuracy of the contents of the appraisal, only that it has been received and understood as the appraiser's view.

The employee should then be allowed to comment in writing in the space provided on the appraisal. Should the appraisal warrant an increase in pay, such notation would be made on the front side of the PAF as should a notation-as to when the next appraisal is due.

Special appraisals

Special appraisals should be conducted in a similar manner as regular appraisals, except that the occasion would be to either note routinely outstanding performances or substandard performances. Poor performance should be appraised before the employee's performance becomes unsatisfactory. This allows for corrective action before the possibility of termination. The PAF, may be used to document that a verbal warning has been issued or to document an official written warning. When poor or questionable performance must be appraised, a technique known as levelling should be used. The levelling technique is carried out as follows:

1. Conduct levelling sessions on a one-to-one basis. There are rare exceptions when a third person should be present to validate conditions or observations; one-on-one is usually more open and conducive to agreement and future commitment.
2 Be completely honest and straightforward. Do not

use the levelling technique if less than total honesty is contemplated.

3. Deal with the problem as soon as possible. Immediate action is much better than delayed action. Delays in dealing with a problem infer a weakness on the part of management and a lack of willingness to deal with unpleasant issues when they occur in hopes that problems will go away. They usually do not.
4. Set up the room so that nothing is between the evaluator and the employee. Move out from behind a desk and sit as an equal with the employee. Do not stand while the employee sits, or vice versa.
5. Go immediately to the problem. No small talk or jokes are appropriate.
6. Send "I" messages. "I" messages show concern without inferring that the employee is necessarily a bad person. Statements such as "I am concerned about your repeated tardiness for work" or "I am troubled because you are having difficulty adjusting to your fellow workers" are not so likely to put the employee on the defensive but will likely cause the person to open up and talk about problem areas.
7. Give honest positive reinforcement when deserved, but never patronize.
8. Listen. Half of communication requires listening, understanding meanings, and determining where people are coming from when they talk.
9. Avoid references to past mistakes if they are not relevant to current issues. (Past mistakes should have been dealt with in the past. It is *now that counts.)*
10. Arrive at a mutual decision or understanding as to what future actions or behaviour may be expected.
11. Reconfirm understandings by providing written

notes of discussions and decided actions; do this for the record and provide a copy of such notes to the employee (may be a copy of a written warning).

12. Keep the entire encounter professional and free of emotion on the part of the evaluator. Should the employee become emotional, allow the employee to calm clown before proceeding with the appraisal.

Employee performance appraisal is one of the most important aspects of personnel administration in which the executive housekeeper will become involved. A manager gets things done through people. TO understand this requires a commitment to the understanding of human dynamics and a desire to be a professional in the task of supervision.

Communication and training

Good management requires an absolute understanding of proper delegation and how such delegation brings about commitment and involvement on the part of employees. Successful commitment cannot be attained by being secretive about matters that employees have a need to know out of concern for jobs to be performed or about matters that they want to know, which indicate that employee performance is contributing to the success of the company Commitment and involvement stem from thorough orientation, individualized training, and regular meetings through which the employees get the word.

Departmental meetings

On a regular basis (at least monthly), departmental meetings should be scheduled. They should be interesting, informative, and productive. Praise for jobs well done is always appropriate in departmental meetings where individual praiseworthy performances may be recognized in front of others. Announcements about upcoming events and the success (or failure) of past events are appropriate, as well as management observations about certain happenings.

A portion of meetings should be devoted to the presentation and discussion of new hotel policies, as well as the regular and periodic review of existing policies. Guest comments as to service (both good and bad) need to be presented; however, specific comments about poor individual performance arc best presented in private. Meetings should allow time for questions from employees, whereby management may learn about matters concerning employees.

The executive housekeeper should allow junior managers and supervisors to chair meetings but should always be present to convey management's control over meetings. Team leaders should conduct regular (simplified) meetings with team members, keep notes of such meetings, and discuss the results with the executive housekeeper.

Long-range planning

There are many cases in which budgets are presented to executive housekeepers that dictate how much labour and supplies will be expended in the performance of tasks. Such budgets, which originate with top management and are handed clown, seldom draw the commitment of operational managers because little or no planning was contributed at the department level. The participation of the executive housekeeper in formulating the operational budget for the house keeping department is essential if managers are to commit themselves to successful accomplishment of the long-range plan known as the budget.

Top management must be involved in the budgeting process: Company expectations should be stated and national trends analysed; criteria should be established regarding standards to be met in the use of supplies; marketing plans must be finalized for the upcoming year; and budget guidance is essential. Once these tasks are done, however, each department of the hotel should begin the task of assembling from a zero base, requirements for the expenditure of man-hours, materials, and money to produce the service or product that will be creating revenue.

After identifying expected sales and related costs, top management should critique the budget, indicating where adjustments must be made in order that company or corporate objectives will be met. If modification of the budget is necessary, it should be revised by the operating departments until agreement is reached.

The operational budget cycle usually requires several months from the onset of planning until critiques and adjustments are finalized. The budgeting process must therefore be begun well in advance of the beginning of the budget (fiscal) year. Operational budgets usually reflect periods of the fiscal year. Some hotel operating budgets are constructed with each of the 12 months reflecting a period. Other systems reflect 13 (28-day) periods, each of which is made up of four consecutive weeks. The 13-period system seems most appropriate because periods will start on the first day of a scheduled workweek and will end on the last day of the following fourth workweek. It allows for the comparison of revenues and costs on a consistent basis each period.

Budget periods based on calendar months create two months out of 12 where an extra payday will Occur, causing a distorted comparison of wage cost against revenues. Such distortion will not occur in 13-period systems. In addition, set days of each period will always occur on the same days of the week in each period, allowing for systematic comparisons of similar days. For example, assume that workweeks begin on Saturdays and end on Fridays. The first day of every period will then occur on a Saturday. The sixteenth day of every period will similarly always be the third Sunday of each period. Except for special holiday periods, hotel revenues and resultant costs of operations will more likely reflect similarity by days of the week than any other statistical criteria.

Each budget planning cycle is commenced by those involved in budgeting room sales. Schedules indicating the volume of room sales to be expected on each day of the upcoming year are prepared and finalized before operational cost budgeting is begun by any department affected by fluctuating occupancy (such as housekeeping).

Most schedules of expected: room sales will also show a comparison of the upcoming budget year with the existing year in order that growth can be analysed. Not only will growth in the sale of guestrooms be significant, but changes in average room rate and expected period revenues will later prove significant in the development of statistical targets for the housekeeping department.

Since man-hour utilization represents the highest housekeeping cost of operation, the greatest detail in justification will be required in the development of man-hours to be expended. Recall that man-hours for the various types of work performed within the housekeeping department arc classified for accounting purposes. In our earlier example, man-hours worked by GRAs were classification, hours worked by section housekeeping aides were, those worked by supervisory personnel were, and those worked by public area, linen room and utility personnel do not fluctuate and are therefore classified as fixed hours. Other classifications of man-hours to be performed in a rooms department include front office personnel, which would be under the control of the front office manager. The executive housekeeper needs to explain how man-hour requirements are established for each wage department. Usually a standard form for man-hour justification is prepared and included as part of the budget submission package.

The executive housekeeper man-hours will be required to service this Occupancy for the model hotel. Statements about method of operation as related to the GRA wage department (07) are based on the least number of man-hours that will accomplish the servicing of budgeted occupied guestrooms. Note that night operations are identified separately; training costs are also identified separately but are not included at this point. Training cost will be added with other property training costs and summarized separately. In the example, it is estimated that four employees will be replaced each period at a training cost of 24 nonproductive hours per employee replaced per period.

If a critique challenge is made by top management to the detail expressed in the budget justification, a clear statement as to what service will be discarded or downgraded before hours can be reduced must be made. If profits must be increased but services maintained at the level specified in budget justifications, average room rates would have to be increased to improve revenues and resultant profits. Such may be the topic of discussion during budget critiques.

The budgeting of other controllable items, although not as detailed as man-hours, will require the same effort. Note the format by which current year actuals and projections through the end of the current year are compared with next year's budget. The final budget is divided into six parts: total sales, total salaries and wages, total employee costs, total controllables, control profit, and statistics. The presentation of wage cost is by wage department, the balance of which has now been added for the entire rooms department.

The total employee costs refer to costs over and above salaries and wages, including benefits averaging about 20 percent of salary and wage cost. Controllables refer to the various supply cost accounts where monies will be needed. Not all cost accounts fall under the purview of the executive housekeeper, but those that do are obvious. They include cleaning supplies, guest supplies, laundry expenses, linen costs, and parts of several other accounts, including general expense. Each controllable cost may also be expressed as a percentage of revenue. For example, cleaning supplies might approximate three-tenths of 1 percent of revenue and guest supplies approximate six-tenths of 1 percent of revenue. Such statistics have a tendency to vary with type of hotel, type of market, expectations for excellence, and other specific factors.

Once the budget has been developed, it will be critiqued as we described earlier. Once approved, the major long-range operational plan is now in place for the upcoming year. As the budgeted year progresses, period statements will be produced by the accounting department in a form almost identical to that expressed in the budget. New actual costs are next to what has been budgeted. The executive housekeeper is expected to explain any serious negative deviations from the plan and how these deviations will be corrected. This type of control is one of the major challenges to expert professional housekeeping.

3

Lodging Operations

Lodging establishments can be classified by size and type of service, ranging from the small, humble bed-and-breakfast inn to the colossal megahotels and resorts that offer luxurious accommodations and services. These lodging properties can be independently owned, franchised, or run by management companies. Students in hotel and restaurant management programs must be aware of the advantages and disadvantages of working for small companies as well as for multi-unit corporations.

Lodging operations are an intrinsic part of the hospitality trade and perhaps the most important of the segments into which this industry is divided. To lodge means to furnish guests with room or quarters, generally on a temporary basis. This broad definition implies that the lodging industry is quite diverse, for the renting of living space can range from a simple room in a boarding house to a spacious suite in a luxury hotel or a bungalow in a lavish resort.

Since the beginning of recorded time, people have travelled and therefore have been in need of lodging. For instance, the excavated ruins of Pompeii in Italy include houses of rest and solace where, as long ago as 79 A.D., wayfarers and seamen of the time were able to relax and be entertained for a fee. Lodging facilities that were used for economic purposes were built along transportation routes where travelling parties found it convenient to make rest stops en route to their destinations. In Marco Polo's time, rest areas were strategically placed at a distance of a day's ride by caravan. Polo was able to travel from Venice to the Mongol Empire of Kublai Khan in Central Asia by making scheduled stops along the way, where food and safe shelter were available.

Chaucer's Canterbury Tales, written around 1390 in England, contains lively descriptions of inn-keeping practices of the time. In Don Quixote, many of Cervantes' ideals are put into practice at an inn in La Mancha, Spain. What we know today as inns had their origin in England some centuries ago, the term meaning "a public house that provides lodging for travellers and others." These taverns with rooms for rent were usually located along highways to provide a convenient overnight stay for those travelling by coach.

The introduction of railways in the nineteenth century created the need for a large number of these hostelries along the numerous lines that crisscrossed the country. Today, the term inn implies a small hotel, although properties called "inns" often contain a large number of rooms; for example the Holiday Inn Crowne Plaza in New Orleans has 439 guestrooms.

The term hotel derives from the French hostel. The modern French word hotel suggests "a more or less commodious establishment with up-to-date appointments," though this was not necessarily true one hundred years ago. Today, the term hotel defines a lodging establishment offering accommodation, food and beverage, and amenities to guests.

The New Orleans' Windsor Court Hotel, which consumers have rated as one of the best hotels in the United States, advertises meeting facilities, outdoor pool, health club, ballrooms, concierge services, five-diamond dining room, chamber music, and 24-hour suite service. Nightly rates at the Windsor Court range from $320 for regular guestrooms to $990 for two-bedroom suites.

The first spas were operated in Europe and consisted of resorts located by mineral springs, which were believed to have curative powers. Today, spas offer a wide array of health-related services ranging from curative massage and mud baths to weightloss programs.

Types of lodging establishments

Besides hotels, motels and resorts the lodging industry today offers a variety of establishments aimed at fulfilling the needs of the current market. The most common are:

— Bed and Breakfast Inns

— Time-Share Condominiums

— Cruise Ships

— Institutional Lodging Establishments

— Casinos

Bed-and-breakfast inns are usually small, privately owned establishments located in suburban and rural locations. They are often uniquely appointed converted private homes that cater to travellers seeking a homey, personal environment.

Time-share condominiums are apartments, villas, or bungalows usually built near popular vacation spots (such as ski resorts, beaches, or Disney World, for example) that are sold to individual owners who use them or rent them out to transient guests. Time-share owners also have the option of trading with other owners of units located in different parts of the country or the world.

Cruise ships can be described as floating luxury hotels/ resorts that provide most of the same services and amenities as properties located on land. Having become quite popular in the vacation and convention markets, cruise ships are one of the fastest growing segments of the hospitality industry.

Institutional lodging is provided by housing facilities that are integral parts of institutional organizations, such as hospitals, retirement homes, universities, and colleges. In some cases this type of lodging requires limited services, such as weekly cleaning or catered meals, which are provided by contracting companies.

With the adoption of gaming by a large number of Native American tribes, casinos have grown in popularity in many states of the United States. Casinos are generally first-class hotels that provide elaborate facilities for gambling, ranging from the ubiquitous slot machine to the sophisticated baccarat or roulette tables. These highly profitable establishments often offer luxurious lodging and lavish entertainment at low cost to attract potential customers.

Lodging properties can be independently owned, owned by a multi-unit chain, franchised, or managed by a management company.

Properties that are independently owned are not affiliated with any multiple -property entity and are usually managed by their owners. This type of property still represents the largest segment of the lodging industry.

A typical in dependently owned establishment is small in size and is located in a relatively small community. There are advantages and disadvantages to independent operation: on the positive side, independent lodging establishments can provide guests with unique, personalized service while saving royalty and management fees that otherwise would have to be paid to franchisors and/or management companies.

On the negative side, such properties may not have name recognition to travellers, they lack collective advertising power, and they are unable to benefit from a national/international reservation system.

Often, independently owned and managed properties join reservation referral systems and marketing associations, such as Best Western International, Leading Hotels and Resorts, or Utell International.

Chain properties operate under the direct control of the chain's headquarters. Establishments belonging to the same chain display the same logo and offer identical services by category.

For instance, a Hilton four-star hotel must provide similar service and amenities whether it is located in Florida or in Oregon. This assures guests of consistency in price, room layout, menus, sports facilities, and so on. There exist a large number of chains in the world, such as Ritz Carlton and Loews in the United States, Four Seasons in Canada, and Grupo Sol Melia in Spain.

An effective way for owners of lodging properties to take advantage of the marketing and central reservation power of chain systems is to contract the right to conduct business displaying the logo of the chain by franchising. However, once the franchise is granted, the franchisee must comply with the corporation's requirements regarding service and amenities to be provided to guests. When hotel owners lack the operative expertise necessary to manage their properties efficiently, they may choose to contract with a management company. In this case, the owner signs a contract delegating the property's operations to such a company in exchange for either paying a basic fee or allowing the management company to retain an agreed-upon percentage of the revenue or income, or a combination of the two.

Classification by size

Lodging facilities can also be categorized by size. An arbitrary classification can be:

— *Small*: up to 75 rooms

— *Medium*: from 75 to 200 rooms

— *Large*: from 200 to 500 rooms

— *Very large*: more than 500 rooms

The size of a property can be used to estimate the amount of work required of the housekeeping department on a daily basis to maintain the property. For instance, while a 100-room property can be serviced with a relatively small number of housekeeping employees, the Sheraton Hotel & Towers in New York City, with 1,750 rooms, will require over one hundred section housekeepers to service the guestrooms at 100 percent occupancy.

Classification by type of service

Lodging properties can also be categorized by service. Economy or budget properties focus on meeting the basic needs of the travelling public-that is, clean, comfortable rooms that are not expensive.

The market segments typically attracted to economy properties are guests travelling with children, bus tours, and budget-minded retirees. Many of these properties do not offer food and beverage services except for breakfast, although they all feature TV and some have a swimming pool, whirlpool, and tennis courts.

Mid-market properties offer all the amenities expected in a "home -away-from -home setting." Restaurants, coffee shops, bars, luggage service, meeting rooms, health club, and room service are generally offered in such properties. The quality of bed linen, towels, room furniture, lobby decor, and customer service must be good or very good.

Travellers who frequent properties of this type are business people, individual tourists, conventioneers, and guests wishing to receive a guaranteed level of excellent service. Often, mid-market properties feature suites that consist of a bedroom, adjacent living room, and a kitchenette with refrigerator. Suites are very appealing to families with children or to two couples travelling together.

Luxury properties offer world-class service, which includes any type of convenience that would be expected by any traveller in any country in the world. Committed to the ultimate in hospitality, luxury properties may feature extravagant amenities like Godiva or other imported chocolates, speciality toiletry items, slippers, silk robes, and special services like executive floors, concierge, foreign language translators, nanny, and private secretary.

The American Automobile Association (AAA) is the most common rater of lodging establishments in the United States. As a service to its members, this organization provides travel guides that are updated annually describing the properties and evaluating their services.

The ratings are determined by field inspectors who base their decisions on thorough evaluations of the properties' design, decor, fittings, comfort, and of their levels of service, cleanliness and upkeep. In general,

AAA awards three diamonds to economy establishments while mid-market properties are assigned four diamonds. Invariably, luxury hotels and resorts receive a rating of five diamonds. In some countries, an official branch of the government performs the classification of lodging properties to ensure that the quality of their lodging establishments is consistent.

Housekeeping department

A characteristic common to all lodging establishments, regardless of size and category, is the need for housekeeping services, which can range from very sophisticated to a simple matter of "refreshing" rooms once a week.

For instance, a luxury hotel, casino, or resort usually requires that the rooms be impeccably clean, that the bed linen is changed every time the bed is used, and that turndown service is provided daily. On the other hand, the service for a university residence room might consist in just providing the tenant with a fresh set of sheets every Monday morning.

Mid-range service hotels generally require that guestrooms are thoroughly cleaned daily, that bed and bathroom linen is changed every day, and that 24-hour housekeeping service is provided seven days a week. In any case, because housekeeping services must always be provided, the management of the housekeeping department in every lodging establishment is of critical importance to the success of the property.

It is essential that future graduates of hospitality programs understand the options that the industry offers regarding housekeeping management positions. Graduates wishing to achieve the position of executive housekeeper in a relatively short period of time should keep in mind that a small or medium-sized property does generally offer the best opton for candidates to reach their goal. In large or very large establishments, where housekeeping operations are quite complex, it will take longer for candidates to become managers of the department.

In any case, the position of executive housekeeper will always be a challenging and rewarding one as well as an adequate springboard from which to work toward the goal of becoming the property's general manager.

When looking for their first job, hospitality graduates should understand the difference between working for properties that are independently or chain-owned, franchised, or run by management companies.

An independently owned establishment might not offer substantial opportunities for advancement, as the owners do not usually have any other properties. In this case, the waiting period for reaching an executive position can be a long one.

On the other hand, chains offer limitless job opportunities, as these corporations generally expand nationally and internationally by building new places or merging with other companies. If a management company manages a large number of properties, the possibilities for advancing could be as large as those offered by chains.

However, it is not unusual for these companies to be rather small, in which case not many openings will occur regularly. Often, independent operators own franchised properties. In this case working for a "Marriott" or "Sheraton" hotel doesn't mean that you will be working for these corporations, as the owners have merely contracted with the chains the right to display their commercial names.

The room division

Lodging is an integral part of the hospitality industry. Hospitality involves the reception of guests and the provision of services to them with liberality and kindness. The task of providing hospitality and services to guests in a friendly and efficient manner falls mainly on the property's rooms division. The overall success of an operation depends on the profitability of the rooms division, which generally accounts for a large share of a hotel's sales while generating a gross profit percentage from 70 to 80 percent of the revenue.

Besides providing lodging, and professional services such as check in, luggage handling, and room upkeep, rooms division personnel must provide the "home-away from-home" feeling so cherished by travellers who are temporarily separated from their families.

Offering tastefully decorated guestrooms and public areas and impeccable cleanliness in a subdued, relaxing atmosphere is also of the utmost importance.

Large properties are divided into operational units called divisions. Two of these divisions-Rooms, and Food and Beverage are revenue-generating centers, while the others are considered to be support centers.

The executive in charge of the rooms division is the Rooms Division Director, who in some properties may be called resident manager, executive manager, or senior assistant manager.

The rooms division director reports directly to the property's general manager. As a member of the executive committee, the rooms division director takes an active part in policy-making decisions related to operations. Other members of this committee generally include: the Food and Beverage Director, in charge of the food and beverage division; the Sales Director, who deals with sales, marketing, and public relations; the Controller or chief financial officer; the Human Resources Director, in charge of personnel matters; and the Plant Manager, responsible for the engineering and maintenance needs of the property.

Of the rooms division, which is divided into departments, the front office and housekeeping departments are of critical importance to the property. The Executive Housekeeper is the head of housekeeping and is therefore directly responsible for managing what is in most cases the largest department of the establishment.

The position of executive housekeeper in the organizational chart is that of department head, equal in rank to the front office manager, the security manager, and the remaining managers in charge of departments in other divisions.

In smaller properties, the division directors do not exist; instead, department heads manage the different units and report directly to the general manager.

The housekeeping department is an integral part of all the areas into which a lodging operation is divided. Although housekeeping's primary communication takes place with the front office and engineering departments, a strong relationship must exist with an the other units of the property as well.

For instance, room service, a department in the food and beverage division that delivers food to guestrooms, must be in direct contact with housekeeping for the removal of trays and carts. The sales department, which often must have access to ready rooms to be shown to meeting planners or tour operator representatives, must communicate this need to the housekeeping department.

Communication with the front office

Guestrooms in lodging properties are sold by the front office. The front desk must know at every given moment what rooms have been cleaned and are available for occupancy. Housekeeping must provide the front desk with a listing of rooms that are ready for occupancy so guests can be checked in.

If the communication between the two departments is poor or breaks down, delays in guest checking will occur or people will be checked into rooms that are thought to be ready but that in fact are occupied or not ready. If this happens often, the property's reputation will suffer.

The cycle of communication begins early each day, when the front desk provides the housekeeping department with a written (or computer-generated) report called the night clerk's room report.

The purpose of this report is to inform the housekeeping department very early in the morning of the status of all guestrooms in the property as it appears on the front desk records.

The housekeeping employee in charge of opening the house transfers the information received from the front desk into forms to be distributed to the housekeeping supervisors who, in turn, will notify the room attendants before they begin to work in their respective sections.

As guests check in and out of the hotel throughout the day, the front desk notifies housekeeping. As rooms are cleaned, housekeeping notifies the front desk that rooms are available for selling. As soon as it is possible, an *A.M. guestroom check* is performed by housekeeping to ascertain whether the information provided in the night clerk's report was accurate.

When discrepancies are found between the status of rooms received from the night clerk and the physical inspection of the rooms, the front desk is immediately notified. For instance, if the front desk reports that a certain room is vacant and housekeeping finds it occupied, a discrepancy exists and the front desk should be notified. There are several reasons why discrepancies may occur. The most common are:

— A guest switches from one room to another and the front desk neglects to change its records.

— An error is made by the night clerk when filling out the night clerk's report.

— A guest is given the wrong room key by mistake.

— The room is used by an unauthorized employee.

— The room is sold by the front desk without being recorded, and the money is pocketed by the clerk.

— A guest checks in or out between the time the report is made and the check is conducted.

The *P.m. room check* is conducted by the housekeeping department just before the end of the morning shift. This guestroom check consists of entering every room in the house at approximately the same time in order to generate a report showing the status of all guestrooms. The report is brought to the front desk and compared with the front desk records.

As with the A.m. report, if discrepancies are found, they are immediately investigated and the records corrected. Besides reporting whether rooms are occupied, vacant, out of order, or ready, the report should provide the front desk with information that can help this department better control the guest records. The most common symbols used are:

B = slept out (guest did not use the room but baggage is still in the room)

NB = occupied, no baggage

DND = do-not-disturb sign on door

LO = lock out (room has been locked by management so that guest cannot re-enter)

As the evening progresses and the room attendants on the evening shift continue to clean rooms from late check-outs and day rate occupancy, the front desk is notified of the rooms available for sale.

Other communications between the front office and the housekeeping department involve information about occupancy forecasts, the arrival of VIPs, the early check-in of groups, the closing of certain sections for deep-cleaning or repairs, delivery of guest laundry, lost and found items, special guest requests, and so on.

The communication between the housekeeping department and the front desk is greatly improved when the property uses a computerized system. For instance, when a guest checks out, the front desk clerk enters the departure in the computer and it appears instantly in the housekeeping monitor.

When housekeeping has rooms ready to be sold, the information is entered in the system and it too shows up quickly in the front desk terminal.

Communication with Maintenance

The relationship between housekeeping and the maintenance department -must be as close as that with the front office. Every piece of equipment, fixtures, and furniture in the guestrooms, hallways, linen and laundry rooms, public areas, and employee locker rooms must be in perfect working order at all times.

The number of items that may be in need of repairs in a single guestroom can be substantial: beds, chairs, desks, TVs, radios, lights, doors, toilets, faucets, walls, heating, air conditioning, and so on. It is therefore imperative that good communication between the two departments exists at all times. For instance, if a guestroom lock is broken, maintenance must be notified, the room must be put out of order, the work performed, the area cleaned, and the room put back in vacant ready status.

There are two types of maintenance performed by the engineering department in hospitality properties. Regular maintenance is performed when an item is broken and needs to be repaired. In this case, a three-part work order form is filled out by a housekeeping employee who forwards two copies to engineering and keeps the duplicate filed until the work is completed. When work is completed, one of the copies is returned to housekeeping for comparison, the work is inspected, and the area cleaned.

When a problem is urgent and engineering does not promptly address it, housekeeping generates a second request work order to remind that department that the work must be completed. If the repair needs to be done in order to be able to sell the room that day, an urgent request is sent to engineering so that the work is given priority over other nonessential jobs.

The orderly flow of information between housekeeping and engineering about items or areas in need of attention is of critical importance. As the housekeeping department staff is directly involved in cleaning most sections of the property, they are in the best position to find areas in need of maintenance or repair.

Preventive maintenance consists of inspecting guestrooms and other areas on a regular basis to identify repair and maintenance needs. In most hotels, the executive housekeeper and the chief engineer cooperate in combining room cleaning with preventive maintenance programs. This involves conducting a thorough maintenance inspection of all rooms in the property two or three times a year.

Communication between the housekeeping and human resources departments is necessary when considering personnel staffing. When an employee is needed in the housekeeping department, an employee requisition is filled out and sent to human resources to initiate the process.

After receiving the request, human resources advertises for the position, pre-screens the candidates, conducts the first interview, and checks references. The final candidates are then sent to housekeeping for a second interview and hiring selection.

Human resources is usually also involved in the orientation of new housekeeping employees, at which time the company's philosophy, compensation package, pay schedule, and rules and regulations are explained in detail to the new worker. This department also ensures that the new employee fills out all necessary forms related to legal residency, income tax, and personal information. Good communication with human resources will result in hiring the right employees to fill housekeeping vacancies.

Communication with food and beverage

Food and beverage is the second major revenue center in the property after the rooms division. The food and beverage division in large hotels comprises the property's kitchens, restaurants, coffee shops, cafeterias, bars, lounges, banquets, catering services, clubs, and room service. In large hotels, the housekeeping department should only be indirectly involved in the cleaning of food and beverage outlets.

However, the communication between food and beverage and housekeeping is necessary in some specific areas. There must be good cooperation regarding the pickup of room service material from guestroom areas. Housekeeping must see to it that hallways are free from trays and carts placed there by guests and section housekeepers; therefore, calls to room service must be regularly placed to remind this department to clear all areas.

The laundry room must provide the food and beverage department with clean napery on a daily basis. This often means that the laundry manager must request that the soiled linen be delivered to the laundry room on time, properly sorted out, and free from food scraps and table debris.

Furnishing clean uniforms to cooks, waiters, and bartenders is also usually the responsibility of the housekeeping department. As communication with food and beverage service personnel is traditionally difficult, efforts must be made to establish good relationships between departments.

Communication with sales and marketing

The primary goal of the sales and marketing division is to sell the products and services offered by the property. Given that cleanliness is one of the most important reasons for guests to choose a particular lodging property, the onus of providing this critical service falls on the housekeeping department. There must be good communication between sales and housekeeping if customer satisfaction is to be achieved.

For instance, if sales and marketing has guaranteed late check-out to a large group of guests attending a convention without notifying housekeeping, some of the rooms might not be cleaned in time to be available for a tour group scheduled to check-in that same evening.

If sales and marketing has promised that forty rooms will be available for early check-in to a company attending a conference at the property and housekeeping has not been notified, there might not be enough manpower that morning to clean the rooms on time.

Communication between sales and housekeeping is also necessary when specific rooms or suites must be available for inspection to meeting planners who are considering the property for a possible convention. If the rooms in question have not been impeccably cleaned, the company executive might well take their business elsewhere.

Communication with the accounting office

It is seldom acknowledged that communication between housekeeping and the accounting office is of great importance, yet there are several reasons why this is so. For instance, in large properties, the purchasing agent often reports to the controller; therefore, the executive housekeeper is communicating with the accounting office when placing orders for equipment and supplies for the department.

4

Staffing Patterns

The housekeeping department must prepare the rooms for incoming guests as soon as possible. Although guests are expected to check out around noon and to check in after 2 P.M, this is not always the case. It is not uncommon for convention and resort properties to have most of the guestrooms in the house depart at midday and receive a large number of guests right at the same time.

When one considers that the rooms must be thoroughly cleaned and inspected in such a short period of time, it is clear that the scheduling of employees in lodging properties can be very difficult indeed. Because labour is the largest housekeeping expense, the executive housekeeper must be sure not to over-schedule the department's work force, for calling too many employees to work results in decreased departmental profit.

On the other hand, not having enough section housekeepers to quickly turn over ready rooms to the front desk will result in incoming guests having to wait in the lobby until enough rooms are available for check-in. Thus, under-staffing the department to save on labour expense may also cause guest dissatisfaction and an eventual loss of business. When scheduling workers, the executive housekeeper must combine the need to provide adequate coverage to clean the guestrooms effectively with ensuring fairness to employees and achieving an adequate departmental profit.

Scheduling employees for guestroom cleaning and laundry operation is done taking into account the property's daffy occupancy. If the establishment is full today and at three-fourths capacity tomorrow, all guestroom cleaning and laundry personnel will be scheduled to work tomorrow but only 75 percent of the workers should be asked to work the day after. For example, a 400-room property that has 16 of its rooms cleaned by one section housekeeper in one 8-hour shift will schedule the room attendants on a particular week as follows:

Day of the Week	Percentage Occupancy	Rooms to be Cleaned	Section Housekeepers
Monday	80	?	?
Tuesday	100	320 (400 × 80)	20 (320 ÷ 16)
Wednesday	75	400 (400 × 1.0)	25 (400 ÷ 16)
Thursday	90	300 (400 × 75)	19 (300 ÷ 16)
Friday	40	360 (400 × 90)	23 (360 ÷ 16)
Saturday	40	160 (400 × 40)	10(160 ÷ 16)
Sunday	90	160 (400 × 40)	10 (160 ÷ 16)
Monday	?	360 (400 × .90)	23 (360 ÷ 16)

Criteria for workloads

The number of rooms to be cleaned by each section housekeeper in an 8-hour shift varies from property to property, depending on factors such as the size of the rooms, number of breaks permitted per shift, the time allowed for lunch, the average number of people occupying one room, and the standard of cleanliness to be achieved.

The section housekeeper workload may range from 12 guestrooms in suite hotels to 20 in budget motels. In this last case, allowing one hour for lunch and breaks, a section housekeeper must clean rooms at a rate of one for each 21 minutes (21 × 20 = 420; 420 ÷ 60 7 hours) Executive housekeepers should compile a section housekeeper need table establishing the number of room attendants required for each level of occupancy. The table can also be extended to include the number of hours that section housekeepers generate per day, per week, and per month. This information may be valuable to anticipate the cost of labour in any specific period of time.

The cost of labour can be determined by multiplying the number of hours by the average hourly wage paid to section house -keepers. The accounting office provides the average hourly wage to the housekeeping department on a regular basis.

Standing schedules

The function of scheduling workers in the housekeeping department is of great importance. The manager must juggle several factors in order to protect the interests of the company, fulfil the individual needs of the workers, and provide guest satisfaction.

To protect the company's interests, the manager must schedule the minimum number of workers to achieve an optimum labour cost percentage, because the more employees called to work, the greater the payroll cost will be.

At the same time, employees have all types of individual requests; some of them may prefer to have weekends off, others may insist that they will not settle for less than rotating days off, others will need fixed days off every week to match those of their spouse. In any case, scheduling must always be done keeping in mind the ultimate goal of providing efficient service to the property's guests. The first step in housekeeping scheduling is to prepare a matri × showing the scheduled consecutive days off for the guestroom cleaning teams, laundry teams, and relief teams.

Adjusted daily schedules

The purpose of standing schedules, as described above, is to designate which days the working teams are off and which days they are scheduled to work. However, in most cases guestroom occupancy in the lodging industry is never constant. For this reason, whenever occupancies are below 100 percent, the number of section housekeepers must be adjusted down accordingly.

The adjusted schedule includes the laundry team whose workers are also scheduled according to the property's occupancy. The standing schedule must be posted the day before, prior to the end of the morning shift so that the workers know whether they are scheduled to work the following day. The estimated occupancy for the day is obtained from the front office, which usually is able to provide an accurate forecast based on reservations on hand, weather conditions, events taking place in town, and historical data from the same day in previous years.

On some occasions, however, upon opening the department early in the morning it may be found that the actual occupancy of the hotel differs substantially from the estimated forecast posted on the adjusted schedule the previous day. In this case, the opening supervisor should attempt to adjust the number of workers required to clean the number of rooms actually sold. This is usually done by calling the workers by phone.

When the actual occupancy is above the forecasted estimate, the supervisor needs to ask those section housekeepers who were given a day off to come to work;

when the actual occupancy is below the forecasted estimate, the supervisor needs to ask some of the scheduled section housekeepers to stay home. If, after all attempts are made, the number of workers is above the maximum needed, they can be assigned to extra work in the department; for instance, deep cleaning of rooms or public areas. If the number of workers is below the maximum needed, the supervisor can assign janitors, housepersons, laundry or linen room personnel to clean guestrooms.

When the employees of lodging properties are unionized, daily .scheduling must comply with the specifications of the contract in force. For instance, the contract may stipulate that workers are guaranteed 40-hour work weeks or that employees are not allowed to do any type of work other than that which they were hired to do.

Rotational schedules

An alternative to standing schedules is rotating forward the teams' days off by one day each week. This means that if Team One was off Monday and Tuesday this week, next week the team will be off Tuesday and Wednesday. The only advantage of rotational schedules is to ensure that all teams will eventually have a weekend off.

The disadvantages are substantial; workers will not be able to commit themselves to activities outside the workplace, they will not be able to secure stable baby-sitting help, or it will be impossible for them to have the same day off as their spouses. For example, a student who must attend classes on Tuesdays and Wednesdays will not appreciate having rotating days off at work. A working mother who relies on sending her child to a nursery Monday through Friday might not be able to find child care on weekends. A worker who needs

Wednesday and Thursday off to match her husband's days off will not be willing to work these days.

Alternative scheduling methods

Four day work week

Some large lodging properties have adopted a four-day work week system consisting of 10-hour shifts each working day. This type of schedule enables housekeeping employees to have more leisure time, to reduce time and expenses commuting back and forth to work, and to decrease child care by one day per week. Companies can benefit too by decreasing employee meals and uniform cleaning costs.

However, the system, raises the question of whether workers can endure 10-hour shifts without decreasing their normal productivity and quality of work. A section housekeeper who must clean 16 rooms in 8 hours (30 minutes per room on the average) would have to clean 20 rooms with the 10-hour shift system, which could affect the morale of the employees in the long run. Some properties have found that using the four-day work week system has not decreased guest satisfaction while showing positive responses from their staff and substantial payroll savings.

Part time workers

Lodging properties may resort to hiring employees who are willing to work less than 40 hours per week, such as semi-retired people or college students. In this case, the company will profit by reducing costs for items such as employee benefits and overtime. On the other hand, part-time workers are usually less reliable because their stake in hi the job is less substantial than that of full-time workers, which may create scheduling difficulties.

Flexible work hours

In smaller properties employees may be allowed to begin and end their shifts at times convenient to them. Needless to say, this system will appeal to workers and increase their morale. On the other hand, the coordination of tasks in the department can become a nightmare if the employees are allowed too much flexibility. The system of flexible work hours could be adopted in properties where the arrival and departure of guests is predictable, such as in small highway motels where most check-outs take place early in the morning and most check-ins occur late in the day.

Job sharing

The purpose of job sharing is to allow two or more employees to accomplish a job regardless of who does it at any particular time. Although this system may be quite appealing to workers, the loss of supervisory control is very obvious. Job sharing could be adopted in small properties when the employees are well known to the manager and have proven to be reliable.

Guestroom team cleaning

Some recent surveys of housekeepers have shown that pairing room attendants for guestroom cleaning may improve productivity and enhance morale. On the other hand, guestroom team cleaning may have the risk of collusion and lower productivity by having two largely unsupervised workers in each other's company.

An advantage of team cleaning could be improved security, as having two housekeepers working together may deter assaults by other employees or guests. In cases where the two workers are a good complement to each other, team cleaning might achieve higher levels of productivity and increased levels of morale, while in instances where the personality of the team members is incompatible the results would be the opposite.

Extended time off

Some properties experience intense occupancy fluctuations during the year. While all workers are needed during peak season, during off-season there might be only sufficient occupancy to require a skeleton crew. One way to solve this problem is to schedule workers on the basis of seniority, but this would necessarily result in losing those employees being laid off. A better arrangement is to have the staff agree on sharing the work.

The structural planning of the housekeeping department beginning with the definition of its areas of responsibility are described in this chapter. Although in small properties executive housekeepers may be in charge of servicing most areas, in large establishments the areas of responsibility should be limited to guestrooms, offices, public areas, back-of-the-house spaces, employee locker rooms and cafeteria, laundry and linen rooms. Once the areas of responsibility have been established, the executive housekeeper needs to determine how often they are to be cleaned, and to what degree. The purpose of this planning activity is to provide workers with specific guidelines about how the different cleaning tasks should be performed.

Areas of housekeeipng responsibility

When organizing the internal structure of lodging properties, the identification of cleaning and maintenance responsibilities for every area of the hotel is a prerequisite. All spaces of the property must be assigned by upper management to the different operating departments that are then charged with keeping their respective areas in a perfect state of cleanliness and maintenance.

Ideally, in order not to leave any space unassigned, the various cleaning and maintenance area boundaries are marked on a copy of the property's blueprint. The areas of responsibility of the housekeeping department will be different depending on the size of the property. In small lodging operations the executive housekeeper is usually in charge of the cleaning and upkeep of most areas. In this particular case, very close cooperation between housekeeping and other departments is necessary to have the job done efficiently.

For instance, if housekeeping is in charge of cleaning the banquet rooms, the manager needs to know the type and time of functions in order to provide the necessary service. In some cases, because the preparation and service of food begins very early in the morning and ends quite late in the evening, the cleaning function in food and beverage areas must be provided late at night.

In large properties, the division of work by area is spread out among the different operating departments. Often some of the cleaning functions-such as cleaning the kitchen, restaurant, and grounds-are contracted out to outside companies.

Before contracting out cleaning tasks, it is important to obtain cost estimates from two or three different sources based on the size of the areas and the type and frequency of the cleaning desired. Once the contract has been signed, it is essential to check the quality of the work performed by the contractor. In no case should the cost of the services contracted be substantially higher than the cost of the same services performed by in-house personnel.

An ideal division of work in large properties would keep the housekeeping department from having to clean areas that are operated by the food and beverage or engineering divisions. There are several reasons for this: the housekeeping department usually does not have the necessary technical resources, the time, nor the expertise to clean ovens, walk-in refrigerators, kitchen hoods, and swimming pools or to prune palm trees and trim rose bushes.

Once the cleaning and maintenance responsibilities for all the areas of the property have been established, the respective department heads must plan the activities necessary for the upkeep of their areas, secure sufficient resources, and provide personnel to service them effectively.

Area cleaning inventories

The first step in planning the upkeep of the different areas assigned to the housekeeping department is to establish a list of the items that need to be regularly cleaned and maintained.

A cleaning inventory list for guestrooms, for instance, will include all items that need to be cleaned, checked, and maintained in each room. The list should follow the sequence that section housekeepers keep when servicing guestrooms, for example, beginning with the entrance door to the rooms, standing lamps, window sills, furniture, and so on and ending with vacuuming the carpet.

Another example of cleaning inventory would be that drawn for the lobby of the hotel, which might include not only furniture and fixtures but a water fountain, plants, bookcase, chandelier and so on. Area cleaning inventories can be combined with cleaning frequency schedules, including what needs to be cleaned and how often the items must be cleaned in one single document.

Cleaning frequency schedule

Once the area cleaning inventory lists have been

prepared, the frequency for cleaning and maintenance of each item should be established. Figure 3.1 shows a sample of area cleaning inventory and frequency schedule.

Generally items need to be cleaned daily, biweekly, weekly, monthly, and so on. Examples of daily service in the lobby area would be the windowsills; plants could be dusted twice a week, the water fountain polished once a week, the air vents on the wall once a month, and so forth.

Besides cleaning items on a regular basis, most areas are deep cleaned once or twice a year. In this case, the cleaning crews scrape and scrub every nook and cranny until all surfaces are spotless. Deep cleaning projects generally coincide with low occupancy periods and are coordinated with repairs being done in the area by the engineering department.

Table 1
Sample area cleaning inventory and frequency schedule lobby

Item	Activity	Frequency
Carpet	Vacuumed	Daily
Furniture	Dusted	Daily
Furniture	Polished	Weekly
Chandelier	Dusted	Bi-monthly
Lamps	Dusted	Daily
Wood Panelling	Polished	Monthly
Sconces	Dusted	Weekly
Water Fountain	S/S Cleaned	Bi-weekly
Sand Ashtrays	Cleaned	Twice daily
Air Vents	Dusted	Monthly
Hallway	Stripped/Waxed	Monthly

Performance standards

After compiling cleaning inventories and frequency

schedules, performance standards must be established. Performance standards are used to inform subordinates of the equipment and supplies they must use to clean an item, of the method or way of doing the job, and of the expected cleaning outcomes.

It is not good enough to tell section housekeepers and janitors to "clean well." "Cleaning well may mean different levels of cleanliness to different people. An example of performance standard to clean a vanity top could be: Spray all-purpose cleaner on the vanity top and wipe the surface clean with a sanitized rag, wiping it dry until no spots, marks, or specks remain."

The development of cleaning performance standards should be established keeping in mind the direct input of the workers who are assigned to do the cleaning.

The written cleaning standards should be a part of the department's standard operating procedures (SOPs) and strictly observed during the training period of new employees. Properties that have written cleaning standards in place are able to measure employee performance by comparing the worker cleaning outcomes with the established standards.

Division of guestrooms

The assignment of guestrooms for daily cleaning is usually done randomly in small hotels. That is, the section housekeepers and gathered at the beginning of the shift and giver, a number of rooms to service on an individual basis. In large hotels, however, house keeping teams should be formed to which the same sections of rooms are consistently assigned.

There are several advantages to allotting the guestrooms to teams. Individual housekeepers take ownership of the rooms they clean day in and day out, showing pride for the work they perform, which increases their morale. Teams create a sense of unity, of common interests and responsibilities (esprit de corps) by which room attendants are less likely to let their partners down by calling in sick, thus improving attendance. A team may consist of four or five section housekeepers, a team supervisor, and a houseperson.

The section housekeeper cleans guestrooms while the supervisor coordinates the work of the teams and inspects rooms. The housepersons assist in the work by providing the team with supplies, hauling the trash, vacuuming the hallways, moving heavy objects around, and so on.

Guestrooms are divided by creating a pictorial representation of all rooms and allocating a certain number of them to every section housekeeper of each team. The criteria for guestroom cleaning workload vary from hotel to hotel depending on the size of the rooms, the number of furniture and fixture pieces to be cleaned, and the level of quality that management wishes to provide. Generally a property with small rooms allocates about 18 rooms per section housekeeper for an 8-hour shift. Properties with average-size rooms assign around 16, while establishments with large rooms or suites allocate about 12 units per shift. As an example, a 400-room property that assigns 16 rooms to one section housekeeper and that groups the section housekeepers.

The 80-room floor of this property has been broken down into 5 sections of 16 rooms each section in teams of 5 would have the following workload distribution at 100 percent occupancy.

Number of teams: 5 (400 ÷ 16 = 25; 25 ÷ 5 = 5)

Number of section housekeepers: 25 (400 ÷ 16 = 25)

Number of team supervisors: 5 (one per team)

Number of houseperson: 5 (one per team)

In this particular example, the assignment of five teams to clean the rooms works perfectly. But what would happen if the hotel continues to operate at 100 percent occupancy for some time?

As the workers need to be given two days off per week to avoid overtime, the department will need a larger number of workers to substitute for those who are off. The problem becomes more complicated if the property operates an on-premise laundry.

Let us suppose that this is the case and that the laundry is operated by one fun team consisting of five section housekeepers, one supervisor, and one houseperson.

In this case, as the hotel is open seven days a week and the employees work only five, the total number of teams, section housekeepers, supervisors, and housepersons needed to clean the guestrooms and operate the laundry will be as follows:

25 section housekeepers needed to clean the rooms + 5 to operate laundry = 30 workers

30 workers × 7 days per week of operation = 210 man/days

2 10 man/days -1- 5 days per week employees work = 42 workers needed

The minimum number of teams and workers needed to cover guestroom cleaning and laundry operation is now:

Number of teams: 8 (42 ÷ 5 = 8)

Number of section housekeepers: 42

Number of supervisors: 8

Number of housepersons: 8

The distribution of teams on any given day that the hotel is full will be:

Teams assigned to guestroom cleaning: 5
(400 ÷ 16 = 25; 25 ÷ 5 = 5)

One team to operate laundry: 1

Two teams off duty: 1

Total teams $\frac{1}{2}$

This example property will need eight teams to operate efficiently.

Staffing matrix

The internal organization of the housekeeping department follows the same pattern as that of the property as a whole. The chain of command begins with the executive housekeeper and goes on to encompass all employees in the department.

Besides the section housekeepers, supervisors, and housepersons needed to clean the guestrooms, and the laundry room workers, the housekeeping department needs additional personnel to service other areas of the property, such as offices, public and back-of the-house sections, and linen room.

The employees in the department's work force can be classified into management, fixed, evening, laundry, and guestroom cleaning teams. The executive housekeeper, housekeeping manager (assistant to the executive housekeeper), and laundry manager fall under management.

These employees are salaried and are required to work a minimum of 40 hours each week. The housekeeping fixed employees are the janitors and the linen room attendants. These workers are usually hourly employees who are guaranteed 5 days' work regardless of guestroom occupancy. The reason for guaranteeing fixed work is that whether or not the guestrooms have been sold out, lobbies, offices and other front and back-of -the-house public areas must be serviced on a daily basis. The evening team takes over the duties of the department at the end of the morning shift when all regular teams clock off.

The jobs generally assigned to the evening shift are cleaning late checkout and day-rate guestrooms, providing turndown service, counting soiled linen, servicing public and back-of-the-house areas, preparing carts for the morning shift, washing guestroom glasses, and filling out guest requests as the evening progresses. As with the janitors, the evening team is composed of hourly employees who are guaranteed 5 days of work regardless of occupancy.

The guestroom cleaning and laundry teams are also composed of hourly employees, but the number of hours they are scheduled to work depends on the number of guestrooms sold daily. For instance, if the hotel is full all section housekeepers who are not off duty that day will be needed to clean all guestrooms, but if the occupancy drops to 80 percent, only enough section housekeepers to clean 80 percent of the guestrooms with be called to work.

5

Inventory and Equipments

Housekeeping material is divided into two major categories: fixed assets and operating assets. Fixed assets comprise housekeeping items that have a long-term life span, generally over one year. Fixed assets usually cost over $ 100 and are depreciated at the end of the fiscal year. Depreciation means that the company reduces the value of assets during the period of the assets' estimated useful life. For tax purposes, depreciation is a tax allowance that can be set aside by the company year after year for replacing the items once they can no longer be used. Fixed assets are subcategorized into F.F.&E. (furniture, fixtures, and equipment), software, and department equipment. Items that have a 5- to 7-year life span are categorized under F.F.&E., such as beds, chairs, paintings, mattresses, and television sets that are used in guestrooms, public areas, and staff areas.

Software items comprise guestroom fixtures of a textile nature that are not bed linens or bath linens, such as curtains, bedspreads, pillows, and blankets. The life span of software items is usually 3 to 5 years. Heavier, mobile equipment used in the housekeeping department for cleaning or transportation purposes is generally classified under department equipment. The life span of these items is between 3 and 7 years. Included under this subcategory are items such as vacuum cleaners, shampoo machines, glass washers, and so on. Operating assets include items under the control of the executive housekeeper that are generally used in the day-to-day operations of the department. They are considered cost items whose money outlay is charged to operating expenses.

An important characteristic of operating assets is that it must to be regularly inventoried. Operating assets are usually categorized into cleaning supplies, linens, uniforms, and guest supplies.

The category of cleaning supplies includes every one of the items used for cleaning purposes, for example, cleaning solutions, disinfectants, polishers, brooms, mops, and rags. The classification of linens encompasses the subcategories of bed linen and bathroom linen. The subcategory of bed linen includes sheets and pillowcases and that of bathroom linen comprises towels, washcloths, bath mats, and washable shower curtains.

The category of uniforms is self-explanatory, including apparel used in the housekeeping department by supervisors, section housekeepers, housepersons, laundry, and linen room personnel. Operating assets items used by guests are listed under guest supplies. This category is usually subdivided into two classifications: nonreusable and reusable items.

Nonreusable guest supplies include soaps, pens, paper items, mints, etc. Items that can be used again, such as ashtrays, clothes hangers, and wastebaskets fall under the reusable subdivision.

Capital expenditure

Every lodging property is allocated with the necessary fixed and operating assets prior to its opening to the public. The costs of the initial allocation of material are itemized on a pre-opening budget that includes all inventory requirements to open the property and commence operations. Once operations begin, budgets for fixed and operating material items necessary for operating the property during the next twelve months must be prepared. The budget used to record the fixed assets needed for the upcoming fiscal year is called the capital expenditure budget. This budget is relatively easy to compile; it consists of a list of the number of fixed assets (F.F.&E., software, and department equipment) required by the housekeeping department, their individual prices, and the sum total for all items listed.

Operating budgets

Operating budgets are also prepared annually for the property's fiscal year operation. In large properties, the housekeeping operating budget is part of the rooms division operating budget, which includes both the front desk and the housekeeping departments. Unlike capital expenditure budgets, operating budgets have a direct relationship to the day-to-day revenue resulting from the sale of guestrooms. The rationale behind this approach is to limit operating costs to a predetermined percentage of the generated revenue. For example, assuming that the housekeeping department is expected to expend 1.2 percent of sales on guest supplies, if the daily room revenue is, say, $20,000, the cost of guest supplies should be $240 (20,000 x 1.2%). If the revenue is $18,000, the cost should be $216 (18,000 x 1.2%), and so on.

The cost percentage assigned to each operating budget expense category is based on the cost history of the property, the quality of the products used, and the pay scale and types of benefits that employees receive. The housekeeping categories used by the housekeeping department usually include: housekeeping salaries and wages, payroll taxes and benefits, and other expenses. Salaries and wages include those of the entire housekeeping department; payroll taxes and benefits include the operator's share of additional costs related to payroll; the category of other expenses encompasses any other cost incurred by the housekeeping department that is not payroll-related.

Purchasing house keeping materials

The function of buying goods in lodging institutions is a highly specialized job. Buyers must be knowledgable about the items they purchase, be familiar with the market, and know how the materials are produced and marketed.

The process of buying material for the housekeeping department involves finding the best sources of supply at the most satisfactory prices and obtaining the quality and quantity that the property requires. Although cost is always an important consideration, it should not take precedence over the quality of the product and the service of the company that sells it, Buyers should understand how to conduct value analyses. First, the performance of the products' components is evaluated by identifying their essential, desirable, useful, and unnecessary characteristics. Then the buyer must find the products with the most essential and desirable quality factors. The value function can be quantified by the ratio Q/P, where Q = quality and P = price. Although not always possible, the goal of the buyer should be to keep the value of products as high as possible by increasing Q while keeping P down.

The buying function in lodging chains is often centralized. Items like soap, linen, mattresses, pillows, furniture, and fixtures are procured by the company's purchasing department and shipped to the different units on request. Purchasing in large independent properties is done by the purchasing agent, who is a specialized buyer in charge of procuring products for all departments in the property. Smaller properties often allow the department heads to purchase goods for their respective areas of responsibility. In any case, it should be the job of the executive housekeeper to always pretest and approve all items used in the housekeeping department and decide the quantities and the specifications of the products to be bought. It should not be the job of the purchasing agent, or any other person for that matter, to purchase material and supplies without the consent of the executive housekeeper.

It is also important to solicit the input of janitors, section housekeepers, housepersons, and laundry personnel on the appropriate characteristics of the items that in the end are to be used by them. All merchandise purchased should have precise specifications, which are descriptions of the products' quality and factors that should reflect precisely the performance needs for each particular institution. Specifications should be stated clearly, giving the information needed to assure proper identification.

For instance, a luxury resort does probably require the best bed linen money can buy, while a small, inexpensive motel may just need bed linen of fair quality. Before buying a product, prices should be obtained from at least three different vendors.

Product price and vendor dependability and service should be reviewed once or twice every three months. Purchasing decisions should be made based not only on price but on quality, suitability, and storage availability as well. There may be three types of entities involved in the purchasing function: producers, middlemen, and consumers.

Producers manufacture the items to be sold and sometimes sell the products directly to the consumers. Middlemen may bring the different commodities to their own warehouses from which they distribute them to consumers or act as order takers and have the goods shipped directly from the manufacturer. Middlemen always add a charge to the product's price.

Usually, the fewer middlemen through which a product passes, the lower the price. However, although purchasing directly from the manufacturer may be less expensive, very often lodging properties benefit from buying through brokers (middlemen) because these can provide better service and in some cases employee training at no cost. Another disadvantage from buying directly from manufacturers is that they often require the purchase of large quantities of goods. In this case, the money saved because of lower price is upset by the cost of having assets tied down for long periods of time. There is great competition among purveyors of cleaning and guest supplies. Some will lower their prices initially to obtain the property's account. Others may offer prizes or kickbacks to get their foot in the door.

Executive housekeepers should be aware of these often unethical tactics and decline any "free" personal gifts. If the executive housekeeper needs to order products directly from a manufacturer, filling out a formal purchase order may be necessary. The purchase order is, in essence, a sales contract stating the specifications of the product to be delivered and the conditions involving payment. When the merchandise has been previously bought by the property's buyer and stored in the main storeroom, the housekeeping department usually needs to fill out a requisition form before the products can be obtained.

Executive housekeepers should always be on the lookout for new items on the market. Testing for new, better, or less expensive products often leads to improving the department's bottom line.

Inventory control

Functions of purchasing, receiving, storing, issuing, and accounting for housekeeping material must be managed efficiently. The range of inventory used in the rooms division of lodging operations is quite large, varying from textiles, guestroom furnishing and amenities to sophisticated department equipment and supplies.

The executive housekeeper must control the function of purchasing by defining clearly what is to be procured, who will be in charge of the buying, what specifications are to be considered, and what quantities will be needed. The person in charge of purchasing must consistently provide the needed quantities of products in housekeeping inventories. Although in some cases purchasing is done by the corporate office or by the property's purchasing agent, the executive housekeeper is ultimately responsible for the cost and results of what is purchased.

For some products, linen for instance, pars need to be established; for others, for example soaps and paper products, maximum and minimum quantities are set up. Pars can be defined as the number of required on-hand items to perform housekeeping operations. In the case of linens, for instance, the optimum number of pars is 4.

This means that ideally the property should have on hand one set of sheets and pillowcases set up in the guestroom beds at any given time, another set being laundered, an additional set ready to go in floor closets and room attendant carts, and one final set on reserve. For guest and cleaning supplies, the maximum quantity is the greatest number of units that should be in stock at any given time, while the minimum quantity refers to the fewest number of units. For example, the maximum and minimum number of cases of soap could be 35 and 25 respectively. That means that if at any given time the soap inventory is above 35, the product is overstocked. On the other hand, if the number of cases falls below 25, additional supplies must be ordered. This system eliminates the risk of overstocking or of running out of products. The receiving function of goods ordered must also be controlled.

Unless adequate inspection and receiving procedures are used, the best purchasing system may fail because it is at this point that determination must be made of whether or not the products meet the specifications and quantities of the order previously placed. Failing to inspect the merchandise adequately may result in higher costs, lower quality, theft, and fraud.

On receiving a shipment, the goods should be compared with those listed on the receiving sheet or purchase order to verify the correctness of the delivery. If the goods meet the prearranged requirements, they are accepted by signing the invoice or delivery memo. If the products do not meet inspection requirements, they should be refused and a notation indicating the reasons for refusing the delivery made. The function of storing merchandise must also be controlled adequately.

Access to storerooms must be limited to authorized personnel only. The storeroom should be locked off -hours and a record should be kept of the person entering it and of the merchandise taken. Valuable items like towels and some guest supplies should be stored in an area that remains locked at all times. The storage area should be designed to hold the specific products stored in it; bottom shelving levels should be at least 10 inches off the floor to ensure adequate ventilation and to allow for cleaning underneath.

A rotation system should be established by which oldest stock is placed in front and issued first. In large properties, housekeeping items may be stored in the main storeroom. In this case, the housekeeping department will need to fill a requisition form to request products. Every requisition should bear the signature of a person designated by the executive housekeeper to sign it. Nothing should be requested without an approved signature.

When products are stored in the housekeeping department, issuing controls must also be established so that the merchandise is handed out to authorized personnel only. Floor closet storage should also be locked at all times and access limited to the section housekeepers, housepersons, or supervisors in charge of the area.

To account for the cost of housekeeping operating assets used, physical inventories are conducted regularly, in most cases monthly. Linens, uniforms, and cleaning and guest supplies inventories are taken by counting all items on hand and listing them on a physical inventory form.

Laundry chemicals may be included in the cleaning supplies category or counted separately for better control. The purpose of taking physical inventories is to find out what amount of items for each category is on hand and to work out its current market value.

Once the value of items used is ascertained, the costs are expensed against the revenue produced for the same period and the percentages obtained compared to the amounts budgeted for the different categories.

The cost of items used is determined by adding the total purchases during the month to the opening inventory and subtracting the merchandise on hand as per the physical inventory for every category.

Physical inventories are difficult to conduct as all items that need to be accounted for must be counted one by one. In the case of linens, for instance, linens are found in guestrooms, laundry room, linen room, floor closets, room attendant carts, etc. To keep tight control on valuable items, for example imported chocolates for special guests, a perpetual inventory system may be implemented.

Housekeeping F.F.&E., and Department Equipment

Executive housekeepers must administer and maintain their proprieties' fixed assets classified as Furniture, Fixtures and Equipment (F.F.&E.), Software, and Department Equipment. Although new establishments are usually handed over to the management team equipped with allitems needed for operation, the executive housekeeper is directly involved in the replacement, refurbishing, and upkeep of most fixed asset items in the property. For this reason, executive housekeepers must have appropriate knowledge of the assets that are under their control.

Design

Regardless of their type of service, lodging properties must maintain interior design consistency standards throughout the building. Whether a property has been classified as economy, mid-market, or luxury, its guestroom and public area design, colour patterns, fabric and upholstery quality, and overall appearance must befit the category they represent. Doing piecemeal refurbishing or renovating must always be avoided. Colours, for instance, must be complementary.

In general, blue is a complement of orange, green of red, and yellow of violet. Using several light tints and shades of the same colour makes rooms seem larger, while full-intensity hues tend to make the room seem compact. Adjoining walls should be painted the same colour to provide a sense of continuity.

When covering -walls, smaller prints should be used in small rooms and in all cases, colour patterns should be complementary in fabrics, wall coverings, and carpets.

Earth tone colours which often used in *art deco* design, such as ocher, mauve, and burgundy, are quite popular in guestroom and lobby outlines. These soothing colours, when combined with terracotta vases, lamp bases, and statuettes, are often found in classic settings and are generally pleasing to most guests.

Surfaces look better and last longer when finished with durable materials like marble, granite, and corian. Public areas should be attractively decorated and furnished with special touches to please guests. For instance, lobbies may be fitted with fireplaces, bookcases, and live plants to make them seem more homey and inviting to travellers.

Furniture

Executive housekeepers are generally responsible for the refurbishing and upkeep of the furniture in guestroom, public, and employee areas. Furniture should be solidly built, easy to maintain, functional, and attractive. It is not advisable to purchase pieces of furniture directly from a catalogue; instead, the executive housekeeper should carefully examine samples to ensure that the products have been built to withstand repeated rough use.

All furniture tops should be plastic-laminated or finished with water-repellent polyurethane to avoid scratches, rings, and stains caused by abusive treatment and spilled liquids. Desk chairs should have padded backs to provide comfort to guests and prevent wood from hitting desktops. Furniture dotted with glides or casters will prevent carpet damage when pushed or pulled around the room.

Luggage racks are better if built-in and fitted with wall-protecting panels, as there is a greater likelihood that the luggage will bump against and deteriorate walls when detached racks are used. Desks should be large enough to accommodate a desktop computer and a fax machine.

TV/VCR units should be an actual piece of furniture, rather than simply a conventional metal stand, and should be fitted with 180-degree swivels so that guests can see the screen from anywhere in the room. Case furniture such as chests of drawers, credenzas, armoires, desks, and bureaus also should be purchased with durability in mind.

Drawers should be equipped with nylon ball bearings and slide glides so that they don't jam when opening and closing. In general, guestrooms should provide a warm residential look; for instance, love seats and armchairs can replace the standard chairs so often found in hotel rooms.

Upholstery

Upholstery fibers may be natural, synthetic, or plastic. Natural fabrics, such as cotton, linen, silk, and wool, are rich looking and long wearing but expensive and delicate to maintain because they stain easily. Synthetic fibers are less expensive and easy to clean but they are less elegant and more likely to generate static electricity. Often, upholstered materials are a blend of natural and synthetic fabrics. The greatest advantage of upholstery plastic materials such as vinyl is that they can be easily cleaned by just wiping with a soapy cloth; however, they generally have a duller appearance than natural or blended materials.

Upholstery fabrics should be strong enough to withstand repeated shampooing. Treating fabrics With soil-retardant sprays can decrease the need for dry-cleaning the material. It is also important that upholstery fabrics be treated with flame-retardant finishes. Before putting upholstered furniture fabrics into use, they should be pretested to ascertain the best way to clean the pieces without causing shrinkage or discoloration. Some fabrics can be cleaned with solvent, others can be cleaned with water and detergent, and some only allow for vacuuming.

In general, synthetic fabrics such as nylon and plastics such as vinyl are the most stain-resistant and easy-to-clean upholstery materials.

Beds

Beds are the central attraction in guestrooms and often a big selling point for travellers when choosing a lodging property. When asked to pay an average of $70.00 per night per room, guests expect to receive a clean, well-maintained sleeping area and a comfortable bed. In commercial operations, beds consist of a frame to support the springs and mattresses and unattached headboards.

Bed frames usually consist of metal bars with legs attached to each corner or of a metal or wood platform. The main advantage of platform frames is that room attendants don't have to vacuum underneath the box frame, thus saving time when cleaning the room. Headboards are mounted on the wall and should match the general design of the room's furniture. It is important to know the composition of the bed structure of each property in order to figure out the maximum member of people that the property can house. Knowing the different types of beds and how many guests can stay in the rooms will help executive housekeepers plan for bed and bathroom linen and supplies. Table 6.1 shows the different types of beds normally found in lodging properties.

Another type of sleeping equipment is the mobile bed. Families on vacation and travelling high school or college groups often require additional sleeping accommodations in guestrooms. The rollaway, or bed on wheels, consists of a folding frame with an attached bed spring body.

The mattress in rollaways must be made of latex foam or have very light, flexible innersprings so that they too can fold with the frame. Because rollaways are unable to provide a comfortable surface to hold the weight of an adult person, they should be recommended only for children or young people to avoid legitimate complaints about the property's not providing adequate acco-mmodation.

Cribs are also essential to have in order to accommodate infants or young children. While cribs should be collapsible to save storage space, their extension mechanisms should be kept in good working order to prevent the crib from collapsing when being used.

Dual-purpose sleeping equipment is common in guestrooms. These pieces of furniture provide both seating space and extra sleeping capacity, eliminating the need to roll in a mobile bed on short notice. Sofas, couches, chair-beds, and in-wall beds are the most common dual-purpose pieces of furniture found in lodging properties. Sofas, couches and chair-beds convert into beds by removing the cushions and pulling out the folding frame and mattress or by dropping the back to the level of the seat. In-wall beds, also called Murphy beds, are concealed in the wall behind a panel, giving the room the appearance of a studio or parlour rather than a bedroom. The wall is balanced in such a way that it can be swung open with a gentle pull on a handle.

Table 1
Sample Bed Structure In Lodging Properties

Type	Standard Size (inches)	Number of People per Bed
Single	38 x 74	One
Twin	42 x 76	One
Double	54 x 76	Two
Queen	60 x 80	Two
King	76 x 84	Two

Box springs

The main purpose of bed box springs is to act as shock absorbers between the mattress and the bed frame itself. Box spring coils are more rigid than those of mattresses to provide a firm base for the mattress to rest on. Besides cushioning the mattress, box springs increase the height of beds, giving them a more elegant look.

Mattresses

Surveys of favourite guest amenities conducted regularly by hospitality magazines consistently show that guests put comfortable mattresses at the top of the list, second only to cleanliness.

Most mattresses used in lodging operations are of the innerspring type; they have metal coils that support the weight of the sleepers while conforming to their body contours. The strength and number of coils determine the mattress firmness, which may range from medium to super firm. Heavy-gauge steel wire coils are best, allowing for weights to flex down a specific area without disturbing the space surrounding the pressure points. This allows for two persons of different weights to lie side by side and each get different levels of buoyancy. The firmness of the mattress is determined by the gauge of steel used, the number of turns of each coil, and the way the coils are attached to the mattress frame.

Preferably, the springs should be encased in fabric pockets to provide independent coil action, rather than being attached to each other with wire or hooks.

Good mattresses have sufficient padding to cushion the springs beneath and provide a smooth surface. The padding should be nonallergenic and comply with the government flame-spread regulation, which states that a lighted cigarette should not be able to ignite the insulation.

The recommended way to purchase mattresses is to inspect a cutaway section to make sure that the padding is sufficiently dense, that the coils are of fine quality and closely spaced, and that the covering fabric is well attached to the main body.

Lodging properties may also use foam mattresses, especially for their rollaway beds. The synthetic material used in this type of mattress is usually latex foam or urethane.

Although less expensive, rubber mattresses do not provide the adequate firmness expected by an adult guest, nor do they last nearly as long as those built with innersprings.

Water-filled mattresses (waterbeds) became quite popular with the public when they were first used in the 1960s, but they soon proved to be inconvenient with lodging operators because they often leaked and because the water had to be heated, which became costly. Although today's waterbeds are efficiently built with individually filled cells that do not need to be heated because of an insulating foam layer, there doesn't seem to be a great demand for them from lodging guests.

Lodging properties, however, should have a few waterbeds to fulfil the request of interested travellers.

Fixtures

Guestrooms and lodging property lobbies are also furnished with accessories such as mirrors, decorations, pictures, and lights, to complement the furniture. The colour and style of fixtures should be balanced with the overall room decor; a vermilion vase, for instance, will probably not match a surrounding of pale yellow hues.

The amount, style, and quality of furnishings will dramatically affect the appearance of rooms. For instance, strategically placed mirrors can give small rooms an illusion of depth; serene motifs in paintings will provide a feeling of tranquillity; triple magnification make-up mirrors and wall-mounted hair dryers in bathrooms are a welcome amenity; a well-stocked mahogany bookcase in the lobby will provide a homey feeling to guests who enjoy reading.

Carpets

Beautiful carpeting can enhance the appearance of lodging properties and make a lasting impression on guests. On the other hand, discoloured, worn, or dirty carpets are usually sources of guest complaints. The first step in selecting the right carpet is to match its colour, texture, and pattern with the design of the area where it is to be installed.

Then, other factors need to be considered, such as determining the anticipated level of wear and tear caused by the intensity of traffic, the location of the carpet, and the budget allocated for it. When heavy traffic is expected, carpets should feature strong resistance to abrasion, as well as texture retention and anti-soiling and staining characteristics. The location of the carpet should determine specifications such as enhanced colourfastness, antimicrobial protection, resistance to snags, and resilience under rolling loads. Besides durability and stain resistance, carpets in lodging properties should be capable of withstanding repeated cleaning treatment.

Before purchasing carpet, be sure you fully understand the warranty coverage offered by the manufacturer or installer.

Warranties for commercial carpets should include protection for wear and tear, colourfastness (fading from sunlight and atmospheric contaminants), tuft bind deterioration, static charges, backing strength, ravelling of seams and edges, and any other manufacturing defects.

Carpets must be professionally installed in order to comply with the manufacturer's instructions. If carpeting is not installed properly, it will buckle and wear out fast. One important component of the installation process is to use a quality carpet cushion or pad that will prolong the life of the carpet.

In general, denser, thicker pads yield better results than thinner, softer ones by holding their shapes longer and being more resistant to dirt and stains. In back-of-the-house areas that are subject to traffic of heavy carts and where an impression of luxury and coziness is not necessary, carpets may be glued directly to the floor.

Carpets should be dense to the point of not showing the backing when bending a piece with both hands with the pile facing up. In woven carpets the density of the pile is measured by the number of lengthwise yarns in a 27-inch width of carpet.

In tufted carpets, the density (gauge) is measured by the number of tufts per widthwise inch expressed in fractions where the numerator of the fraction indicates the number of inches and the denominator the number of tufts. A gauge of 3/40, for instance, indicates that there should be 40 tufts in every 3 inches of carpet. Another way of ascertaining the quality of a carpet, all things being equal, is by its face weight, or its number of ounces of yarn per square yard. The greater the face weight, the better the quality.

Two types of fibers are used in carpet construction: natural and synthetic, each one having peculiar characteristics and a number of usage advantages and disadvantages.

Wool is a soft-to-the touch, durable, resilient but expensive natural fiber that has been used in carpet making for centuries. Because of its absorbent fibers, wool is susceptible to damage from strong chemicals and has poor abrasion resistance. Most fibers used in carpets today are made of nylon, which has a high crush resistance and therefore long life.

Nylon also has a high melting point, which prevents marks caused by objects dragged across the carpet. Nylon fibers can be treated with chemicals to effectively prevent their soiling and staining.

Carpets made with a blend of wool and nylon offer an excellent combination of the best qualities inherent in these fabrics.

The best characteristic of polypropylene (olefin) is that it doesn't absorb moisture, thus resisting stains and eliminating the need for much of the otherwise required maintenance.

Because of its resistance to sun fading, olefin is recommended for outdoor carpeting. In general, solid colours in all carpets, especially light colours, show more dirt, which requires frequent vacuuming.

Executive housekeepers should have sufficient

knowledge of carpet construction to ensure that the right carpet is selected for each area in the property. There are three main elements in the composition of carpets: the pile, or face; the backing, or material to which the pile is secured; and the padding, or cushion on which the carpet rests.

Most commercial carpets are tufted, that is, the yam is threaded through the backing material to form loops. The backing material usually is woven jute or polypropylene with a layer of adhesive latex extended over the material to anchor the tufts. Knitted carpets are made by interlacing together the pile yam and the backing.

The process of embedding the pile fibers electrostatically into a layer of adhesive material applied to the backing is called flocking. Weaving is the old-fashioned way of making carpets using conventional looms. The yarns are interlaced together to form the pile and the backing.

As with linen, the yams woven lengthwise are called the warp and the yarns going across are the wefts. The process of making carpets by compacting the fibers and the backing by mechanically punching them together is called needle punching.

Lighting

Improper lighting in rooms may discourage guests from staying in a particular establishment. Guests, particularly business travellers, expect to find adequate lighting to be able to work over flat surfaces such as tables and desks, or to read in bed or sitting on a couch or armchair.

Lights of adjustable intensity should be placed strategically so that guests can arrange their preferences to suit their needs; for example, subdued lighting for relaxation or bright lighting for working or entertaining friends. Having three-way lamps or lights activated by rheostats give guests the option to set the mood of the room to their liking. Floor lamps are not recommended in guestrooms because they can be easily knocked over and they create tripping hazards.

Desk lamps should have the on-off switches at the base to reduce the risk of guests burning their fingers on the light bulb or upsetting the shade's balance when reaching around to locate the switch. Lampshades should be made of plastic rather than paper or fabric for longer life.

When choosing fluorescent lighting, warm rather than cool light-giving units should be installed to avoid harsh tones of light. Pink incandescent light bulbs provide tones that enhance the appearance of guests when they look at themselves in the mirror. One advantage of fluorescent lights is that they use less energy and last longer than regular bulbs. In all cases, sufficient wattage must be provided in lamps that guests will use for reading or working purposes.

Equipment

Long gone are the days when hoteliers could sell rooms equipped with a minimum of basic features. Today's business traveller is putting a new spin on the concept of guestroom equipment. Lodging chains that cater to corporate clientele offer in-room or satellite office support services including computers and fax and copy machines.

Guestrooms are often equipped with multi-line telephones complete with voice mail and PC compatibility; some hotels even provide cellular phones and 24-hour access to translators and information in other languages. Office centers are fitted with hightech office support equipment, such as computers with desktop publishing, video room, and drafting center. Most hotels today offer TV in-room movie channels, and several chains have added VCRs in the rooms, together with video tape movie vending machines located in the lobby that guests can operate with their credit cards. Refrigerators and microwave ovens are quite common in suite hotels, and coffee-makers, together with selections of coffee and tea blends, are now available in the rooms of most properties.

Wide-screen television sets and high-quality clock radios are a must in four- and five-diamond properties, as are in-room safes.

In-room strongboxes are seen as a last-ditch defence for the guests' personal belongings, including items as large as lap-top computers. The locking systems of in-room safes range from ordinary keys to programmable push-buttons, magnetic-lock devices, and the guest's credit card.

Some microprocessor safes automatically lock for 30 minutes after four false attempts to open them. Besides being a great convenience for guests who don't want to line up for safety deposit boxes, in-room safes are effective against thieves and even employees who may use stolen keys to burglarize rooms.

Valuables can be stored by guests themselves and remain secure during trips to the pool, jogging around the block, or going out to dinner. Some safes have built-in memory, which enables the front office personnel to read the date and time of the most recent safe openings and closings. This can provide convincing evidence in case of a loss claim against the property.

Some up-scale lodging properties, particularly resorts and first class hotels, offer minibars in their guestrooms and suites. Stocked with beverages and snacks, minibars can be profitable because guests are often tempted to have a last drink before going to bed or first thing in the morning. Fully automated minibars can electronically sense when an item is removed, sending the corresponding charge to the guest's room account. Non-automated units must rely on the honesty of the guest to notify the front desk just before checking out if goods have been consumed.

Software

Depreciable fixed assets that are not furniture or equipment, such as bedspreads, mattress covers, blankets, pillows, and window coverings may be categorized under the classification of software.

Bedspreads

As with mattresses, bedspreads should be purchased with the qualities of durability, comfort, maintenance, and fire safety in mind. Bedspreads are an important component in the decor of guestrooms and should complement the motif, colour, and design of the room. Fabrics made of 100 percent polyester offer excellent resistance to fading, staining, shrinking, and wrinkling.

Woven fabrics perform better than knitted ones, which can make pattern colours appear faded if the knit loosens. Polycottons, a blend of polyester cotton, are less expensive than fabrics made of 100 percent polyester, but their life span is shorter, they have fewer fire-retardant qualities, and they fade more easily. While the normal recycling life span of a good bedspread should be at least 5 years, polycotton bedspreads only last from 2 to 3 years.

Other factors to consider when specifying bedspreads are their fill and seaming. Fill is one of the key elements that determines the appearance of bedspreads. The number of ounces of fill per square yard should be 7 or more. Non-compressed fills are better than mechanically packed fills because of their ability to spring back to its original 'loft is greater.

Wide, seamless bedspreads are preferred to those constructed with seams because they don't come apart as easily. Bedspreads can be large enough to reach to the floor or just to cover the mattress.

In this case a pleated cloth skirting called a dust ruffle may be placed between the mattress and the box spring to extend around the sides and foot of the bed. Washable bedspreads should be purchased with the guarantee that they will not shrink, fade, or wrinkle. Par levels for bedspreads should be one plus 10 percent to allow for washing and replacement.

Blankets

The purpose of blankets is to act as insulators. A heavy blanket does not necessarily keep the warmth of the body from escaping through it. On the other hand, a material (even if it is light) that is tightly woven will retain body heat. However, all blankets should be porous enough to allow any moisture buildup under them to escape to the surrounding air. Wool is a delicate natural fiber that is very warm but that requires extreme care when laundered.

Cotton, on the other hand, washes easily but it is a poor insulator and shrinks up to 15 percent if not purchased preshrunk. Synthetic fibers such as acrylics and polyester, if properly constructed, are suitable to commercial operations. Acrylic fibers are warmer than polyester but not as strong. Because guests may fall asleep while smoking in bed, blankets should be fire retardant. The size of the blanket should be large enough to cover the length and width of the mattress and have some additional inches for tucking.

Mattress covers

All mattresses should be fitted with moisture-proof covers at all times to prevent staining. Vinyl plastic covers are impermeable and can be washed like any other fabric. Their use is recommended for cribs or small cots for young children and hospital beds. Felt pads made of moisture-proof, flame -retardant, 100 percent polyester resist shrinkage and are quite durable. Quilted all-cotton pads are very comfortable but have a tendency to shrink and pucker after a few washings.

Pillows

Comfortable pillows are a necessary complement to comfortable mattresses. It is advisable to provide two pillows per person for most guests like to prop them up high to watch television in bed.

Most commercial pillows axe filled with synthetic fiber, mainly polyester. Synthetic pillows are quite common in commercial properties because they are inexpensive, easy to launder, and nonallergenic.

When purchasing pillows, it is important to make sure that the fill is of good quality so that it springs back into shape easily; lumpy, heavier fills are an indication of inferior grade. The synthetic covering of the pillow must be fire retardant and stain proof and able to withstand frequent washings.

Pillows with natural fills such as down and feathers are very expensive, particularly goose down. Lodging properties should stock a few natural-fill pillows to meet the occasional request for them.

Because of the price, down and feather pillows should be provided to guests on a loan basis, that is, a record should be kept in the housekeeping department of the room number where the pillows were delivered and then should be recovered after the guest's checkout.

Wall coverings

The first consideration for selecting wall coverings is that they match the general decor of the room; the second, and just as important, consideration is their durability and ease of maintenance. The two most common forms of wall coverings are paint and vinyl.

The paint used to finish walls should be easy to wash with soapy water and of very good quality so that the surface doesn't require repainting after a short period of time. Vinyl wall coverings are available in several thicknesses to suit the area to be covered; for instance, walls covered with thin layers are vulnerable to bumps from baggage and carts and should be used only to cover no-traffic areas. Heavier vinyl can withstand heavy impacts and can be used over surfaces susceptible to abrasion.

Although far more expensive than paint, vinyl wall coverings generally pay for themselves because they require very little maintenance. Vinyl coverings are made by laminating the material to cotton or polycotton backings and are glued to walls using an adhesive paste.

To prevent mildew from loosening the vinyl from the adhesive, the glue should contain a mildewcide. Fabric wall coverings can provide rooms and hallways with a luxurious, elegant look but they should be avoided in commercial operations because of the difficulty of cleaning or replacing them when soiled. Wallpaper should be used only if it is stain and water-resistant and allows for damp cleaning with soap and sponge.

Service areas, busy hallways, and elevators where carts and dollies may gouge the wall's should be protected with rubber or heavy vinyl cove base and wall guards. Corner salients should be reinforced with thick plastic corner guards.

Window coverings

Most windows in guestrooms are covered with curtains and sheers. Windows in offices, lobbies, and employee areas are usually fitted with vinyl blinds. Because of their susceptibility to fading, fabrics used for curtains must be resistant to direct sunlight. As curtains attract dust and odours, they require frequent washings and dry cleaning; for this reason, it is advisable to purchase good-quality, vinyl-coated fabrics that can retain their shape and colour for long periods of time. Curtains should be flame retardant to comply with local fire departments specifications. Drapery can be simple or quite ornate. Valances, and shirred or pinch-pleated fabrics, can add elegance and warmth to rooms, although they will require more cleaning time to keep them dust free. In all cases, the curtain rods and cords must be sturdy to avoid damage; having batons instead of cords may reduce the chance of breakage.

Department Equipment

The housekeeping department needs major pieces of equipment to clean guest, public, and employee areas and to transport clean and soiled linen, trash, and supplies. In all cases, the department equipment used in housekeeping should be of heavy-duty quality, able to withstand rough and continuous use. Often, purveyors of chemical supplies also carry a complete line of equipment. In some cases, manufacturers have their own representatives who will describe the machines and demonstrate their performance. Perhaps the most significant piece of housekeeping equipment is the housekeeping cart.

Usually, one cart is assigned to the cleaner of each section of guestrooms (the section housekeeper) and one to each janitor. The cart should be large enough and have enough shelves to carry a full complement of supplies needed in each working shift in order to avoid unnecessary trips to the linen room for additional supplies.

Although sturdy, the cart must be light and maneuverable enough to be pushed by one person from door to door and from floor to floor, including pushing it into and out of service elevators. The cart should be contoured with rubber bumpers to protect walls and wall corners and have casters with brakes of superior quality.

Some carts can be purchased with side panels that can be locked in order to prevent linen and guest amenities from being exposed to whomever walks past them, thus eliminating theft. If fitted with laundry and trash bags, these should be made of heavy-duty material to withstand hard use. Plastic baskets or caddies containing guest amenities and cleaning supplies are generally placed on the top shelf of carts.

Vaccums

Several types of vacuum cleaners are used by housekeeping. One requirement common to all of them is that they be heavy-duty and powerful enough to provide efficient, one-pass cleaning. The typical vacuum cleaner used in guestroom carpet cleaning is upright, with one or two motors. The dual-motor type has one motor to drive the beater brush and another to provide the suction.

Some useful characteristics of commercial vacuums are as follows: having collector cups or zipper receptacles instead of paper bags (some models can be messy and difficult to empty, in which case it is better to use disposable bags), long electric cable, wraparound bumpers, secondary filters to protect the vacuum motor, adjustable brush settings, three-position handles, and self-lubricating brushes. Some vacuums are incorporated into the housekeeping cart. This arrangement, however, may cause some difficulties. Because the hoses must be long enough to reach all corners of the room, suction power may be reduced. And since the vacuum must be operated in hallways, the noise permeates throughout the area. Also, because the machine is attached to the cart, repairs and maintenance are more difficult to perform on site than in the engineering shop.

Large-area vacuums are used in hallways and lobbies that contain extensive areas of carpeting. In very large ballrooms and meeting rooms, vacuums with 30-inch brushes should be used. These high-power machines can operate at 1,200 rpm and are able to service 14,000 square feet of surface per hour.

Wet/dry vacuums are designed for wet pickup on any type of hard flooring surface. Equipped with a wide squeegee, they can be used to remove liquids when hard floor& are stripped or for any kind of liquid absorption. Back vacuums worn by the housekeeper, are convenient for dusting and cleaning vertical or high surfaces and fixtures, especially curtains, drapes, and wall coverings. Back vacuums are light, quiet machines equipped with adjustable straps and hoses that can be expanded to three times their normal length.

Floor machines

Floor machines are designed to mechanically polish, buff, strip, scrub, grind, sand, burnish, and shampoo surfaces. Usually one multipurpose machine can be used for several tasks by changing the pad as needed to accomplish the task at hand. Burnishers are used when the property has large areas of terrazzo or tile floor. These machines are capable of burnishing up to 30,000 square feet per hour. Polishers are heavily weighted machines used to grind, sand, and polish marble and other stone floors.

Scrubbers are used to automatically scrub hard or resilient surfaces by applying a stripping solution and recovering the liquid as the machine is pushed along the surface. Large scrubbers feature 40-gallon stripping solution and recovery tanks, a 34-inch self-propelled scrubber, 37-inch squeegee assembly, and can service 44,000 square feet per hour. Extractors are used to clean carpets and rugs.

The simplest and least expensive consists of a machine with two tanks-one that holds the cleaning solution and one that collects the suctioned liquid. A better version has a beater brush attached to the wand to deepen the penetration of the cleaning solution into the carpet fabric.

Self-contained extractors are very convenient to operate as they don't require a wand or hoses. The best models have four-phase cleaning action (spray, scrub, rinse, and extract in one pass) with a spray power of 100 PSI. Self-contained carpet extractors are also available with dry foam instead of liquid solution.

When large lodging properties use drinking glasses made of glass (rather than plastic), glass washers are necessary. The practice of washing housekeeping glasses in the kitchen's dishwashers is not an effective one as it is usually seen as an "encroachment" by the food and beverage department personnel.

When operating a glass washer, the right type of detergent and the correct water temperature as determined by the local health department must be provided. Rather than transporting trash, soiled linen, and supplies in plastic bags, lodging properties should use light trucks or hoppers. This is preferable to hauling material in bags carried over the shoulder, especially along public hallways.

Cleaning supplies

Cleaning supplies are categorized under operating assets and are included in the property's operating budget.

Cleaning supplies comprise the chemicals necessary to perform the myriad cleaning jobs throughout the property and the nonchemical utensils needed to apply, scrub, rub, cleanse, wipe, etc.

The chemicals onto all types of surfaces. There are several hundred manufacturers of cleaning chemicals, each of which markets and sells countless products. The responsibility of selecting and using the right chemicals rests with the executive housekeeper.

Purchasing supplies

In large properties, the purchasing function, including housekeeping products, is performed by the purchasing agent. However, it should be up to the executive housekeeper to determine what products to use in the department, and to inform the purchasing agent of the specifications and characteristics required for the supplies to be bought.

Because marked differences exist among products, before choosing cleaning supplies they should be tested by the employees who will use them regularly. Janitors, housepersons, and section housekeepers must agree that the products chosen will be effective.

An agreement should be made between the department and the vendor to train workers, at no cost, on how to use the cleaning supplies properly. As with many other products, price should be only one of the factors regarding the purchasing decision, the others being availability, service, and quality.

For instance, if a product is difficult to obtain, if the purveyor doesn't provide training and technical support, and if much larger quantities than a more expensive one have to be used, you might not obtain the expected value from it. Shopping for cleaning supplies must be done competitively; that is, trying to obtain the best price for the same or comparable product.

When asking for a product quotation, the executive housekeeper must be very specific regarding its packaging, composition, and concentration.

It is important to designate specific days and time to receive sales people. Placing orders by phone can help save time, although direct contact with vendors is essential as they generally are specialists in their fields and therefore are able to suggest the solution to severe cleaning problems.

Periodic shipments of supplies may be arranged for those products used in large quantities; however, in no case should vendors be allowed to place an order without the direct approval of the person in charge of purchasing.

Because the cleaning supplies market is quite competitive, it is common for vendors to offer free items and personal prizes to the person in charge of buying. It is only ethical to assume that any discount or give-away should benefit the property and not the buying individual.

Accepting gifts or kickbacks should be prohibited, so for example if a vendor gives the purchasing agent tickets for an upcoming football game, the tickets should be rejected or, if accepted, raffled off among all employees.

Bulk purchasing of chemicals generally allows for great savings in price to the housekeeping department. There are, however, serious disadvantages with buying chemicals in large quantities. For instance, over-buying products may mean having to store them for long periods of time, tying up resources and space. Chemicals may also deteriorate while in storage and actually be more labour intensive. For example, decanting a liquid from a 55-gallon drum into smaller containers may take a considerable amount of time.

Human error when mixing concentrates and water or causing spills may also be a considerable disadvantage.

Although pre-measured chemicals are ready to be used as purchased, thus not requiring much handling, their higher cost is a disadvantage. The fact that they generate a lot of trash as they are used is also an inconvenience.

In-house chemical dispensers or mixing stations can be a good alternative to both bulk and pre-measured products. The dispensers, plumbed to hot or cold water, can automatically mix bulk chemicals, eliminating human error and labour cost from the process.

Housekeeping chemicals

The three major purposes of chemicals used in the housekeeping department are to remove dirt, to destroy harmful microorganisms, and to preserve and beautify furniture, fixtures, and surfaces.

Chemical cleaners are manufactured to remove soils from surfaces through chemical action. The stronger the chemical is, the better effect it will have on getting the job done. The strength of cleaning chemicals is measured on the pH scale. pH is the symbol for the logarithm of the reciprocal of hydrogen ion concentration in gram atoms per liter.

For example, a pH of 5 indicates a concentration of.00001 atoms of hydrogen ions in one liter of solution.

The scale goes from 1 to 14, 1 indicating a very acidic solution, 14 a very alkaline solution, and 7 a neutral solution.

Cleaning chemicals that have been enhanced with alkalis or acids to strengthen their cleaning powers can be dangerous to humans and often cannot be used on certain surfaces. A neutral cleaner can be used for all types of jobs but its cleaning power is limited.

The executive housekeeper should have adequate knowledge of the department's needs to select cleaning chemicals appropriate for each type of cleaning job to be performed regularly in the housekeeping department.

Generally speaking, high-alkaline cleaners are effective degreasers while acidic cleaners are good for fighting lime and rust, which are always found in urinals and toilets.

Another name for cleaners is detergents. Detergents act chemically to emulsify dirt, holding it in suspension so it can be removed away from the surface. Synthetic detergents are easy to rinse off and often have excellent cleaning, deodorizing, and germicidal characteristics.

Most cleaning detergents are made from mineral oils. All-purpose cleaners have neutral pH-balanced formulas for general-purpose cleaning jobs. They usually are synthetic detergents, often vegetable oil based, of which pine oil is very popular because of its pleasant scent and strong deodorizing power.

All-purpose cleaners may have corrosion inhibitors to protect metal surfaces. Single-purpose cleaners are heavy-duty cleaners used for specific cleaning jobs. Abrasive cleaners are cleaning powders or pastes combined with silica for tough cleaning jobs. These cleaners will scratch soft surfaces like fiberglass or porcelain. Gentler cleansers made with nonscratching calcite instead of silica greatly reduce their abrasive action.

Degreasers are highly effective cleaners, often biodegradable, that remove grease, tar, ink, food deposits, smoke film, fats and other grimy soils. Degreasers can be highly effective on concrete floors. It is important to remember that some products advertised as degreasers may be toxic and therefore not suitable for use on kitchen surfaces.

Although most all-purpose cleaners can be used as deodorizers, stronger chemicals are needed to counteract stale odours. Deodorizers, or air fresheners, should neutralize odours without adding strong perfume scents in the space to be deodorized.

Deodorizers can be purchased as mists, wall and urinal blocks, cup and wick, and aerosols. Glass cleaners are ammonia- and alcohol-based products that clean and provide a protective coating to glass surfaces.

Glass treated with good-quality glass cleaners resist fogging caused by moisture and temperature changes and in some manner repel dust, dirt, fingerprints, and smudges.

Most glass cleaners can also be used as multipurpose cleaners on chrome, stainless steel, enamel, formica, ceramic tile, and other washable surfaces. Metal cleaners are nonscratching products that remove rust, tarnish, corrosion, and grime from metal surfaces and fixtures.

These products can be used on brass, stainless steel, copper, chrome, and aluminium materials. Metal cleaners, can be purchased as liquids, aerosols, pastes, and cotton wadding.

Another purpose of housekeeping supplies is to beautify surfaces and fixtures. Furniture polishes are liquid waxes or oils or silicone-based sprays designed to protect and give shine to wood, leather, vinyl, metal, and plastic surfaces.

When pigments are added to liquid furniture polish, the product helps cover nicks and scratches in wood furniture, panelling, and floors.

Most metal surfaces can be dusted, cleaned, and polished with metal polishes. Strong liquid metal polishes can remove rust, corrosion, tarnish, and grime from brass, stainless steel, copper, chrome, and aluminium. Cream polishes are quite effective in cleaning sterling silver, silver-plated utensils, nickel, and pewter.

Restroom and bathroom cleaners

Strong acidic cleaners are needed to clean away lime and rust deposits in restroom and bathroom fixtures. Bowl cleaners may contain hydrochloric or phosphoric acid to cut scale and calcium deposits with little or no scrubbing.

Milder bowl cleaners are nonacid and nonabrasive, designed not to etch or pit porcelain fixtures, but their cleaning power is lower. Most toilet cleaners kill bacteria and viruses, including the HIV- I virus, on contact.

Janitors and section housekeepers should be trained well in how to handle these powerful products. Acidic bowl cleaners, for example, should not come in contact with metal attachments, stone, or tile surfaces. Public and employee urinals are usually deodorized and disinfected with paradichlorobenzene blocks that neutralize offensive odours.

Graffiti removers consist of a gel formula that effectively effaces ink, crayon, lipstick, some spray paints, magic marker, and bumper stickers from most hard surfaces. These powerful products should not be used, however, on rubber, vinyl, plastic, or painted surfaces.

Besides cleaning, housekeeping chemicals can be used to control and kill pathogenic bacteria by sanitizing and disinfecting surfaces and utensils. Disinfectants are germicidal chemicals that kill microorganisms and prevent them from multiplying.

Often, germicides are combined with chlorinated liquid detergents to act both as germ killer and cleanser, making them effective against many forms of microorganisms, including salmonella, fungi, and a broad range of viruses.

Aerosol disinfectants are generally much stronger as they are able to eliminate most bacteria and viruses such as herpes simplex, influenza, and HIV-I. Hand soaps are also important in fighting contagious diseases.

Liquid soaps used by employees in back-of -the -house areas should be antimicrobial and capable of reducing nosocomial infections caused by the fungal organism candida albicans.

Guest liquid soaps should be formulated with emollients to soften the skin, have a pleasant fragrance, and produce a rich lather.

Floor care chemicals

Hard and resilient floor cleaners must be pH neutral, that is, mild enough to clean dirt from surfaces without affecting polymer finishes, sealers, and shines. Floor cleaners are water- or vegetable oil-based and can be applied to synthetic surfaces, marble, terrazzo, and other washable floors. Stronger solvent-based cleaners, capable of erasing heel marks, rubber burns, tar, and grease from concrete and hard wood surfaces are very effective but will affect the floor finish when applied.

Strippers are chemicals used to remove and clean old floor finishes prior to rewaxing, resealing, or refinishing them. These products penetrate and emulsify worn wax buildup, polymer and acrylic finishes, and surface dirt deposits.

After the floor has been stripped, the alkaline residue should be neutralized with a neutralizer rinse prior to applying a new finish. Floor sealers are used to protect porous surfaces such as concrete, terrazzo, wood, and marble from staining.

Stronger sealers have a substantial amount of solids and are formulated to fill scratches and provide a base for floor finishes. Some sealers can coat and polish surfaces at the same time. Resilient floor finishes usually contain detergent-resistant acrylic polymers. Good products are burnishable and resistant to scuffing and black marks, acting both as sealers and finishes.

Carpet chemicals

Carpet shampoo is marketed under many commercial brands, and its composition can be different as well. Some shampoos are water-based and are a blend of polymers, biodegradable surfactants, and solvents. Soil-retarding carpet shampoos provide a fluorochemical barrier to protect against dirt, dust, spills, and stains.

Defoamers are silicone foam suppressors used to eliminate foam from the recovery system of steam cleaners. Antistatic sprays are designed to eliminate static electricity buildup on wool and synthetic carpets caused by foot traffic or low humidity. Spot removers are concentrated formulas used to pre-spray carpets before shampooing to remove tar, grease, lipstick, graffiti, and food or beverage stains.

Cleaning accessories

The number of nonchemical cleaning supplies in the

housekeeping inventory can be substantial, ranging from broom to wringer. Upright brooms are sold under several denominations, such as janitor, warehouse, household, lobby, porter, and whisk brooms. In all cases, upright brooms should be heavy duty and have wire bands to help retain their shape.

Push brooms usually consist of a combination of horse hair and synthetic fibers. For durability, the broom block should be attached to the handle by a sturdy metal brace. Wet mops also come in a variety of forms: four-ply cotton-synthetic fiber blend mops have good absorption; mops with looped ends are more durable than cut-ended.

Some brands feature mildew- and bacteria -resistant mops with scrubber headbands and double banding. Tight twisted, string-style eight-ply mops are specially designed for floor finishing applications. Mop buckets / wringers come in different shapes and forms as well.

Dual bucket systems consist of two overlapping buckets mounted on a mobile platform with casters; one bucket holds the cleaning solution and the other carries the rinse water for better sanitation. Heavy-duty plastic buckets are preferable to zinc ones as they are quieter, have no corrosion, and will not dent.

Storing chemicals

Hazardous materials are dangerous as they can harm both workers and property. Knowing how to safely handle, mix, and store them can protect employees, guests, and the company from explosions, fires, environmental contamination, higher insurance premiums, and costly litigation. Besides being dangerous, chemicals are expensive and strict guidelines should be followed to hold employees accountable for their proper dilution and use.

Hazard Communication (HazComm)

In order to protect workers from unsafe working conditions, the occupational Safety and Health Administration (OSHA) requires that employees handling chemicals are informed of the risks that these chemicals pose and that the employer provides appropriate training on how to use them safely.

Failure to comply with OSHA's HazComm regulations may result in fines if inspections of the property indicate that the directions have not been followed. HazComm requires that a list of all hazardous chemicals used in the housekeeping department be compiled and kept updated.

The executive housekeeper must then develop a program to let all employees be aware of, and alert to the hazardous materials they will come in contact with, teaching them about their specific characteristics and dangers.

The program may include lectures provided by distributors of chemical products, videos, discussions, and hands-on demonstrations. Other important steps include ensuring that all containers of chemicals are properly labelled and that workers follow approved disposal procedures.

The label must state the name of the chemical, hazard warnings, and the manufacturer's name and address. Because people who work in housekeeping maybe unable to understand English, labels with colour codes or signs are strongly recommended.

Workers should wear the right personal protective equipment when handling certain chemicals-mainly gloves, face masks, and goggles. Mixing or combining hazardous materials must be done strictly following the manufacturer's guidelines. Acids and caustics, for instance, can cause violent reactions when combined. Transferring liquids from one container to another can produce flammable vapours that can ignite easily.

Worker exposure to hazardous materials may cause allergies, such as eye, nose, and throat irritation, skin rashes, anxiety, and nausea. In severe cases, chemicals may cause dizziness, vomiting, blindness, and even death.

Besides complying with OSHA's regulations, the housekeeping department must display a list of all the chemicals used, specifying information about the manufacturer, the product's hazardous ingredients, its physical and chemical characteristics, flammability, recommended handling, health hazards, and what to do in case of ingestion, fire, or explosion.

This information is obtained from the manufacturers' material safety data sheets (MSDT) provided when the product is purchased. Employees working with chemicals should be required to read and understand product warning labels. The list must be updated and made available to employees at all times.

Chemicals should never be stored near food products but in separate storage, preferably under lock and key. Flammable liquids and sprays should be stored in a cool, dry place away from heat and sunlight. Enclosing them in metal lockers is best, in order to avoid possible fires from spreading.

Guest supplies

Lodging companies provide their guests with guestroom items intended to make their stay as convenient and comfortable as possible. These items also raise the guests' perceived value for the rate paid when occupying a room or rooms.

Non-reusable supplies

Also called amenities, non-reusable supplies are items that guests are expected to use up or may take away with them when at the end of their stay.

Tables 2 and 3 are limited lists of bathroom and guestroom amenities commonly supplied by lodging properties. Finding the right amenities for a property must be a calculated endeavour; the higher the room rate is, the more luxurious amenities should be.

Conversely, rates paid by guests in economy properties do not allow for providing them with extravagant supplies. But, in all cases, today's travellers have come to expect the best possible amenities for the type of establishment they patronize.

For example, guest surveys indicate that about 75 percent of respondents rank bathroom amenities as "extremely" or "very desirable" attributes when travelling on business, second only to the property's full-scale services.

Overall, a property's amenities figure very high in the total sum of what a particular establishment represents to the traveller, who often equates the facility's image with the amenities provided.

Table 2
Sample Bathroom Amenity Items

Aftershave lotion
Bath gel
Bath salts
Bath soap
Body lotion
Body powder
Cologne
Cosmetics
Deodorant
Fabric wash

Table 3
Sample Guestroom Amenity Items

Bathrobe	Mints
Candy	Notepads
Chocolates	Pens
Coffee and tea	Postcards
Cookies	Sewing kit
Corkscrew	Shoe horn
Flowers	Shoe mit
Fruit	Slippers
Laundry bags	Stationery
Matches	

Bathrooms amenities

Some lodging properties offer guests their own private-label products, stamped with the company's logo, because they can be customized to fit their clientele needs or because in most cases the cost is less. Others opt for adopting brand names, arguing that guests instantly recognize and prefer the quality of national and international brand amenities.

The basic bathroom amenities for most properties are deodorant and hand soaps, shampoo and conditioner (often provided combined in one container), shower caps, and paper products.

Soap bars should be of reasonable size, usually 1.5 ounces for bath and 3/4 ounce for facial. Shampoo and conditioner should be provided in easy-to-open bottles with large tops or snap caps, as packets are very difficult to tear open with soapy hands. Shower caps are a necessity for guests to shower or bathe without wetting their hair if they so desire.

Luxury properties usually provide sophisticated products like almond oatmeal and glycerin soaps, fancy toiletries, all-inclusive lost luggage kits, and ecologically sensitive, all-natural items, packaged in recycled paper printed with soyabean inks and wrapped in parchment to emphasize minimal paper use. Paper products must be of premium quality. The facial tissue must be soft, absorbent, and durable, preferably with 2-ply rather than one. Bath tissue should have a large number of sheets per roll so that less time is spent refilling dispensers. Adequate thickness and strength, as well as softness, are also necessary.

Guestroom amenities

Upscale lodging establishments outdo each other by offering a vast range of amenities aimed at pampering their guests while they relax in their rooms. Today's hoteliers view personal-care amenities as a positioning tool for their lodging properties, in that the more plentiful and novel they are, the higher value for the rate paid is perceived by guests.

Coffee makers, together with several blends of gourmet and decaffeinated coffee and a variety of teas, are common. Besides the typical candy placed on the pillow at turndown-service time, companies are adding speciality confections, such as Belgian and Italian chocolates or fancy fortune mints described as "rectangles attractively wrapped with witty fortunes and/or proverbs inside the wrappers."

Chocolate chip and oatmeal cookies, cosmetics, and safe - for-all -fabric stain removers are just a few of the $300million-a-year products that the industry invests in indulging guests.

Reusable supplies

Depending also on the quality of lodging establishments reusable supplies can range from the barely essential items offered by economy properties to the highly sophisticated, state-of-the-art technology found in first-class establishments. Supplies provided by most lodging properties are coat hangers, ice buckets, waste-baskets, ashtrays, Bible, and, recently, electronic equipment. Coat hangers should be made of wood or hard plastic instead of flexible wire. Hangers with ball tops rather than hooks are usually not taken by guests, although some travellers find it difficult to fasten them to the lip on the closet rod.

Women's hangers with skirt clips are designed for garments that hang better clipped than on a bar. Hangers are also available with clamping trouser bars to assure guests that the clothing will stay in place. Ice buckets are preferable if they are insulated with polyethylene liners and have a lid; stainless steel buckets are very durable and have a stylish look.

Providing tongs with the ice bucket is a nice touch. Rather than plain-looking rectangular rubber waste-baskets, oval fireproof ones made of metal with simulated grain leather are more elegant. For smoking rooms, heavy crystal ashtrays with bevelled edges are best.

The Gideons, a non-profit organization, provide free of charge guestroom Bibles on request. The appearance of all guest supplies is greatly enhanced by imprinting the property's or chain logo on them. The cost of logo items taken as souvenirs may be compensated by the advertising effect they will have when seen by members of the family and friends proudly displayed in the guests' own residences.

Today's guests, particularly business travellers, expect to find a wide selection of in-room electronic equipment. Computers with Internet access, fax machines, voice mail, videocassette players, and high-quality stereo receivers are an important part of the selection of amenities that technology- minded guests hope to find in lodging properties.

Uniforms

Uniforms for section housekeepers and housepersons should be functional, good-looking, and comfortable, with sleeves that allow for ease of movement. Badly designed, unstylish uniforms can affect the workers' morale and lower the property's image. Because of turnover, smocks, shirts, and pants must be easily alterable and able to stand frequent washings.

While 100 percent cotton uniforms are comfortable to wear, they usually shrink, wrinkle, and cost more. Polyester/ cotton blends are wrinkle-, shrink-, and soil-resistant, less costly, and easier to wash. It is important to establish an adequate par of employee uniforms so that each worker is provided with a clean, fresh-looking outfit each day. The executive housekeeper should have on band enough sizes of uniforms to fit all employees at any given time.

The sight of large-frame employees clad in small-size clothing and small-frame workers wearing large-size uniforms should be avoided. In large properties, when the housekeeping department is in charge of keeping and maintaining uniforms for other departments, it is advisable to assign a specific employee for this particular task. In this case, a large, secure storage space and a commercial- size sewing machine for repairs and alterations should be provided.

Uniformed departments, such as front desk and porters, often require outfits that need dry cleaning. Having uniforms dry-cleaned outside of the property can be quite expensive, so the purchase of a dry cleaning machine for employee and guest clothing should be considered. In order to save space, capital investments, and labour costs, some properties may resort to having uniform services provided by companies that furnish a five-par of uniforms for each full-time employee on a weekly basis. Although quite convenient, this service may cost the property a considerable amount of money. The executive housekeeper must analyse the cost of purchasing, laundering, and maintaining uniforms in-house and that of having the service provided by an outside contractor, if the cost of the latter is substantially greater, the service should be conducted on the property. One way to maintain adequate control of employee uniforms is to make each worker responsible for his or her outfit. A good procedure is not to issue a clean uniform unless the soiled one is returned.

6

Cleaning and Laundry Room Management

The primary function of the housekeeping department is to keep its areas of responsibility clean and functional. Every cleaning function must be set in detail in the department's standard operating procedures (SOPs). These procedures describe the routines associated with the daily functions of the department. Specifically, standards are determined to equalize employee workloads, to ensure that employees know what is expected of them, and to maintain high quality services.

Guestroom cleaning

The essence of the lodging industry is to provide guests with impeccably cleaned rooms and bathrooms. Students of hospitality programs must understand from the beginning that guests do not patronize establishments in which the cleaning function is not conducted effectively.

Sequence of housekeeping functions

The housekeeping department is usually opened very early in the morning by an assistant manager or senior supervisor who receives the front desk report from the front office department. The front desk report, which is usually prepared by the night clerk or night auditor, consists of a computer printout, or written form if the property is not computerized, specifying the status of each guestroom in the house, the number of rooms occupied the previous night, and the rooms that are expected to check-out and stay-over. This report is an exact copy of the guestroom status found in the front desk computer, or the room rack if the property is not computerized. A code beside the numbers of all rooms in the house describes whether the rooms are occupied, vacant, ready, out-of-order, expected to check out today, and so on.

The supervisor receiving the front desk report first verifies whether the number of department employees scheduled yesterday to work today is sufficient to service the number of rooms occupied. If not enough workers were scheduled, the supervisor will have to telephone around to ask people to come to work.

On the other hand, if too many workers were scheduled for the occupancy reached, calls will be made to ask some employees to stay away that day, saving them an unnecessary trip to work. Having the right number of workers each day to service the rooms occupied prevents higher than necessary labour costs due to overstaffing or to overtime wages for not having enough employees to do the work in 8 hours.

The information received on the front desk report is then transferred on to the team supervisor work report to inform all team leaders of the status of all guestrooms in their respective sections.

Each team supervisor will then communicate the status of the rooms in each section to the team's section housekeepers using a section housekeeper work report which is given to them at the beginning of the shift. When the property is not at 100 percent occupancy, and not all section housekeepers are called to work, the occupied rooms of the sections that are open are assigned to the section housekeepers who are working that day.

Beginning daily activity

At the beginning of the working day, housekeeping personnel congregate in the linen room where they clock in and receive a briefing on the day's activities. Generally, daily activities in the housekeeping department start at 8:00 A.M., although in some cases this time may be different depending on the type of establishment, day of the week, or special functions taking place at the property.

For instance, most of the guests in business hotels do get up early for meeting purposes, to catch an early flight, or attend a convention.

On the other hand, on Saturdays and Sundays, guests traditionally get up late and like a late check-out. Also, if the guests of a large convention have been granted permission to check out late in the afternoon, most of the housekeeping work force will be needed to work late to prepare the rooms for that day's arrivals.

The day's work begins with the section housekeepers collecting their fully equipped service cart and work report and signing for the passkey for their respective sections on a key control sheet. In high-rise buildings, all housekeeping personnel should use service elevators only.

The work report indicates the status of all rooms in the respective housekeeper sections. Instead of knocking on doors at random, section housekeepers should follow a logical order so that guests are not woken up or disturbed while still in their rooms.

Rooms that have already checked out should be serviced first, followed by rooms showing requests for early service, expected checkouts, stay-over rooms, and requests for late service. Last, usually after check-out time, the status of "do -not -disturb" (DND) rooms must be ascertained. It is important to verify what is behind a DND room lest a guest in need of help is unable to use the phone. This situation can occur if the guest is unconscious or in a coma.

The first attempt to contact the guest should be done by phone; if the guest answers, the section housekeeper should ask if a cleaning of the room is required. If there is no answer, the section housekeeper should knock at the door and try to enter the room. If there is no answer and the room is double-locked, a manager should enter the room using a master key.

In situations when the room is finally opened and the security chain is on, the chain must be cut with a chain-cutter. It is important to remember that in connecting rooms, the guest could have left the DND sign on, double-locked the door, and set the chain in one of the rooms while exiting from the room next door.

Also at the beginning of the working day, hallways stairwells, vending-machine areas, elevators, and floor closets and vestibules should be inspected by the houseperson of each team.

Common problems found early in the morning are leftover room service trays, spills, overflowing wastebaskets, and signs of vandalism. After correcting these flaws, the housepersons proceed to help the section housekeepers in their respective teams by providing them with supplies, moving heavy pieces of furniture, taking soiled linen to the laundry room, and so on. The housepersons usually finish their shift by vacuuming the public areas assigned to each of their teams.

Room status verification

As the daily work progresses, section housekeepers should notify their team supervisors if any discrepancy is found between the status of rooms as shown in their work report and the real status of the rooms. For example, if the section housekeeper work report shows that room 105 is occupied and there is no sign of guests in the room, the front desk report might have been wrong. In this case, the front office must be immediately notified of the discrepancy.

Some lodging properties require that the housekeeping department file a status report for the accounting department as a cross-reference to the occupancy report submitted by the front office. If the front desk is selling rooms and pocketing the money or if they let employees or friends stay in guestrooms for free, the problem is soon discovered.

At about 10 o'clock, the A.M.. room check is conducted by all teams entering the guestrooms at about the same time. All relevant discrepancies found from the front desk report must be communicated to the front desk as quickly as possible.

As work progresses, the team supervisors coordinate the activities related to the rooms in their sections, such as communicating to the front desk the rooms that are vacant and ready to be sold, notifying section housekeepers of guests changing rooms, communicating the need to clean rooms for early arrivals, VIP treatment, and so forth. In most properties, team supervisors are also in charge of inspecting guestrooms.

Guestroom cleaning procedures

Section housekeepers should knock at the door with their knuckles, announcing themselves as "housekeeping," at least twice prior to entering the room. The door should remain open, With the service cart blocking the entrance for safety reasons. This way, if someone attempts to pull the cart to enter the room, the section housekeeper would be alerted.

All lodging properties have standard operating procedures for guestroom cleaning; however, these procedures differ from property to property.

Usually, section housekeepers are asked to air out the room by opening windows and turn on all lights to make sure that they are in working order. The TV set and the heating/ air-conditioning units are then checked, resetting the thermostat to the lowest comfortable setting. The section housekeeper ascertains that no items are missing, broken, or vandalized. If that is the case, the team supervisor should be notified immediately, who in turn will call the front desk so that the guest is charged accordingly. If out-of-order or not working equipment is found, a work order is filled out and sent to the maintenance department. If the guests have checked out of the room, the section housekeeper should ascertain that no personal belongings have been left behind. If they have, the team supervisor is notified as soon as possible, who, in turn, will notify the front desk and security department. If the guests have not checked out, all scattered clothing items, papers, documents or magazines should be placed away neatly, making sure that nothing is thrown away that may be useful to the guest.

The first step in cleaning the bedroom is to empty out the trash in the refuse bag of the service cart, changing the waste-basket liners with new ones and cleaning the ashtrays. The bed is stripped, keeping items off the floor and handling the linen carefully lest guest items have been left there. Special care must be taken with sharps (needles) that may be in the sheets.

At this time, the mattress, box spring, blanket, bedspread, pillows, and bed pads are carefully inspected for stains or torn spots and replaced as needed. The soiled bed and bathroom linen is placed in the service cart receptacle for fast delivery to the laundry room for processing as seen as the bag is full. In most properties, the house-person regularly empties the receptacles into a hamper for transportation.

Basic bed procedures

The first step in making the bed is to place the bottom sheet smoothly on it, tucking it at the head and sides. The bottom and top sheets and blanket are then metered at the foot of the bed and tucked along the sides. The bedspread is then placed over the blanket, turned about 15 inches back from the headboard, and the pillow(s) placed over it.

Both bedspread and pillow(s) are then rolled back toward the headboard. The bedspread should be smoothed out so no lumps or creases show after the bed has been made. Section housekeepers should be trained to make beds moving around them only once in order to save time and energy.

Dusting and wiping the bedroom

Lamp shades are brushed with a dry cloth or feather duster. All furniture, fixtures, and doors are lightly sprayed with a cleaning solution or furniture polish and damp-wiped with a dust cloth. Air vents, windowsills, light bulbs, telephones, the top of thermostats, and closet shelves are also wiped clean with a damp cloth. Drawers are wiped out and inspected for cleanliness and ease of operation. If the drawers are difficult to open (or close), a work order should be filled out. All recycled items should be meticulously cleaned or replaced. The property or chain literature and phone books must be kept as new, without marks or creases.

Missing clothes hangers should be replaced and those not belonging to the property removed. Mirrors and TV screen should be sprayed and wiped with a dry cloth. All drapes, lamp shades, and pictures must be centered and balanced. The carpet is then vacuumed, including under the bed, starting at the far end of the room and ending at the door. Finally, deodorant spray is applied to curtains and carpet before leaving the room. This procedure is particularly necessary in "smoking rooms."

When the guestroom has a balcony or patio, the floor is swept and the door and furniture dusted. If the room is at floor level, the patio door should be properly secured by setting the security bar in place. Properties offering suites with kitchenettes require considerable labour to service the living, cooking, and dining areas. Dishes must be washed, cooking equipment and utensils scrubbed and polished, and refrigerators, cupboards, and drawers wiped clean.

Some lodging properties have experimented with guestroom team cleaning; that is, having two section housekeepers dean guestrooms at the same time. Although team cleaning may be preferred by housekeeping workers, it usually is not labour-cost effective. In practice, a room that is serviced in 30 minutes by one room attendant cannot be finished by two room attendants in 15 minutes.

Bathroom cleaning

Section housekeepers should wear gloves when cleaning the bathroom for chemical and germ protection. After checking all lights, inspecting the faucets for leaks, and dumping the waste-basket, the commode is cleaned inside with bowl cleaner and a toilet brush and outside (including the tank) with a germicidal solution.

The bath area should be cleaned by the section housekeeper standing inside the tub on a rubber mat placed at the bottom of the tub to keep from slipping. The bath walls, soap dishes, plumbing fixtures, and shower doors are cleaned with all-purpose cleaner and wiped dry with a cloth. The tub is cleaned, using mild scouring powder/liquid if necessary. The tub stopper should be pulled out, freed from hair, and wiped clean.

The vanity and sink are cleaned with all-purpose cleaner and wiped dry. The sink stopper should also be pulled out and wiped clean. The mirror should be cleaned with a damp cloth or sprayed with a mirror-cleaning solution and wiped dry.

The bathroom floor should be wiped with cloth and germicidal, including behind the door. Any lint in the bathroom ventilation vent or fan grill should be removed. All supplies and guest amenities should be replaced as needed. Towels should be neatly folded in racks or hanged properly from towel bars.

Toilet and facial tissue should be replaced if less than one-quarter full. A second toilet tissue roll should be left in the bathroom as reserve. It is a good idea to have section housekeepers place a card stating that the room was serviced by them; this increases pride and identifies the worker with the job performed; for example, "Hello, this room has been serviced by Erika. Have a pleasant stay with us." After the room has been cleaned, the section housekeeper notifies the supervisor that the room is ready for inspection. In some properties, section housekeepers may use codes through the telephone or the television set to inform the housekeeping office that the rooms have been serviced.

Lost and found procedures

All items found in a lodging property are usually

deposited in and controlled by the housekeeping department, given that most articles are left behind by guests in the property's guestrooms. Standard operating procedures for lost-and-found items must be in place and made clear to all employees. In all cases, when articles are found anywhere in the property they must be taken to the housekeeping department (usually to the linen room) and adequately tagged and logged for fast identification.

The lost-and-found logbook must include the date on which the item was found, its description, the place where it was found, the person who found it, and the number assigned to the tagged item. At times when the housekeeping department is closed, the article will be securely kept at the front desk and brought to the linen room first thing in the morning.

Items containing multiple articles, such as bags, wallets, or purses, should be inventoried and their content described and verified by two employees. All tagged items must be kept under lock and key for security reasons.

All inquiries regarding lost-and-found items should be addressed to the housekeeping office. After proper identification, the items are returned to their owners. If the inquiry is made from out of town, the property should send the item free of charge to its owner by mail or UPS package.

Valuable articles should be sent by registered mail or insured for their approximate cost. It is customary in the hospitality industry that items not claimed within a reasonable period of time, generally three months, are given to the employee who found them or given away to a charitable organization.

The P.M. Housekeeping report

Prior to the end of the morning shift, all section housekeepers conduct a check of all the rooms in the house simultaneously. Each room attendant records on a blank daily work report the status of each guestroom in his or her section. The reports of all section housekeepers are recorded on a blank front desk report and delivered to the front desk. The front desk will then compare the housekeeping room status with the status kept in the front desk's computer, or room rack if the property is not computerized.

Any discrepancy between the room status provided by the housekeeping department and the room status at the front desk is quickly investigated and corrected. For example, if the housekeeping room report indicates that room 101 is occupied and the records at the front desk show that the room is vacant, the room is checked as to whether housekeeping or the front desk was in error.

At the end of the morning shift, the housekeepers of every team restock the floor closets assigned to them with clean linen and guest and cleaning supplies, they vacuum hallways, tidy vending areas and stairwells, and dump all trash. If time allows, section housekeepers refit service carts for the following day and store them for the night.

Inspection of bedrooms

The general rule in lodging properties is to have all guestrooms inspected by qualified staff before they are handed over to the front desk for renting them to guests. This control function is important for properties with quality assurance programs, as inspectors are the last employees to catch any errors made during cleaning before guests arrive.

Small properties with no or very low turnover may

decide to trust their section housekeepers and leave to them the job of inspecting the rooms just after they have been cleaned. Large properties, however, should have a rigorous system of inspecting guestrooms prior to their being rented to guests.

Usually, the guestrooms are inspected by the supervisor of each team; some large hotels have designated inspectors whose only job is to check rooms.

In all cases, standards should be set to help section housekeepers and inspectors work toward reaching the same goals of cleanliness and room appearance. Often, inspectors give scores to the section housekeeper responsible for cleaning the room that determine, after a certain period of time, whether the room attendant qualifies for bonuses or rewards attached to superior performance.

On the other hand, substandard scores will lead to retraining room attendants or disqualifying them for the job. Inspectors should be trained to do fair andaccurate inspections. Some properties enter the data collected on a computer to show performance over the long term.

The data may show that the performance of a particular team is low in a specific area, for example bathrooms. In this case, additional training in bathroom cleaning should be emphasized to bring the team up to bathroom-cleaning standards.

Vacant -and-ready (VR) rooms should be inspected first so they can be turned over to front desk for assignment to early arrivals. The person who inspects rooms must be well trained to detect errors and make sure that everything in the room is in perfect order. Well-trained inspectors can perform this function very quickly and effectively without having to use checklists.

Some inspection programs include the preventive

maintenance inspection of guestrooms in order to anticipate mechanical or functional breakdowns before they may occur. When deficiencies are detected, a maintenance work order is filed and sent to the engineering department for immediate attention. Maintenance work orders should be in triplicate-two parts going to engineering and one kept on file until the job is completed. If the deficiency is not corrected after a reasonable amount of time, a second work order request should be initiated. The order form for emergency repairs, such as broken guestroorn door locks, should be marked "urgent" and delivered to the engineering department in person for immediate action.

The evening shift

The housekeeping evening activities in medium-size properties are usually conducted by a team consisting of a supervisor, a house-person, a reduced number of section housekeepers, and one or two janitors. In large and very large properties, a greater number of employees is necessary.

The evening team receives the housekeeping P.M. report showing the status of all the guestrooms at the end of the morning shift and continues with the task of cleaning late check-out and day-rate rooms so these can be rented to guests. If the property offers turndown service, the evening team will perform the tasks of unfolding the bed, drawing the drapes closed, and refreshing the room by emptying the trash and replacing used towels.

The evening section housekeepers also fill guest requests, such as delivering extra pillows or blankets to rooms, providing cribs or roll-a-way beds, or bringing extra towels. The evening teams also wash drinking glasses, restock service carts and caddies (portable cleaning-supply containers with a handle), clean public restrooms and, if necessary, process soiled linen in the property's laundry.

It is important to provide beepers to members of the evening team so that the front desk or manager-on-duty can effectively communicate with housekeeping personnel. The service carts are also stocked in the evening to facilitate operations and avoid confusion the following morning. Each service cart is supplied with bed and bathroom linens, paper supplies, guest amenities, and recycled items.

The cleaning supplies commonly placed in caddies are cleaning solutions, brushes, scrubbers, sponges, and cleaning rags. The service cart is equipped with trash and soiled-linen bags.

A broom and dustpan and a vacuum cleaner are also placed on the cart. If the property uses keys instead of guestroorn entry cards, the cart should also have a locked bolted-on metal box with a slot where the leftover keys are placed. Its purpose is to avoid leaving guestroorn keys on top of the cart where they are easily accessible to thieves.

Guestroom deep cleaning

Section housekeepers are usually allotted an average of 30 minutes to service a stay-over or check-out room. Periodically, room attendants are given extra time to clean guestrooms in depth, performing tasks such as brushing carpet edges, rotating mattresses, vacuuming drapes, and cleaning under the furniture.

In order not to tie up guestrooms for long periods of time, deep cleaning should be combined with maintenance tasks conducted by the engineering department, such as recaulking tubs, changing air conditioning filters, or performing minor repairs.

Deep cleaning of guestrooms should be intensified during low-occupancy periods. Generally all rooms in the house should be deep cleaned at least once a year.

Public areas and back of the house cleaning

The housekeeping department is also in charge of the cleaning and maintenance of offices, public and back-of -the-house areas. Potential guests and visitors have a first-hand opportunity to judge the cleanliness of the property from what they see in the "on-stage" public areas.

Public and employee areas are cleaned by janitors, who are scheduled to work regardless of the property's occupancy, because the front- and back-of-the-house areas must be kept clean, whether the property is full or not, 24 hours a day. The cleaning of public areas is conducted following preestablished area cleaning inventories and frequency schedules. Thus, the janitors will know exactly what and how often all their assigned areas must be cleaned.

For instance, while the chandelier in the lobby of the property usually is dusted every two months, the carpet in the same area is vacuumed daily (or twice a day).

Besides cleaning, janitors should keep public areas in good order by straightening the furniture, emptying ashtrays, trashcans, and cigarette urns, and taking away empty glasses and used newspapers. The handset of public telephones should be wiped clean with a germicidal solution and the telephone book replaced if it has scribbled lines on it.

Special attention must be given to the foyer and lobby where guests will get a first impression of the property upon entering the establishment. Handprints and smudges on glass doors are common, as well as footprints and traces of mud on the carpet when the weather is inclement. Appropriate matting and runners must be placed strategically to protect the appearance of the lobby's floor.

The presence of dust, cobwebs, smudges, dull-looking water fountains, or unpolished wood surfaces in the public areas is unacceptable. Elevators, including service elevators, require frequent attention as bell carts and heavy suitcases do often bump against walls and floor, scratching or marking their finish.

Just as important as public areas is the cleaning of employee areas and other sections at the back of the house. The employee locker room and restrooms are areas where vandalism and graffiti marks frequently occur. The upkeep of these areas, hallways, and the employee cafeteria is a reflection of the care and concern that the company bestows on its employees, which may positively or negatively affect the morale of the property's work force.

Restroom cleaning

Public restrooms require special and dedicated attention, as they are not only used by guests, but also by visitors, restaurant and bar patrons, and people attending meetings or conventions in the property.

Public restrooms must be constantly checked, cleaned, and stocked with high-quality sanitary, paper, and soap supplies. Restrooms should be fitted with automatic air fresheners or other method of odour control. Battery-operated wall cabinets can automatically deliver fragrances using 30-day cartridges.

Men's urinals should be equipped with screens and deodorizing blocks containing chelating agents to prevent mineral deposit buildups. Basins and counter tops should be sanitized with a germicidal cleaner.

All chrome fixtures should be wiped clean and polished. Toilets should be brushed inside with an effective bowl cleaner and the tank cover (if any) and body of the bowl wiped dean with cleansing solution. Special attention must be given to graffiti and lipstick marks, so common in public spaces. Mops used in restrooms should be sanitized with a strong disinfectant solution added to the water in the bucket/wringer.

Surface cleaning

Surface coverings may be classified into resilient and nonresilient according to their hardness. Cleaning and maintenance of floors and walls depends on the composition of the surface's material. Surfaces must be preserved from deterioration as much as possible by protecting them from wear and tear. Once the surface shows signs of wearing away, it must be redone to bring it back to its original state.

The first step to redo floors is to remove the worn out finish. This process is called stripping. Commercial floors are stripped using a stripping solution mixed with water and scrubbing the surface with a rotary floor machine. The resulting mixture is picked up with a wet vacuum or mop and bucket and the floor rinsed with clean water.

After the floor dries, porous surfaces are treated with a sealer to protect them from wear and tear and liquid spills. The last step is to apply a finish to the surface to make it slip resistant and give the floor a glossy, shiny look.

Often, sealer and finish are combined into one product. Finished surfaces are maintained by polishing them with rotary floor machines which clean, buff, and burnish the floor using different types of pads.

The most common resilient surfaces found in

lodging operations are made of synthetic rubber, vinyl, wood and, of course, carpeting. The most common hard floors (nonresilient) are ceramic, marble/terrazzo, epoxy, and concrete. The composition of the floor determines the kind of care it should receive. For instance, while porous surfaces require sealing, the sealing of nonporous floors is unnecessary.

Synthetic rubber floors

Floors covered with synthetic rubber tiles are nonporous and therefore waterproof; however, liquids containing oil, solvent, or grease may cause the material to crack and deteriorate. Rubber floors are easy to maintain, as they just require mopping to keep them clean.

The cleaning solution used should be pH neutral, as alkalies and acids would mar these surfaces. These types of floors do not require sealing. Synthetic floors can be kept shiny by buffing them with a water emulsion floor polish. When wax or dirt buildup is embedded in the finish, the floor should be stripped with a mild de-waxer.

Vinyl floors

These are nonporous surfaces resistant to most chemical spills. Thick vinyl material is quite durable and can be purchased in a variety of patterns to resemble natural products. If the material is treated with special seals when made, it can be resistant to scratches and abrasions.

No-wax vinyl surfaces do not need sealing, stripping, or finishing. Conventional vinyl floors can be treated with solvent-based waxes and buffed to a rich luster. Wax buildup can be removed with a mild de-waxing stripper. Dusting and daily mop-and-rinse will remove most dirt and grime.

Wood floors

Wood floors are not common in most modern lodging

properties, where carpeting, ceramic tile, and synthetic surfaces are the norm, but they may be found in older establishments and in some ski resorts and hunting lodges. Because of its porosity, wooden floors must be well sealed to prevent stains; once stained, the surface needs to be thoroughly sanded to remove the marks. Wood floors can also be damaged by mobile equipment with metal rollers and by moving heavy furniture without first protecting the surface. These surfaces can be treated with a combination sealer/finish made of water-borne polyurethane. When properly sealed and finished, wooden floors just require an occasional buffing to keep them shiny.

Carpets

Preventing staining and wear is more important for carpets than it is for other types of floor coverings. For example, if the lobby of a lodging property is carpeted, the slush, mud, and gritty soil tracked in by guests quickly become embedded in the carpet fabric, causing it to stain and wear very fast. The best prevention for carpet deterioration is adequate protection. Placing walk-off mats in doorways and plastic runners over the most high-traffic sections of the carpet will lengthen its life and save labour hours in cleaning and maintenance.

Scheduled daily vacuuming of carpets is probably the best way to extend their lives. Most of the soil tracked into a building is dry-the kind that can be controlled by vacuuming.

The absorption of dust, sand, and grit particles by vacuuming will prevent the erosion of fibers when they are compressed by the weight of traffic from people and carts. Vacuums with top-loading bags are preferable, as they ensure that the vacuum does not lose effectiveness as the bag fills.

Marks and stains can be removed by bonnet cleaning, by which carpet shampoo is sprayed on the surface to be treated and a rotary floor machine equipped with a bonnet is passed over until the stains finishing. Conventional vinyl floors can be treated with solvent-based waxes and buffed to a rich luster. Wax buildup can be removed with a mild de-waxing stripper. Dusting and daily mop-and-rinse will remove most dirt and grime are removed.

When surfaces are heavily soiled, deep cleaning is necessary. Heavy soils can be treated using water extractors that automatically apply the cleaning solution and pick it up with an attached wet vacuum system that recovers water and soil in a holding tank.

Carpets should be cleaned with hot water, except for wool fabrics that require cold water. Dry foam and dry powder methods are less effective than water extractors, but it takes less time for the carpet to dry so the area can be used sooner if necessary.

Some products applied regularly to carpets are antimicrobial solutions to prevent the growth of bacteria and fungi, antistatic sprays to eliminate static electricity caused by low humidity or high winds, and fluorochemical treatments that resist soiling and prevent spills from becoming hard-to-remove stains.

Upholstrered surfaces

Upholstered armchairs and couches can be spot-cleaned with most of the same products used on carpets. Machines with special attachments are needed to apply the spot removers to narrow surfaces. Some spotters are fortified with enzymes to treat organic compounds; tougher soils, such as crayon, fresh paint, ink, and gum, require solvent formulas to dissolve the stains.

Ceramic floors

Because ceramic floors are very resistant to water spills and easy to dean, they are quite common in bathroom and kitchen. Usually, the terracotta that forms the tile is covered with a glossy coat that makes the surface 100 percent waterproof. A disadvantage with this type of floor is that they can be very slippery when wet. These surfaces are cleaned by sweeping and damp mopping. Sealing or finishing of ceramic floors is not necessary, except for the grout between the tiles.

Marble/terrazzo floors

Marble is a crystalline limestone that is capable of taking a polish. Terrazzo is a floor material of broken stone (marble or granite chips) and cement that can also be easily lustered. Although very hard and durable, these surfaces are very sensitive to oils and acid and alkaline cleaners. A mild detergent is all that is needed to keep them clean. Because of their porosity, marble and terrazzo floors must be sealed, and when stripped, alkaline products should be avoided. The surfaces can be burnished to obtain a mirror-like finish.

Epoxy floors

Epoxy is a synthetic material that is durable, abrasion-resistant, and easy to maintain. Alkaline compounds diluted in water are used to clean epoxy floors. Epoxy surfaces can be kept shiny with a light finish application. Alkaline products are needed to strip the finish.

Concrete floors

Concrete floors, made with a mixture of cement and sand, are usually used as outdoor surfaces, such as driveways, loading docks, and pool-side areas. Cleaning is done by sweeping and hosing with water. Concrete is a porous compound that should be sealed to prevent liquid stains from seeping into it. Urethane -fortified products resist water and help protect against graffiti. An alkaline product diluted in water is required to strip the sealer.

Walls and ceilings

Some wall and ceiling coverings that are different from those normally used on floor surfaces are paint, plastic laminate, fabric, vinyl, and wallpaper. Painted surfaces can be cleaned with mild detergent and water.

Dusting and damp-wiping are all that it is required to keep plastic laminate clean, as it is nonporous and will not absorb stains. Fabric materials are very susceptible to mildew and stains. Walls covered with fabric should be spot-cleaned with chemicals rather than with water and detergent to avoid shrinkage. Vinyl covering can be purchased in many decorative motifs. It is durable and easy to clean with mild detergents.

On the other hand, most wallpaper coverings cannot be cleaned with water, so they must be replaced if they are marked or stained. Written procedures for all aspects of daily maintenance of surfaces should be established. In general, grease and dirt are acidic in nature and they are best cleaned with alkaline products. The more grease and dirt on a surface, the more alkalinity is needed in the cleaning compound to treat the area.

Design of the laundry room

Setting up a laundry room requires a detailed analysis of the property's needs. Poor planning may result in inadequate space to perform daily operations, insufficient equipment to keep up with the volume of linen to be washed, too small drains to funnel away the discharged water, poor working conditions caused by inadequate ventilation, and so on.

The first step in designing the laundry consists of building a facility that has enough capacity to process the maximum amount of linen that the property can generate per day. Ample space should be allocated to install all equipment required and to provide an area large enough for dean and dirty linen to be easily separated. The space allocated varies with the size of the property and can range from 1,000 square feet in small properties to over 20,000 square feet in larger operations.

The laundry room should be equipped with enough washers and dryers to process all items that the rooms and food and beverage divisions will require at 100 percent occupancy without incurring overtime or running the laundry operation round the clock. The design should anticipate all mechanical, electrical, and ventilation installation connections for the equipment as well as identify the optimal location of drains for washers and soak sinks. If water restriction in the area is severe or if the water costs are high, a system for recycling washer rinse water can be installed. These water recovery systems route rinse water from the washer's dump valve into a recovery tank to be reused in the wash cycles. Over 25 percent of water usage can thus be saved.

The selection and specifications of the equipment depend on the type of linens to be laundered. For instance, a lodging property with restaurants and banquet department should have extra washers to process food and beverage napkins and tablecloths; a property offering in-house dry cleaning service will need to install dry cleaning equipment; an establishment that uses no-iron sheets may not require a mangle to iron these items. Choosing the right linens will result in substantial savings of equipment and labour costs.

Most nylon and polyester/cotton blend fabrics require less washing and drying time, and do not need to be ironed. One negative aspect, however, of synthetic fibers is their sensitivity to high washing and drying temperatures.

Once the equipment has been selected it should be installed to allow for the best possible layout. An adequate work-flow pattern should be designed to provide an efficient distribution of space and avoid worker cross-traffic. Ideally, the work flow should follow a circular pattern in the following order: laundry room entrance soak sinks → washers → dryers → mangle(s) → sheet folder stand → folding table → shelves and mobile racks → laundry room exit. Because laundry operations are conducted in a hot, humid environment, sufficient exhaust capacity should be provided to draw out the moist air. Because of frequent liquid spills, the floor of laundry rooms should be waterproofed and consist of a nonslippery material.

Washers

With the introduction of microprocessor controlled machines, washing linens has been greatly simplified. Gone are the days when loading detergent in the machine and setting water temperatures and time cycles were done by hand. Instead, these functions are done automatically by programmed processors that regulate the amount of soap to be injected in the machine, activate thermostats, and control the machines' timers. Smaller washers, for instance 18-pounders, operate on the same principles as conventional residential machines; that is, the soiled linen is placed in the machine's receptacle and agitated through washing and rinsing cycles. The washer finally spins the moisture out and the load is ready to be transferred to a dryer.

Larger washers, however, are built with high efficiency and productivity in mind in order to maximize laundry outputs. Some washer extractors, for instance, feature single-pivot tilts to facilitate loading and unloading, high-speed extract to reduce drying and ironing time, and thermal cool-down to eliminate wrinkles. The tilt feature minimizes operators' fatigue and back stress, helping the establishment keep its people by making the job easier. The incorporation of microprocessors to washer- extractors has also simplified operations and ensured consistent, reliable results.

Some machines offer over 20 pre-set wash programs that can be activated at the touch of a button. These machines can be preprogrammed with washing formulas specifically designed for hospitality linen; thus, a lodging property can have different preprogrammed formulas for bed linen, terry cloth, napery, and greasy kitchen aprons and rags. Large washer-extractors may be comprised of two or more separate pocket cylinders that allow different loads to be processed at the same time. Some lodging chains that operate a central laundry serving several establishments, and therefore process over 2,000 pounds of linen per hour, use tunnel washers. Tunnel washers have several chambers that enable the machine to process multiple loads simultaneously.

Investing in washer- extractors with high G-force (spinning power) can result in as much as 30 percent savings in time and energy. The lower the water retention of the fabrics is, the less time and energy consumption that will be needed during drying and ironing. For example, machines with greater than 200 G-force will reduce substantially the gas or electricity used during the drying process over 90 G-force washer -extractors. Operators of lodging facilities should install washing equipment with extraction flexibility, as all fabrics do not have the same extract G-force requirements. For instance, an extraction force of 90 is ideal for permanent press and blends, while a 140 G-force range is necessary for hard-to-dry items such as blankets, spreads, and mattress pads. Because of the high gravitational force exerted by these powerful machines, large washer- extractors must be professionally anchored onto the laundry floor.

When located near guestrooms, washer-extractors should be well cushioned to avoid excessive noise or floor vibration. Estimating the number and size of washers to be installed in a property depends on the type of linen to be processed, the desired number of hours within which the linen must be finished, and the linen poundage of the establishment. A lodging property with food and beverage facilities should have at least three washers installed, one for bed linen, one for terry cloth, and one for tablecloths and napkins. These three different kinds of linen require different washing formulas because of the different composition of the fabrics and the type of soiling that must be laundered. For instance, napkins and tablecloths are usually soiled with fats and oils, while guestroom linen usually has different types of stains.

The number of hours allocated for daily laundering is also a key factor for sizing laundries. If it is determined that 1, 500 pounds of linen should be processed in 8 hours, it would be necessary to have twice as many washers as needed to launder the same amount of linen in 4 hours. The linen poundage is the weight of one par of linen: that is, the maximum output for peak business period or the weight of all items that need to be processed at 100 percent occupancy.

Using the same example as before, a lodging property with three 50 pound washers and 1/2-hour washing cycles would theoretically require 5 hours to process 1,500 pounds of linen (3 × 50 = 150; 150 × 2 =

300; 300 × 5 = 1,500). If the linen poundage to be washed in the same period of time had been 3,000, a double number of washers would have been required.

Dryers

As with washers, the number of dryers needed to process one par of linen in a given number of hours depends on the poundage and type of fabrics to be dried. Bed linen that is put through mangles for ironing, for instance, does not need to be passed through dryers. In general, because the drying cycle usually takes double the time of the washing cycle, twice as many dryers of the same capacity are needed to get the job done. In order to save energy, a battery of dryers should be enclosed on the top and sides so that heat is not lost around the equipment. This contained heat can thus be used as warm intake air. When using gab dryers, the outside air intake for combustion should not be larger than needed so that no extra cold outside air is absorbed into the dryer area.

A damper closing the aperture when dryers are not in use can effectively block the outside air from coming into the laundry room. Dryer burners should be cleaned regularly to ensure that lint has not caused the burners to partially clog. The inefficient burning of gas can be identified by a yellowish flame, rather than blue. Dryer lint must often be removed from the dryer ventilation system and the dryers' adjacent areas.

Mangles

Linen can be ironed by feeding it to rollers or by placing it on presses. When done by hand, ironing linen is a labour-intensive, time-consuming process. Sophisticated tandem units on the market today can dry, iron, and fold linen automatically. These flatwork finishers have a built-in folder assembly that can handle items from pillowcases to king-size sheets that require an ironed look. Most lodging properties use no-iron bed linen to avoid the high labour cost associated with pressing. However, they usually have small or medium -size mangles to iron napkins, tablecloths, and pillowcases to add to the facility's image. In this case, linens go directly from washer to finisher, reducing the amount of energy needed to dry them.

Besides washers and dryers, the laundry room must be fitted with additional equipment necessary for linen processing. Soak sinks are needed for spot and stain removal using strong chemical formulas. The soak sinlks should be placed between the soiled-linen sorting area and the washers. Folding tables and folder stands should be placed by the dryers and mangles, close to storage shelving. The folding tables are used to fold terry cloth items and the folder stands to fold sheets, blankets, shower curtains, and bed pads. Only one worker is needed to fold items using the folder stand, while two attendants are necessary to fold them by hand.

Plastic or vinyl-coated canvas laundry hampers can be very useful to transport linen to and from washers and dryers and to hold soiled and clean items while being processed. Stainless steel mobile racks are often necessary to hold the clean linen for later transport to the different floor closets on the property.

Laundry operation

The linen laundering cycle begins with the collection of soiled items from guestrooms and the food and beverage outlets, and ends with the distribution of clean linen to all locations.

Collection of soiled linens

Section housekeepers should be trained to sort bed and bathroom linens in order to facilitate the laundry department's work. If at all possible, the room attendants should separate bed from bathroom items, placing them in different containers. Heavily soiled items should be clearly set apart so laundry workers can initiate the necessary pre-treatment as soon as they arrive in the laundry room. The use of hampers to transport linen, rather than plastic bags, provides a better impression to guests, causes no environmental waste, and saves bagging and unbagging time. When the property has linen chutes, all sorting is done in the linen room. Good communication and cooperation is needed between the laundry manager and the food and beverage director to ensure that napery items are sorted and inspected for debris before they are brought to the laundry room.

Napery mixed with silverware, pieces of bread, and food scraps should not be accepted by laundry personnel for processing. Items heavily stained with butter, ketchup, wine, or sauces should be delivered separately. Kitchen rags and chef's aprons must never be bundled together with napery items.

Once in the laundry room, linen must be sorted out by category and readied for washing. Because each category requires a different water temperature and chemical formula, linens must be carefully separated before being loaded in the washers. For instance greasy kitchen aprons require strong washing chemicals while wool needs milder detergents. Coloured napery should not be processed with bleach, while white bed linens require bleach to kill bacteria and whiten the fabric. In general, bed linen, terry cloth, napery, blankets, and bedspreads should be washed separate from each other.

Besides sorting the linen by category, each batch should be separated by degree of soiling. Items that are not soiled or very lightly soiled require weaker formulas and less agitation than heavily soiled items. Because the number of heavily stained items is usually less, having a couple of small-size washers to process small loads will prevent having to use larger machines for partial-load washings. Sorting personnel should be trained to detect unrecoverable items such as torn, burned, or heavily soiled articles, which should be made into cleaning rags.

Before loading the linen into the washers, special care must be taken to presoak and pretreat heavily stained items. For example, blood, egg, fruit, and dark beverage stains should be soaked in cold water and spot-cleaned with detergent. Grass, paint, and grease stains should be spot-cleaned before washing. All fabrics, however, should be tested for colourfastness before chemicals are directly applied to them.

Washers and dryers should be loaded with the maximum amount of linen that their capacity allows; thus, a 35-pound machine should hold about 35 pounds of dry soiled linen. If the soiled linen is damp, as may happen with bath items, fewer pieces will make up the recommended weight. Not using machines to full capacity will increase the operating cost of the laundry as washers and dryers will use the same amounts of water, chemicals, and energy required for full loads.

Most washing machines in the market today are equipped with several washing programs aimed at processing diverse types of fabrics and degrees of soiling. The programs consist of different washing times, water temperatures, levels of agitation, and amounts of chemicals to be used. These programs, used properly, can help conserve energy and lengthen the life of fabrics. For instance, a program for washing lightly soiled linen will be set to use less time, a lower temperature, and fewer chemicals than a program set to process greasy items. The lighter program will cost less to run and prolong the number of washings that the material can stand. The water temperature needed to wash articles usually varies from 140°F to 160°F.

For example, while greasy kitchen items require the hottest temperature, lightly soiled sheets can be washed at 140°F. Some programs, however, are preset to use cold water as some types of stains do not require hot water for removal; on the contrary, warm water might imprint the stain permanently.

In addition, no-iron fabrics better retain their wrinkle-free characteristics when washed in cold water. Laundry operators should use cold-water programs whenever possible to save the energy needed to heat the water. A sufficient level of agitation is necessary for adequate washing action; not enough agitation due to insufficient washing time, improper water levels, or machine overloading will not provide adequate results. Linens washed with the wrong chemicals or with incorrect amounts of chemicals either will not produce good results or will ruin the articles by deteriorating their fabric composition.

Using too much chemical can also cause damage to linens as well as waste precious budget dollars. Each washing program consists of several cycles, similar to those found in a residential machine. The flush cycle soaks the linen and dissolves the soils; the wash cycle uses soil-breaking products, detergents, and other chemicals to clean the items; the rinse cycle removes chemicals from the linen; and the extract cycle spins the moisture from the load before it is moved on to the drying or ironing phase.

Good water quality is necessary for washing linens. Hard water prevents detergents from releasing their sudsy action to remove soils, leaving a grayish shade and an "unclean" odour in finished linens. Often, lodging properties must install water softeners before they can obtain adequate results. Large quantities of water are used in washing linens; some programs may require one Rush cycle, one break cycle, one washing cycle, one softener cycle, and three rinse cycles. In locations where water is expensive, special care must be taken to minimize the, use of water whenever possible. Partial loads are a waste of water and can cause wear and tear on washing machines. Newer washer-extractors reduce the amount of water necessary to clean linens.

Several factors determine the types of chemicals needed for commercial laundries: these include the water used, the different texture of fabrics to be washed, and the degree of soiling that must be removed. The chemicals commonly used in laundry operations are alkalies that help neutralize acids in the washing solution. Alkalies are often necessary because suds in detergents act better on soils and stains if the washing solution is lightly alkaline. Antichlors are added to rinses to ensure that chlorine bleach is totally removed from the washed fabrics. Bleach is a powerful chemical that is very effective in killing bacteria, whitening linens, and removing stains. Chlorine bleach, however, can destroy some fabrics, particularly certain synthetics, Oxygen bleach is milder and can be used with most washable fabrics, including coloured ones, but it is ineffective on heavy stains. Breaks are heavy-duty, alkaline compounds designed to break soils in the soak cycle. Breaks are used for heavily soiled loads. The washing agent used in the washing process is the detergent.

Detergents containing suspending agents and alkaline builders are very effective in removing grease and oils. Some detergents have water-softening ingredients to increase their cleaning action; others contain enzymes that break down and liquify organic stains such as food, blood, urine, and fats. Softeners are added in the final wash cycle to eliminate static cling, smooth wrinkles, and make ironing easier. Sours are acidic chemicals used to neutralize any alkaline residues left after washing and rinsing linens.

A single product that combines a fabric softener and an alkaline neutralizer may also be used. Starches are carbohydrate compounds that are added to give linens a stiff appearance. This procedure is commonly used to give a crisp look to cooks' uniforms and toques (chefs' hats).

The use of laundry detergents can be substantially reduced by using ozone in the washing process. Ozone is a gas formed by ozone generators by passing an electric current through the oxygen that exists in the wash water. The gas acts as an oxidizing and bleaching agent, disinfectant, and solvent of soils and oils. The chemical reactions that ozone produces make it possible to clean linens with fewer amounts of detergents and at lower water temperatures. Fabrics washed by the ozone method may last longer than when processed with strong chemicals at higher water temperatures.

Although drying times vary with different types of fabric, generally it takes twice as long to dry linens as it takes to wash them. Drying temperatures also vary from item to item; for instance, fluffy all cotton towels require hotter temperatures than thin synthetic fibers. All linens should be loaded into dryers with the minimum moisture possible to reduce drying time. Modern washers are equipped with highspeed spins as a final cycle to remove excess moisture from washed items. Dryers should be loaded to capacity to minimize energy costs.

Items that need ironing are best processed when slightly damp; for this reason, they don't need to be dried. Ironing is a labour-intensive process that should be avoided whenever possible. On the other hand, pressed tablecloths, napkins, and pillowcases create a favourable impression for guests, as do cook and serving -personnel uniforms.

Like ironing, folding is a time-consuming, labour-intensive process, particularly if it is done by hand. Linens should be folded immediately after drying or pressing to avoid wrinkling. Sheet-folding stands can save labour costs, as only one worker is needed to fold the items instead of two employees. Laundry folders should be trained to sort out linen items with imperfections such as tears, fading, stains, and loose seams before they are distributed for usage.

Once linens are folded, they should be handled as little as possible. Folded linen should be shelved in the linen room, placed on mobile racks for transportation to the floor closets, or placed directly onto the section housekeeper carts for ready use. The ultimate goal of a well-run laundry is to obtain optimum results in terms of appearance, odour, and feel. Regarding appearance, the linen must be snow-white (for white items) and free of wrinkles and spots caused by staining. The odour must be fresh and clean, not stale or musty; the feel should be smooth and velvety, not coarse or rough. Laundry accounts can benefit from the expertise of nationwide chemical companies to obtain best results; in some cases, these companies guarantee that the quality of linens processed with their products will be optimum. In order to check quality, their service personnel conduct routine tests for water hardness, iron residue in finished linens, and the pH of washed items. Improper results of finished products include discoloration, stains, abraded fabric, lint specks, excessive wrinkling and shrinking, and fabric pilling

Most first-class lodging properties offer laundry and dry cleaning services to their guests. However, it is common to contract these services with an outside commercial laundry because of the specialization and time-consuming details that valet service entails. Properties that wash and dry-clean employee uniforms and draperies usually process valet service items in-house. In this case, smaller washing and drying machines and dry cleaning equipment need to be installed, as well as additional personnel to tag, process, and bag each guest's articles.

On-premise valet service can greatly encumber housekeeping operations and take up considerable laundry room space. In all cases, good communication between valet attendants and the laundry room must be established, and clear, specific procedures put in place to avoid misunderstandings and complaints. Some of these procedures include setting up times for laundry pick-up and delivery, billing guests promptly after each service, and having a quick response system to compensate guests for lost, misplaced, or damaged articles. Small lodging properties may decide to cop-tract out laundering services rather than installing their own on-premise laundry.

While the disadvantages are numerous, a few advantages of outside laundry contracts include not having to make a substantial initial investment and having the additional space otherwise taken up by the laundry room. In all cases, contracts must be carefully set up between the lodging property and the commercial laundry company to ensure an efficient, reliable service; for instance, requiring delivery seven days a week on peak occupancy period. The contract should specify details regarding delivery and quality, such as days of the week and time of day, emergency service, appearance of the linen, folding specifications, sorting procedures, billing method, and method of inventory.

The cost of operating an on-premise laundry is broken down into the categories of labour, linen replacement, energy, chemicals, and other. Of these, the labour cost is the highest. Although expenses can be largely affected by exceptionally high energy or labour costs, depending upon the location of the property, national laundry cost percentages for a typical laundry operation may be averaged thus:

Labour	45%
Linen replacement	20%
Energy	15%
Laundry chemicals	10%
Other	10%

Under normal circumstances, executive housekeepers can work out rough estimates to monitor expenses using these averages as a benchmark.

Laundry operations in large properties are usually coordinated by a laundry manager who reports directly to the executive housekeeper. Laundry shifts normally consist of one shift supervisor, several laundry attendants, and one utility helper (house-person). Because of the different tasks to be carried out in the laundry room, job specifications must be clearly spelled out. For example, the jot) of wash persons may be to handle the loading and unloading of washers and dryers; the utility helper may preson, count, and shelf linen, others may fold and stack, and so on. An ideal staffing scenario is to have enough equipment and personnel to process the property's poundage in 8 hours, to avoid overtime. In this case, 6 hours could be spent on washing and drying and 2 hours in other laundry activities. When the property, is not 100 percent full, the hours of operation should be reduced or the number of people called to work lowered. If establishments operate with insufficient linen pars, two shifts rather than one may be necessary to turn out enough finished items.

Training laundry workers is of paramount importance, as laundry room operations require the performance of specialized tasks and the handling of sophisticated equipment. Usually the equipment supplier and the company supplying laundry chemicals will provide training assistance. One important training consideration is compliance with OSHA's working standards for laundry workers. Some of these standards specify that all machinery must be equipped with guards to prevent injury to fingers, that steam pipes within employee reach are covered with heat-resistant material, and that power-driven machinery has easily accessible starting and stopping devices. When employing workers who do not read English, safety procedures should be made available in their native language and training workshops should be given by bilingual personnel.

7

Controlling Operation

The control function begins with the compilation of an annual operating budget for the rooms division of the property, of which the housekeeping department is a part. The executive housekeeper must project labour and operating expenses for the upcoming year which, once approved by upper management, become the operational expense parameters. Because most department expenses are a function of occupancy, their totals must be justified. The justification of man-hours for section housekeepers is based on the number of rooms to be serviced and the workload criteria for room attendants. As the year progresses, the housekeeping department receives monthly profit and loss statements showing the revenue of the rooms division and expense totals by category. The director of housekeeping uses the information to monitor costs and readjust expense amounts if they are larger than expected. Statistical information can also be used to control costs and productivity in the department by comparing the results obtained with budget indicators.

Housekeeping operation budget

An operating budget is essentially a financial plan that allocates funds for expenditures by department for a determined period of time, generally one year. It is also a means of control that provides a measure for performance. Budgeting in large lodging operations requires a full cooperative effort of all department heads and the property's controller, who is usually in charge of preparing the final document before it is presented to the general manager for approval. Budgets are generally compiled for one-year time spans and are divided into 12 months, although some companies divide the year into thirteen 28-day periods to avoid distortion in the comparison of working periods (for not all months have the same working days).

Preparation of the operating budget in large lodging properties requires several months of planning and is usually finalized just before the budgeting cycle commences. The budget year can begin on January I (calendar year), or at the start of the company's fiscal year. Once top management has established its guidelines and amounts for each department, the respective departmental budgets are distributed down through each level. One of these levels is the housekeeping department.

The housekeeping department budget is part of the rooms division budget, which also includes the front office. The executive housekeeper's participation in determining the amounts allocated to the housekeeping department is essential if she/he is to be made accountable for the departmental control of expenses. The basic structure of budgets for revenue -generating divisions is:

Revenue (Sales) – Costs (Expenses) = Departmental Income (Departmental Profit).

The revenue of the rooms division consists of the dollars to be generated by the sale of rooms at a certain unit price (number of rooms sold x average daily rate). The costs of the rooms division consist of the expenses incurred by the housekeeping and front office departments.

Typically, include salaries and wages and other expenses. The percent of expenses is obtained by dividing the projected cost of expenses in dollars by the projected revenue. The cost of expenses in dollars is obtained by multiplying the percent by the revenue and dividing by 100.

The first step in the budget process is the compilation of the consolidated room sales summary in which the rooms division director, director of sales, and front office manager are directly involved. The summary is a projection of revenues for the 12 months of the upcoming year based on the forecasted percentage of occupancy and average daily rate. The projections are calculated from the room bookings at hand, historical data from previous years, upcoming local events, state of the local economy and, in some cases, the weather prediction for the area.

Once the division's revenue is forecasted, the executive housekeeper and front office manager ascertain the expenses predicted for the year. Typical expense categories of the rooms division are: front office salaries, housekeeping salaries, payroll taxes and employee benefits, travel commissions, outside services, cleaning supplies, linen replacements, guest supplies, telephone, postage, printing and stationery supplies, uniforms, laundry supplies, customer goodwill, and auto expense.

Of these categories, front office salaries, travel commissions, postage, customer goodwill, and auto expense (airport van) are front office expenses. The categories of payroll taxes and employee benefits, telephone, printing and stationery supplies, and uniforms are shared by the two departments. The remaining categories-housekeeping salaries, outside services, cleaning supplies, linen replacements, guest supplies, and laundry supplies-pertain to housekeeping only.

The amounts to be allocated to each expense category are ascertained taking into consideration the percentages from previous years, and factors such as predicted increases in salaries and wages, adding extra employees to the department, upgrading cleaning and/or guest supplies, replacing an unusual amount of uniforms or linens, and so on. The challenge for department heads when requesting expense allocations is to keep the cost percentages as low as possible while maintaining an optimum level of service and quality.

Once the budget has been finalized and approved by management, it becomes the plan of operation for the upcoming year. The director of housekeeping must henceforth operate the department within the budget's limitations so that the percentages of amounts spent in each expense category do not exceed the percentages budgeted.

It is important to understand that the cost percentages are a function of the revenue. For example, if the projected cost of guest supplies has been set at 2 percent of a $ 10,000, 000 revenue, the dollar allocation for guest supplies for the year will be $200,000 (10,000,000 ×.02). However, if the revenue is less or more than projected, the dollar allocation has to be adjusted accordingly. For instance, if the revenue drops to $9,500,000, the allocation for guest supplies becomes $190,000 (9,500,000 ×.02). If the revenue reached $10,500,000, the allocation changes to $210,000 (10,500,000 ×.02).

Whenever any substantial deviation from the budget occurs, the executive housekeeper will be asked to explain the variance. If the variance is found to be correctable, a plan of action is usually agreed upon between the director of housekeeping and upper management.

The revenue for the upcoming year has been projected 5 percent higher than the current year's to reflect an increase in room rates. The occupancy percentages, however, have been kept the same as in the current year, assuming that a showdown of the local economy does not allow for a larger occupancy. Salaries and wages have been increased by 0.5 percent from last year's in housekeeping and by 0.3 percent in the front office, anticipating a rise in pay. Payroll taxes and employee benefits will be up 0.2 percent overall as predicted by the hotel's controller.

The cost percentages for all categories of "other expenses" have been kept as in 1998, except for "guest supplies" and "laundry supplies." Guest supplies have been increased by two tenths of one percentage point to reflect an upgrade of guest amenities, while the percent cost for laundry supplies has been reduced to 0.2 percent from 0.5 percent following the installation of a computerized chemical feeding system for the laundry washers.

The departmental profit (income) projected is obtained by subtracting all expenses from the revenue. In this example, the income has been projected to be 74.3 percent of the revenue, down from 75.2 percent the previous year. A departmental profit of 74.3 cents for every dollar of room sales is a good target for rooms divisions in the lodging industry.

To justify the expenses for the category of salaries and wages, both executive housekeeper and front office manager must submit a statement showing the amounts needed to pay employees in both departments. The allocation to cover salaries is easy to work out as it consists of adding up the yearly pay of salaried employees. To figure out the wages for fixed employees (those who work regardless of the hotel's occupancy), the executive housekeeper must refer to the property's staffing guide to calculate the number of hours that employees will work per shift and multiply the hours by the average wage that workers are paid. For example, if the hotel schedules four janitors daily at an average hourly rate of $ 6.2 5 and they all work 8-hour shifts, the annual cost for janitors will be $73,000 (4 × 8 = 32; 32 × 365 = 11,680; 11,680 × 6.25 = 73,000). This calculation would be different if, for instance, the number of janitors was fewer on weekends or if the daily hours worked were also fewer. Besides janitors, the category of fixed employees in the housekeeping department usually includes linen room workers and the evening team.

Section housekeepers man-hour justification

To ascertain the wages of section housekeepers, housepersons, floor supervisors, and laundry workers calculations must be made depending on the room occupancy of the hotel, as these employees report to work based on the number of rooms that need to be serviced daily.

The purpose of this statement is to warrant the amount that must be obtained for the concept of room attendant wages in the upcoming budget. The form includes the forecasted occupancy broken down into months, the number of 8-hour shifts needed to service the occupied rooms at the rate of 16 per worker, the total number of work-hours (man-hours), and dollar amounts for each month.

The difference between the amount needed to pay the section housekeepers next year ($ 3 69,413) and the amount stated in the budget. For the concept of housekeeping salaries and wages ($985,321) will cover the expense for salaries and wages of the department's management team, housekeeping supervisors and housepersons, and fixed personnel, as well as cost for overtime, holiday and vacation pay, and bonuses. These expenses will also have to be justified separately. If the property has an on-premise laundry, the cost of labour, based on the projected room occupancy, is usually worked out in the same manner by the laundry manager.

The calculation of the "taxes and benefits" category is generally done by the property's controller and is based on the cost of employee meals, payroll taxes, insurance, and other benefits. In practice, the controller will apply a percentage to the "total salaries and wages" category based on previous years' costs plus any increment to expenses foreseen for the upcoming year.

Profit and loss statement

Once the year is under way, every hotel division and department receives a monthly status report generated by accounting called the profit and loss statement (P & L). This statement shows the hotel's revenue and expenses for the month and includes a variance analysis column which indicates the changes in revenue and expenses from budget by category.

The purpose of the analysis of variance is to alert department heads of percentage changes from budget. If the cost percentages are higher than projected, the causes for the difference must be identified and explained to management and a plan to correct them in the future implemented.

The executive housekeeper will need to investigate the causes for the increases in cost percentages. For the cleaning supplies, there are several possibilities, such as inflated purchasing prices, inferior quality materials, pilfering, improper mixing of chemicals, or overuse of products. The extra cost of outside services could be due to an oversight in budget planning or to an extraordinary expense caused by an unforeseen event.

Productivity control

Productivity is a measure of output compared to input. Examples of output are the number of rooms serviced in a certain period of time or the amount of linen washed in an 8-hour shift. Inputs are the investments made by a business to provide products or services, the materials used to have the job done, and the work of the company's employees.

In the lodging industry, the overall result of productivity is measured by the profit, that is, revenue minus expenses. The average departmental profit of the rooms division in the lodging industry is around 75 percent; that is, for every dollar made from selling rooms to guests, 25 cents should be cost and the remaining 75 cents departmental profit.

Indispensable factors to reach good levels of productivity, apart from the influence of department heads, are appropriate investments in the design, machines, and equipment of the facilities.

The effects of internal factors, particularly those of supplies and labour, on productivity can be controlled by executive housekeepers. Supplies management is a good example of cost savings through efficient techniques. For instance, every dollar saved by purchasing the right product at the right price is an additional dollar added to the bottom line.

Labour management also contributes to increased profits; a worker who has been adequately trained and is motivated to perform effectively can increase the work output by using a minimum amount of time to accomplish the task. Section housekeepers servicing effectively 16 guestrooms in one 8-hour shift instead of servicing 15 will provide better productivity to the company and, therefore, an increase in the company's profit.

Productivity, however, must go hand in hand with quality. It is to no advantage to achieve high productivity if the product is defective. To reach quality control, the housekeeping department must adhere to specifications and inspections.

Inspections take up labour hours and are therefore expensive but, if planned carefully to keep costs low, they can be very effective to ensure proper quality levels. A useful ratio to control productivity in the lodging industry is: revenue ÷ hours of work required = dollars per labour hour. Another indicator of productivity is: hours of work used ÷ units produced = mean hour per room serviced.

Weekly labour forecast

After the labour expense percentages have been determined in the annual budget, labour cost controls must be in line with the preestablished levels of occupancy and employee workloads.

As explained earlier, there are two methods to control the productivity of section housekeepers; one determines the average dollar amount to be generated by one hour of section housekeeper work and the other ascertains the average number of minutes that section housekeepers will need to clean the rooms occupied.

The weekly labour forecast projects the section housekeeper hours needed to service the forecasted occupied rooms for a particular week, in this case, one week in March. By dividing the estimated revenue for the week by the section housekeeper hours, the revenue generated per hour worked is obtained.

Likewise, by dividing the section housekeeper hours by the forecast rooms occupied and multiplying the result by 60, the average number of minutes to clean one guestroom is also obtained. The results are compared to the amounts stated in the yearly budget for the same concepts. If the amounts are close to the budgeted amounts, the number of section housekeepers scheduled for the week is acceptable. If they aren't, a reduction in the number of scheduled hours will be necessary. It must be kept in mind, however, that the control of productivity using the ratio "estimated revenue/section housekeeper' hours could be easily distorted if the ADR differs markedly from the ADR projected in the budget.

Executive housekeepers must develop a formal system of accurate reporting of payroll to the accounting department. The report is a record of hours worked daily by all employees in housekeeping. The system must include a means of control of overtime work.

An effective way to control overtime work is to request that all supervisors obtain authorization for all extra time before it occurs. The hours worked by hourly employees are in most cases recorded on time cards. Workers are asked to punch a time clock in and out at the beginning and end of their shift.

During orientation, these procedures must be explained to employees in detail, such as not clocking in until they are in uniform and ready to work and clocking out at the time they stop working.

Some companies allow for one half hour for lunch on company time; others require workers to clock in and out before and after lunch. Breaks of 15 minutes are always on company time. Management should not ask employees to perform any duties off the clock, as this is against labour laws. Punching a time card in or out for another employee should be cause for disciplinary action. Time machines record hours in military time, starting at 00:0 1 and ending at 24: 00. The actual time worked by an employee is determined by subtracting the smaller time from the larger. At the end of every work week, the summarized hours worked on the time cards are recorded on a time sheet from which actual pay is calculated by the payroll office. Besides the hours worked, time sheets should also indicate hours to be paid for vacation time, sick pay, or overtime pay. If workers are asked to perform duties of a different job category, they should be paid at the higher wage rate for that category, as would apply if, for example, a section housekeeper performs the duties of a supervisor for a certain period of time while the supervisor is on vacation.

Computerized housekeeping management

More and more lodging companies are using automation to manage operations in housekeeping departments. Executive housekeepers can use technology to perform tasks such as controlling inventory supplies, scheduling operational routines, and tracking departmental man-hours and costs.

There are software packages on the market that can perform personnel management tasks such as compiling personnel records, employee absences, training programs, and reports of on-the-job accidents.

Other software applications can be supplements to quality assurance programs to evaluate employee performance. Preventive maintenance packages can schedule tasks well in advance, such as stripping floors and cleaning carpets and upholstery. The computer can be programmed to print daily work schedules.

Perhaps the most useful application of automation to housekeeping departments is the tracking of cleaning and guest supplies, equipment, and linen inventories and usage. If housekeeping can control the use of materials, the purchasing function can be improved by buying the right amount of products to eliminate the possibility of over- or under-stocking supplies.

Other applications of computers are word processing and the ability to produce graphs and charts to help directors of housekeeping organize past-performance data and forecast projections to be presented to upper management.

Word processing enhances the quality of the correspondence generated in the housekeeping department, including reports, memoranda and letters. Computer programs, however, can be very labour-intensive because of the time needed to input data. On the other hand, the pay-offs can be considerable as answers can be obtained by simply striking a key rather than having to perform elaborate calculations.

The management of personnel in the lodging industry is complex. The business requires a large number of workers because most of the functions performed must be done by hand. Some years back, the use of robotics was forecast to be a labour-saving panacea for lodging properties but, although some technological advances have been made, particularly in laundries and front desk operations, beds still need to be made, bathrooms still need to be cleaned, and guests still need to be served by employees.

The industry is notorious for offering jobs that are quite demanding and for paying workers minimum wage, particularly at entry-level positions. Many people enter the field when they cannot find work elsewhere, perceiving their employment as a last resort rather than a career. This creates a chronic shortage of personnel as employees come and go in great numbers. It is not uncommon for lodging properties to experience employee turnover rates of over 100 percent per year.

Today, when unemployment rates are at an all-time low level, the balance of power is shifting from employers to employees, causing a people shortage that is spreading to all sectors of the hospitality industry. It is therefore critical that executive housekeepers maintain low levels of employee turnover and absenteeism.

There are two basic means to reduce turnover and absenteeism effectively: one is to follow the common technical rules of adequately recruiting, selecting, training, and evaluating personnel; the other consists of practising effective methods of employee motivation, compensation, and the creation of an environment conducive to employee satisfaction.

Employee recruiting and training

Ideally, a lodging property should employ only cheerful, good-natured people who smile easily and often, particularly when in contact with guests. Conversely, grouchy people, those who cannot keep their tempers, and who feel sorry for themselves should not be hired at all. In all cases, the success of the operation depends on attracting applicants and placing them in the positions most appropriate to their skills and personalities. Hiring applicants "off the street" may have a very negative outcome. If the wrong person is initially placed in the wrong position, turnover will result, as the person will inevitably leave the company, voluntarily or otherwise.

Recruiting housekeeping employees

Housekeeping hires most of the department's employees on an as needed basis; that is, they are asked to work depending on the daily occupancy of the property. Some employees, who are scheduled regardless of the property's occupancy, are hired full-time, such as supervisors, janitors, or linen room attendants. Part-time employees agree to work usually less than 30 hours per week, generally receiving no major benefits other than wages.

In most cases, part-time workers have an additional

source of income, as they may be retirees, homemakers, or college students. Often, because of cost and fear of overstaffing, businesses turn toward staffing companies for temporary help.

One advantage of hiring temporaries is that it allows the employer to evaluate the temporary employees' qualifications and suitability for the job before offering them a full-time permanent position. Lodging properties should also have a number of people on-call, who are asked to report to work when extra help is needed, such as when regular employees are ill or on vacation.

Unions

Union contracts, however, may have a significant impact on the composition of the company's work force. For example, a union contract may stipulate that all workers must be guaranteed a 40-hour work week; in this case, no part-time employees can be hired. In all cases recruiting new employees is a special concern to both organization and newcomer.

Management expects good performance and cooperation, while the new employee wants fair compensation, to be understood and recognized and, above all, to be helped during the induction process. In large hotels, the human resources department recruits employees. The order to recruit is initiated in the housekeeping department by filling an employee requisition form. This form indicates the position that needs to be filled and describes the specification of the job and the required qualifications of the applicant. The job description is a detailed statement of the tasks required to get the job done.

Each job description should include the minimum employee qualifications required and desired to ensure that applicants will be capable of doing the job for which they are applying. For example, the job description for laundry attendant may require that the applicant be capable of lifting 50 pounds (weight of laundry detergent pails used in the property) and may state that Spanish-speaking workers are preferred (as are most of the other employees in the laundry).

After receiving the employee requisition, the human resources department advertises the position internally (internal recruiting) and externally (external recruiting). An organization that develops its personnel exclusively from within may be limiting itself by having to promote employees who may not be qualified for the position.

On the other hand, capable employees already working for the company should be given a fair option to advance or change positions, and even departments, if they so desire. Thus, the first step is to inform everyone in the department of the job opening. If no one is interested in applying for the position, employees may have friends or acquaintances who are looking for work.

Usually, lodging companies reward workers for their referral of potential employees if these are hired and stay employed for a minimum of 6 months. Friends and relatives are usually well accepted by current employees, who are more likely to help the newcomers adjust to their new jobs.

Another advantage of recruitment from within is that it avoids incurring recruitment costs. When the new opening is for a supervisory position, special efforts should be made to promote from within as a matter of fairness and to provide opportunities for advancement to the employees already with the company.

Charts showing the various opportunities for career progression should be displayed for employees to see. In the housekeeping department, the career path for a house-person could lead from this entry-level position to section housekeeper, team supervisor, assistant to the executive housekeeper, to laundry manager and, possibly, to executive housekeeper.

The most common external recruitment method is newspaper advertising. These ads are particularly successful in attracting the unskilled and young people looking for part-time and temporary employment. The advantage of this is that young, unskilled people can usually be adequately trained to perform the requirements of the job; the disadvantage is that once they have been trained, they may decide to change jobs and leave the department. Radio advertising reaches listeners who do not or cannot read newspapers.

When a supervisory or management position needs to be filled, private employment agencies often provide a valuable source of recruits, but in most cases the property must pay a substantial fee for their services. Public employment agencies may be sources of good employees in some cases. The state employment services are non-fee referral agencies for workers, and so are organizations for the physically impaired.

Most physically impaired individuals are very dependable and efficient in the performance of simple, repetitive jobs. In some cases, companies may benefit from tax credits by hiring workers from federally -supported programs. Schools and colleges are good sources of recruits with special skills. Local community colleges may offer vocational courses in housekeeping or laundry operations.

Most hotel/restaurant management programs require students to complete hundreds of hours in pre-graduation employment in the industry. Bulletin board advertising in these schools usually results in applications for employment. Some colleges and universities have summer internship programs that allow undergraduate students to practice in hotels and resorts prior to graduation. The students can be used as supervisors or management assistants or they can be put in charge of special projects, such as taking inventories, developing job descriptions, or getting involved in clerical work.

Selecting housekeeping employees

The initial contact with prospective employees begins with their filling out an application form. This form is a means of securing standard information about applicants. No person can be denied the opportunity to submit an application for employment; questions to be included in application forms depend on the company but, in all cases, every question asked should serve a purpose. No question should be asked that is not useful for research purposes or for determining the applicant's eligibility for the job.

The U.S. Equal Employment Opportunity Commission has been set up to enforce the Civil Rights Act which protects against discrimination on account of race, colour, religion, sex, or national origin. Because of increased emphasis by state and federal governments to avoid discrimination in employment, application forms must be carefully worded to avoid requesting any pre-employment information that could be considered discriminatory.

Pre-screening

The property's personnel department usually conducts the pre-screening interview. The purpose of this initial interview is to screen out those applicants who do not meet the criteria for the job advertised as specified in the company's job description.

For example, a person who is physically incapable

of servicing 15 guestrooms in 8 hours will automatically be disqualified. The person in charge of pre-employment screening must be well trained in interviewing techniques, as a high percentage of people applying for jobs tend to exaggerate their skills and abilities, to misrepresent their backgrounds, and to conceal or minimize their weakest qualities.

Applicants who are not selected should be notified as soon as possible of the company's decision and their applications kept on file for future reference, mainly for a different job in the company for which they may be qualified.

The personnel department should immediately proceed to check the references of those candidates selected for the interview.

Checking references may reveal issues such as extreme absenteeism, irresponsibility, and not giving adequate notice, or may detect a person who always wants to work in a new property and quit as soon as a new establishment opens.

References may be checked in writing, although in most cases previous employers will be reluctant to put on paper their honest opinion about the worker; written reference checking is usually limited to a verification-of -employment statement.

Telephone conversations can often reveal much more about the applicant, particularly if the person contacted is an industry colleague. Although in most cases it is impractical, the best way to obtain accurate information about applicants is to have a personal meeting with their former boss.

Applicants who are working at the time of the interview may request that their current employers not be contacted for a reference check. This request should be honoured, to avoid putting workers in an antagonistic position vis-a-vis their current bosses.

The interview

Those employees who have cleared the reference check are invited to a personal interview. The goal of an interview is to find the best match between the person and the position to be filled. The interview also allows the candidate and the department head to meet face to face to explore the possibilities of a mutual agreement for employment. In the housekeeping department, interviews may be conducted by supervisors, laundry managers, manager assistants, or by the executive housekeepers themselves.

Interviewers should evaluate the applicant's technical skills, general temperament, and emotional traits. By asking technical questions related to the job opening, the interviewer should attempt to find out if the applicant is (or will be after training) qualified to perform the job in question.

By asking personal questions, the interviewer should try to ascertain the candidate's attitude toward the job and the first impression that the applicant will give in meeting customers and fellow workers.

Some of the technical characteristics may be ascertained from factors such as previous work experience and training, knowledge of the job, stamina, and alertness. Some of the personal traits to be sought after are stability, reliability, initiative, and personal appearance.

In essence, the interview is a two way communication effort in which the interviewer states the nature of the job opening and the applicant presents his or her own qualifications to fill in job. Interviews should be conducted in a private, quiet place where the candidate can be made to feel at ease.

Here are some points to be considered in employment interviewing.

1. A checklist can be helpful to avoid overlooking important information. Questions should be prepared from the job description of the position to be filled.
2. The interviewer should allow at least hall of the interview time to listen to the applicant's statements about himself or herself. To this effect, questions eliciting "yes" "no" answers should be avoided. Make frequent use of 'why?" and "how?".
3. Most housekeeping tasks are tough and require much of the worker's commitment and dedication. Interviewers should not sugar-coat the job to convince the applicant to accept the position, only to find later that the worker finds it unbearable.
4. Interviewers may be swayed in their decision to hire by the neat appearance and smooth talking of candidates (the halo effect), only to discover that they are not capable of performing housekeeping work.
5. Avoid hiring someone who is over-qualified. These candidates often become frustrated with tasks below their ability level, and eventually quit.

The result of the interview should be communicated to the candidate as soon as possible. If the decision is positive, applicants should know immediately so they can give appropriate notice to their current employers and get ready to start work in the new job. If the decision is negative, applicants should be notified so that they can restart their search for a job in other establishments.

Testing

Some lodging companies regularly use tests given to prospective employees as instruments of selection, particularly to those seeking supervisory and managerial positions. However, because tests are only an indirect method of measurement, they are not as valid as the direct measurement of people's abilities. Tests should never be given in lieu of interviews or direct performance observations.

Psychological testing, nevertheless, can be a helpful tool to avoid hiring unqualified candidates. Intelligence tests used in the industry measure vocabulary and arithmetic skills; some are designed for supervisory and managerial positions and a few for workers at an entry level.

Some aptitude tests applicable to the industry measure the applicant's hand dexterity; these are suitable for workers involved in manual tasks; others test clerical aptitude and are recommended for bookkeeping, cashier, and secretarial jobs. Interest tests provide some measure of an applicant's relative interest for certain fields of work.

The lodging industry could use interest tests to examine the candidate's interest in people, as this is a people industry. When using tests as a method of selecting employees, keep in mind that tests have been found to be inherently discriminatory to anyone who has not had the full advantage of a free exposure to American culture.

Hiring

Induction

After being accepted for employment, workers are usually asked to report to the personnel department for their induction into the company. The purpose of the induction process is to fill the necessary paperwork about the new employee, to answer questions, and to make the newcomer feel welcome.

All documentation regarding the new worker should be completed. This procedure includes filling out the W-4 (tax withholding statement), 1-9 (proof of residence), and health and welfare insurance forms. At this time newcomers are provided with the employee handbook. Properties that hire large numbers of employees should use employment checklist forms to ensure that no part of the induction process has been overlooked. The employment checklist includes all prerequisites that need to be completed before employees are sent to their respective departments to begin work.

The induction process continues with the orientation of the new employee. The purpose of orientation is to acquaint the employee and organization with one another.

During orientation, the philosophy of the company is explained, the benefits, pay rate, and deductions are discussed, and the dos and don'ts that the job entails, or general house policies as stated in the employee handbook, are described in detail.

The initial orientation session should be followed with a second meeting after the new employee has had a chance to become familiar with the job-anywhere between two and four weeks later. At this time, any questions that the worker may have are answered.

After the orientation process has been completed at the personnel department, the new employee is escorted to housekeeping where a departmental orientation takes place.

Here, the hours of work and the necessity for calling in as soon as possible in case of illness or emergency are explained, as well as where to check in and out, uniform procedures, grooming standards, and when breaks and meal periods are scheduled.

The employee is then given a tour of the property and is introduced to his or her supervisor who, in turn, introduces the worker to other members of the department. Induction and orientation procedures, if properly conducted, increase substantially the odds of the employee's remaining in the company.

Most new employees in the housekeeping department are hired on a probationary basis, usually 90 days, to allow workers enough time to learn and perform their jobs efficiently. After a successful probationary period, usually when employees reach no fault or no errors standards, they become regular workers and are given a raise as an incentive to continue to perform well and stay with the company.

Induction and peer group

The peer group is an important part of the new employee's orientation. New employees depend on their coworkers for approval and acceptance. For the newcomer, the pressure to conform is very strong. It is a good idea to involve the most representative members of the peer group in the orientation process. This practice will help the old employees and the new person get to know each other as soon as possible.

In fact, the induction process should not be considered as completed until the full acceptance of the new employee by the peer group has been totally accomplished. To end the hiring process, the personnel department should open an individual record file for each employee in which personal information (such as address, telephone number or whom to call in case of emergency) and work data (such as starting wage and title of the position) are recorded. The file is thereafter updated each time a change in status occurs, such as for changes in pay rate, disciplinary actions taken, written warnings, promotions, special recognition, and so on.

Training

The hospitality industry is notorious for attracting large numbers of unskilled workers, especially young workers coming right from high schools and colleges. In addition, members of the hospitality work force tend to change from one job to another, causing a high turnover, and have a relatively low educational background. On the other hand, most hospitality jobs are under the constant scrutiny of the public, hinging on a face-to-face relationship where the inefficiency of one employee may lose a guest forever.

A lodging property cannot afford to have an untrained or disinterested worker on the housekeeping payroll. Training in the housekeeping department should encompass four major areas: technical skills, employee attitude, personal development, and knowledge of the property.

Technical skills training includes teaching workers how to perform the tasks described in their job description without fault or error. In the case of a section housekeeper, for example, it means teaching the person how to service guestrooms, including setup procedures, making beds, vacuuming, dusting, surface cleaning, bathroom cleaning, maintenance of equipment, and security and safety.

The employee will have reached regular performance standards when a minimum number of faults are found by the inspector checking the room attendant's section. Technical training contributes to the success of both the organization and the individual.

Attitude training should create awareness of the relationships between the employee and the guest, other employees, and the company. Workers must be courteous, friendly, and approachable, and show keen attention to detail.

Sensitivity toward fellow workers must be taught, including toward people of other cultures, races, and religions. This will help develop teamwork within a diversified group, which is always the case in housekeeping. Employees should have a positive attitude toward the company and its management by positively representing the property and mirroring the philosophy of the establishment.

Training should also be provided to workers to improve their personal potential and their abilities to make changes in their own lives. This type of training can range from personal grooming sessions to seminars and workshops that will aid in developing their reading and writing skills or to help them increase their perceptions of themselves as functional individuals.

Finally, knowledge training should teach employees the layout of the property so that they can give directions to guests and inform them about hours of operation and main features of the different outlets. For example, a house-person, if asked, should be able to tell a guest how to get to the swimming pool or what type of menu the coffee shop offers.

Lodging properties should have ongoing training programs in place. People in general tend to forget concepts or deviate from standing procedures as time goes by.

Clear indications of the need to retrain personnel include an increase of oral and written complaints by guests. For instance, if management keeps getting negative comments about the quality of guestroom linens, employees in the laundry room should be retrained in washing and/or finishing procedures. Another indication of a need for retraining may be a drop in productivity.

For example, if in the past section housekeepers have been able to effectively clean 16 rooms in 8 hours and lately some of them incur overtime to finish their job, their room-cleaning methods should be examined to ascertain whether the standing cleaning procedures are adequately followed. These performance analyses should investigate the question "could the task be performed quicker, with the same level of quality?" If the answer is yes, the worker should be retrained to increase his or her productivity performance.

There is, however, a difference between deficiency of knowledge, in which the employee doesn't know how to do the job better and should be retrained, and deficiency of execution, in which the employee knows how to do the task but decides not to perform it correctly for his or her own benefit. In this case, the employee should be called to order and asked to do the job according to established procedures.

The most efficient method of training in the housekeeping department is on-the-job training, in which new employees are assigned to watch how the work should be performed, usually observing a supervisor or senior employee. Large lodging operations have designated trainers whose job is to train newcomers or retrain employees who are not performing up to standard.

When employees need to be trained to operate new machines or equipment, vendors or representatives of the manufacturing company often conduct demonstrations at no cost to the employer; in this case the purchaser of the products. Training of supervisors and middle managers can be enhanced by sending them to conferences and workshops where new industry products are introduced and demonstrated.

When employees already in the company are being prepared for advancement, companies should train them in the different operational aspects of the department by following a career ladder or schedule. Thus, committed employees who master each step of the cycle along the way may be promoted to management positions within the property or in other company establishments. Training programs offer distinct advantages to employers and employees alike. The employer will benefit from an increased learning rate, whereby workers will become efficient sooner rather than learning on their own by trial and error. Workers learn to achieve high levels of productivity and quality performance when their training begins with learning only the best way to accomplish jobs.

As training improves performance, employee self-esteem rises, and with it, the willingness to come to work and to increase earning power. Turnover and absenteeism are thus reduced. The simplest and most efficient way to ascertain the effectiveness of training and retraining programs is by obtaining feedback from guest comment cards. If substantial negative comments are received, training programs must be strengthened. Guest comments should be read at employee meetings. Negative comments should be discussed, without naming the employee who caused the problem, and the entire group should be challenged to find an appropriate solution.

Worker motivation

Employees are vital to the success of the lodging industry. A business that requires face-to-face interaction with people requires a work force that is motivated to deliver excellent service. But the work force usually available to the lodging industry has inherent fundamental problems, such as high turnover, a disinterested attitude, and low productivity.

Housekeeping tends to attract individuals with little education who come from lower socioeconomic sources or from minority groups that often do not know how to read and in some cases are unable to speak English. The problem is compounded by the fact that most lodging companies have limited financial resources to increase their employees' compensation beyond inflation rates.

On the other hand, employees look to improve their own quality of life by achieving a satisfactory standard of living through job security and adequate compensation. However, adequate compensation, although necessary, is not enough to motivate the work force.

Maslow's theory of motivation

Abraham Maslow's thoughts on motivation are still quite relevant to employee motivation in the housekeeping department. It can be deduced from Maslow's work that high levels of motivation in employees cannot be achieved unless the employees' basic needs have been met. A worker's physiological needs must be satisfied first; that is, if housekeeping employees are working in very poor conditions, such as in a steaming-hot, non-ventilated laundry room, all attempts to motivate them will fail. Likewise, if the workers' security needs for survival are not granted, motivation will be impossible. This would occur if a housekeeping employee is allowed to work only 28 hours per week and therefore is unable to make enough money to pay for his or her rent. The fulfilment of social needs is also necessary prior to motivating people. A Hispanic employee, for instance, would be unhappy working in housekeeping in the midst of an Anglo-Saxon work force that refuses to accept him or her as part of the group.

Conversely, an Anglo-Saxon worker working among non-accepting Hispanic workers will also be hard to motivate. Self-esteem, the fourth of Maslow's basic needs applicable to hourly employees, must also be satisfied before workers can be motivated. For example, a house-person in the housekeeping department hauling trash to the dumpster all day long, whose job is not appreciated by management and coworkers, will be reluctant to be motivated. Housekeeping managers must always realize that individuals have a scale of needs and that motivating them to be courteous, polite, friendly, or productive does not become pressing to them until their basic needs have been adequately satisfied. Motivation at the departmental level will be easier to achieve if all job descriptions and specifications include both the needs of the organization and the personal needs of the workers.

Herzberg's ideas on motivation

Once employees' basic needs have been covered, housekeeping managers must provide their employees with opportunities that are intrinsically satisfying or that embody responsibility.

Frederick Herzberg proposes that workers can be motivated by recognition, feelings of achievement, job responsibility, and opportunities for advancement and growth. In other words, if employees feel wanted and are happy in their jobs, they will willingly contribute to the goals of the organization.

In a housekeeping department setting, the executive housekeeper can motivate section housekeepers by always assigning them the same section of guestrooms. This individual responsibility will create in them a feeling of ownership and pride.

A career ladder program to promote people from within can be implemented in the department to establish the possibility of advancement from lower entry-level jobs to supervisory and management positions. There is a marked difference between motivation and manipulation of employees. Managers who attempt to influence workers to do what they want done seldom succeed. Niccolo Machiavelli, the cynical sixteenth-century writer, observed that because humans are selfish, greedy, ungrateful, and manipulative, they deserve not to be trusted and must be manipulated in turn, a theory hardly conducive to employee motivation.

Practical motivation techniques

Besides understanding the different theoretic approaches to motivation, executive housekeepers can put in place practical programs and plans to motivate housekeeping employees. Removing obstacles that often hinder performance may help workers to accomplish their tasks. Too much paper work, for instance, may be an obstacle to productivity; another could be a badly designed work area that does not take into consideration the human element.

Lack of communication may create a feeling of uncertainty about what needs to be done, as people only tend to perform correctly when they understand what is expected of them. The simple act of listening often allows managers to hear useful comments from employees regarding work conditions, suggestions to improve work flow, and the existence of morale problems. The fact that the housekeeping department is often the least appreciated in the property may be the hidden cause of low employee motivation.

Housekeeping workers may not gain the same appreciation that the front desk, sales, and accounting people do. It is common for housekeeping to be considered at the bottom of the operational totem pole given that they are paid minimum wage and have little decision-making authority.

On the other hand, these workers must perform the backbreaking job of cleaning 16 or 17 guestrooms in an 8-hour shift. In order to motivate the housekeeping work force, employees must be given credit for the work they do and be respected for what they represent.

Employee evaluation and compensation

The purpose of employee appraisals is twofold: to provide feedback to workers about how they are performing their jobs and to establish a basis for compensation based on the quality level of their performance. The advantages of providing feedback to workers are substantial, as employees who do well need to be recognized for their efforts while those whose work needs improvement must be notified about their specific deficiencies in order for them to be corrected.

Using ratings to determine wage payment and promotions helps motivate employees to work hard so they can reap the benefits awarded to those who do a good job.

To be effective, evaluation methods must be fair, objective, based on preestablished standards of performance, and accepted by those being evaluated. To overcome anxiety or hostility, workers should be involved in setting up the standards of performance against which they are to be appraised, provided that their goals are in line with those of the company.

Rating scales are effective tools for appraisal; they consist of a series of descriptors to which a numerical score is attached to determine the effectiveness of workers in areas such as absenteeism, tardiness, grooming, following instructions, courtesy to guests, and so on.

Most companies ask workers to fill out a rating form after a designated period of time, ranging from six months to a year, while the worker's supervisor or manager also fills out a form on the employee being evaluated. At a scheduled meeting, the perceptions of both the worker being appraised and the supervisor are compared and discussed. From that discussion, goals for the next evaluation period are agreed upon. The goals are again evaluated against actual performance after the next appraisal period has elapsed and new goals are set.

Where performance is difficult to quantify, as in rating assistant managers or supervisors, the critical incident method may be used instead of the rating scale. In this case, the rater may periodically record observations of good or bad performance that are discussed at the time of the rating.

Any appraisal method used in the housekeeping department should be a way of recognizing excellent performance and of identifying areas in which further training is needed, and should be done so that the person being evaluated sees the process as a means of self-improvement. That is, there should be a mutual discussion between superior and subordinate with regard to what conditions must be altered to change or upgrade performance. These changes or efforts to upgrade become the objectives to be accomplished for the next evaluation period.

The first formal appraisal of employees should be conducted at the end of their probationary period. Afterward, evaluation should be done periodically, typically every six months to a year. It is common for lodging companies to have pay scales that start with a probationary rate and go up in accordance with time on the job.

For example, an employee can be started at minimum wage for the first 90 days (probationary period) and then be raised 50 cents to a dollar per year worked to a preestablished maximum hourly rate. Employees who exhibit extraordinary performance are awarded additional increases, regardless of time, based on their positive performance appraisals.

Because performance evaluations are emotionally charged events, reviews should be held in a private, neutral environment, such as in a small conference room. Evaluators should go into the review fully prepared and with an attitude that supports discussion, cooperation, and negotiation. It is better to sit beside the employee rather than across the table from her/him. The meeting should be long enough to clearly delineate the workers' strengths and weaknesses, and show them how and to what degree they must improve their performance.

Compensation

Compensation (pay increases) should be tied to performance. If an employee's productivity is high and the quality excellent, his or her compensation should be greater than that of an employee whose performance is well below standards.

When compensation is tied to performance and the evaluation system is fair and unbiased, employees strive to do well at work in order to obtain better wages and benefits. Most employees establish a relationship between the rewards they obtain from their job and the effort they put into it.

The ideal effort: compensation ratio should be 1: 1, meaning that the effort put into one's work should equal the reward obtained from it. If workers see that other employees in similar positions produce less but receive equal or higher wages than they do, they will soon be de-motivated. Managers should regard equity in compensation as a critical part of the motivational process.

Creating worker satisfaction

One of the underlying purposes of motivating employees is to reduce turnover. Hovering at about 100 percent for line employees and often costing over $3,000 per hourly employee, turnover represents a substantial loss of income to lodging companies. Thus the challenge is to create worker satisfaction so that employees stay with the company for extended periods of time. Besides using motivational techniques and providing equitable compensation and fringe benefits, what else can the executive housekeeper do to alleviate the problem of high turnover? Conducting exit interviews is the first step in attempting to solve high turnover; that is, finding out why employees leave in the first place. Exit interviews help management identify reasons for turnover, paving the way to corrective actions.

During the interview, departing employees should be asked to discuss the company's working conditions, pay rates, training, benefits, job security, and so on. If the turnover is severe, current employees should be surveyed periodically regarding wages, benefits, and working conditions. Once the problem is identified, goals and objectives for a turnover-reduction plan should be set. Some of the most common reasons for high turnover are poor hiring techniques, inadequate orientation and training practices, no opportunity for advancement, poor supervision methods, bad department image, and lack of performance standards.

Besides correcting these technical slips, executive housekeepers must get employees to feel like valuable members of the total team, boosting their self-esteem by making sure that the department does not have an image problem. The creation of a career path program within the department will make employees feel that there are opportunities for advancement.

Encouraging employees to earn professional certification will help them develop the necessary expertise for advancement. Providing literacy classes for those who cannot read empowers workers who then feel more in control of their future. Incentive programs are intended to provide employees with such rewards as recognition and appreciation for the good work they perform.

Commendation letters, gift certificates, bonuses, plaques, complimentary stays in the property, and designated parking spots in the garage are some of the incentives that may provide substantial employee satisfaction at no great cost.

Wellness programs, designed to prevent illness and enhance the wellbeing of employees, are effective in reducing absenteeism. These programs include periodic medical examinations, sessions to improve dietary habits, weight control practices, exercise and fitness sessions, free or discounted meals, stress management workshops, and immunizations.

Employee assistance programs can help retain employees who are substance abusers by helping workers overcome drug and alcohol addiction. Referring affected employees to counselling agencies and supporting them in their rehabilitation will help improve the company's retention of employees.

Transportation assistance can also be an effective incentive in keeping employees in the workplace. Because a great number of housekeeping employees do not own their own means of transportation, in cities where public transportation systems are reliable and can be used by employees to get to work, the company can provide financial assistance to purchase passes.

In localities with poor or no public transportation, employers can provide vans for pickup and delivery of workers to a central location or organize a ride-sharing or carpooling program. With subsidies from state and federal government programs, lodging properties can offer child and prenatal-care assistance for workers, especially to young single parents. The practice of participative management often creates worker satisfaction among employees in that they see themselves as part of the decision-making process.

As they contribute to operative decisions, they become committed to the outcome of these decisions and get involved in the successful accomplishment of common tasks. When everything else has failed the company may resort to create retention bonuses by offering a percentage of a year's pay, spread over a period of several years, to those employees who stay with the company. In sum, any efforts aimed at maintaining high levels of morale, individual attention, and respect for hourly employees will increase service standards and guest satisfaction and reduce employee turnover.

Employee discipline

The implementation of a standard method of discipline is just as important as motivation for employers and employees alike. Corrective actions for unacceptable or irresponsible behaviour must be taken as soon as they occur. Common misconduct cases that take place in the housekeeping department are quarrelling, insubordination, intoxication, excessive unexcused tardiness or absences, theft, and unauthorized or unlawful doings.

Depending on the severity of the wrongdoing, discipline can range from a simple verbal warning to termination. The most effective method of disciplining employees is the counselling session. Counselling sessions should be conducted on a one-to-one basis to ensure confidentiality. In these sessions, the problem or problems should be addressed straightforwardly with the understanding that the only purpose of the meeting is to find a fast, permanent, and equitable solution to the matter in question. Listening to the employee (the other side of the story) is crucial as the worker, not the supervisor, often is in the right.

It is important that at the end of the session a mutual agreement is reached and that there is a strong commitment on the part of the employee to positively correct the situation. Needless to say, if the employee persists in his or her wrong behaviour, the company always reserves the right to apply punitive measures, as the building of positive discipline requires effective disciplinary actions. Once the violation occurs, disciplinary action follows this sequence: oral warning(s), written warning(s), suspension, and dismissal.

Culture diversity

The number of minority hourly employees working in the hospitality industry is very high; in some states, Spanish-speaking people employed in housekeeping are the majority. In some cases, this diversity in the workplace can represent challenging management problems regarding communication, training, and operational performance. In the Southwest, for instance, the entire housekeeping department may be staffed with non-English speaking Hispanic workers.

Cultural differences may also be serious obstacles to traditional management practices. Some minorities are deeply individualistic and resist standardization, in contrast to the Anglo-American inclination to follow clearly defined, established rules of behaviour. While the North American culture has been built around a strong work ethic, with emphasis on the search for efficiency and aiming at constantly improving the current mechanical and technological frontiers, minorities are often preoccupied with concepts like individualism, family, and leisure.

However, language barriers and marked cultural differences do not imply incompetence. There is no valid evidence of differences in most abilities related to the genetics of race or sex.

The vehicle that best promotes understanding is, without doubt, language. Managers and supervisors will be able to bridge the gap between cultures if they are capable of communicating directly with the people they oversee day after day.

An elementary knowledge of the language that can be applied to daily housekeeping operations is therefore invaluable, particularly in establishments in urban areas with large concentrations of minorities. Students in hospitality management programs should elect to study a modern language, particularly Spanish, prior to joining the industry after graduation.

Dealing with multicultural issues can be a rewarding experience. Using effective communication skills and patience, managers and supervisors can successfully reach, and train, a diverse work force. Listening attentively and speaking slowly and clearly in elementary English are a must.

The best method of training minorities with no command of the English language is to follow a "hands on," "learn-by- doing" approach.

One approach to training a multicultural work force

is using pictures, rather than written instructions. For instance, videos or photographs can clearly show how to operate equipment and perform routine tasks, like washing laundry or waxing a wooden floor. This approach eliminates the need for translation, as visual aids are universally understood. It is common today to find vendors who provide demonstration videos about their products free of charge.

When dealing with a diverse work force, setups and stocking consistency helps avoid mistakes. For instance, to create a common language among all housekeeping employees, all floor and janitor closets should always be organized and stocked the same way.

Service carts should also be organized and stocked the same way to create consistency and eliminate confusion. Using colour-coded chemical products and waste receptacles is an excellent way to eliminate safety problems. For instance, the colour red is indicative of infectious waste, green means recyclable contents, and so on.

Cultural awareness is another important aspect of managing a diverse work force. Some groups arrive in the United States with a strong respect for authority and will never discuss or dispute a request if it comes from the boss. Others will never volunteer an opinion if they are not specifically asked to do so. Some are socially shy and may wait until they are away from the group to ask an important question. Some lodging companies have English for Vocational Purposes (EVP) classes conducted at their facilities to teach foreign employees how to communicate with supervisors and peers on the job.

Racial discrimination

Racial problems in the workplace can lead to lack of productivity and costly lawsuits. Productivity can decline if some employees in the housekeeping department harbour resentments; others may decide to leave in search of businesses where racial tension is strongly discouraged.

Lodging companies should have procedures in place to reduce friction between employees of different races and know how to respond when a racial incident occurs. The property must have a written policy that prohibits discrimination based on race, national origin, sex, and physical impairment. It should also forbid discrimination in hiring, promoting, and terminating employees.

Racial remarks or jokes should not be tolerated. The written policy must be communicated to all supervisors and employees, who should also be educated about the company's expectations regarding interracial behaviour. When a racial incident does occur, action must be taken immediately to make sure that it does not escalate to a legal confrontation.

Sexual harassment is a subtle, hard-to-define form of discrimination. It is not unusual to find that as much as 40 percent of women in the work force have suffered some sort of harassment in the workplace in the form of uninvited pressure for sexual favours, of which cornering, touching, leaning over, or sending provocative notes are the most common.

8

Risk Management

Risk management in lodging operations involves the reduction of operational hazards and the minimization of crime. Just as important are the properties' contributions to prevent the continuous decay of the global environment. This chapter deals with the reasons behind the need to involve the housekeeping department in the risk management of lodging properties.

Effective ways to control accidents, eliminate safety hazards, and deter theft are to train employees in risk management and to take specific proactive steps to prevent injury in the workplace.

Setting up safety committees to coordinate efforts aimed at reducing safety hazards and investigating causes of accidents is of critical importance.

Housekeeping departments are in a privileged position of being able to help recover the sustainability of the planet by implementing recycling programs and by the careful disposal of harmful materials.

Source-reduction programs are proactive ways of minimizing waste and pollution by adopting supplies that are recyclable and biodegradable. Lodging properties can also be eco-friendly by asking stay-over guests to request the washing of bed linens and by encouraging them to reuse bathroom linen supplies.

Safety

There are three important reasons why fire and accident prevention for employees and guests are functions of management. The first is legal: the Occupational Safety and Health Act (OSHA) of 1970 requires employers, by law to keep their places of business free from hazards that may cause harm or injury to employees.

The Act assures every working person in the nation safe and healthful working conditions; therefore, housekeeping managers must comply with OSHA regulations to keep workers safe. OSHA inspectors can enter an employer's premises without notice to conduct inspections, review records, and question workers about safety. When serious injury or death is involved, criminal charges can be filed against the property.

Another reason is financial; statistics provided by the National Safety Council indicate that the number of injuries that occur in the service sector is staggering. The average cost of all injuries annually is over $ 100 billion, with an average loss of almost $ 1, 000 per injury.

In addition, thousands of lost workdays cause a huge loss of human productivity and therefore originate a considerable financial burden on organizations. Accidents are the motive for workman's compensation premiums to go up whenever mishaps occur in the workplace. Worker's compensation is insurance required by the states to cover injuries sustained at work.

The worker's compensation insurance premium payments are determined by the employer's safety and health records. Besides, courts of law tend to award substantial amounts of money when injured guests and employees file civil lawsuits against businesses for accidents or mishaps.

As employees and guests expect to find a safe place to work and stay, lodging operators must see to it that their properties are free from harm, injury, danger, or risk and that the organizational climate is conducive to the personal wellbeing of their workers.

The first step toward implementing a safety program is developing job-safety analyses for those tasks that might involve any risk of injury and accident. After describing the potential hazards that the task may involve, safety tips about how to perform the job should be provided to workers. Job analyses are particularly necessary for jobs that involve working with industrial machinery, such as laundry washers, dryers, and mangles.

Safety training programs

Executive housekeepers should institute safety-training programs designed to instruct housekeeping employees in safe work practices. Specific instructions to guard against hazards and dangers unique to their job assignments should also be provided. The National Institute for Occupational Safety and Health (NIOSH), as well as other agencies in most states, provide help, assisting employers in the development of programs on safety standards and practices and providing printed information on regulations and recommendations to maintain health and safety in the workplace.

Some of the safety standards that can be adopted by the housekeeping department may include: keeping working areas safe, maintaining adequate sanitation, eliminating accident and fire hazards, providing first aid supplies and equipment, handling hazardous chemicals correctly, keeping stairs and railing stable, adopting safety factors to operate laundry equipment, having proper grounding for electrical outlets, and so forth.

Examples of specific proactive steps to prevent injury may include immediately fixing loose handles, missing tiles, and torn carpets; avoiding having wet, slippery walkways at all times; and keeping tub and shower surfaces and room furniture in perfect condition.

When accepting the position of executive housekeeper, it is a good idea to request a site inspection by the company's insurance carrier to determine if the department is complying with standard safety regulations.

Implementation of safety programs should start at orientation, when employees should be taught about the safety philosophy of the department (and company), as well as what is expected of them in order to perform their jobs safely.

Programs to improve the department's organizational climate in order to increase the quality of the employees' work life should address the opportunity for personal development, fair compensation, equality, and a comfortable environment.

Job enrichment can be achieved by maintaining a productive balance between what the job offers and what the workers seek. Efforts should be made to minimize job routine by providing employees with job variety (for instance, cross-training), responsibility, and challenge.

Housekeeping departments of large lodging establishments often form safety committees consisting of three or four employees for the purpose of preventing accidents from happening and investigating accidents after they take place in the workplace. Members of the safety committee regularly inspect all areas in the department, such as the linen room, hallways, service elevators, the laundry room, and employee areas, looking for possible safety and fire hazards.

When a potential safety risk is found, the committee requests that the cause be promptly corrected. Examples of potential safety risks are: missing floor tiles, cracked glass panes, inappropriate worker clothing, obstructed fire exits, improperly vented dryers, defective vacuum cleaner cables, wet floors, wrinkled mats or rugs, nonfunctioning fire and smoke detectors, and so on.

Another responsibility of the safety committee is investigating the causes of accidents, establishing and keeping records of occupational injuries, and developing strategies to help prevent future mishaps. Employees should also be trained in how to lift loads safely by keeping loads close to the body, bending the knees, and keeping the back straight.

Fire prevention

Safety programs must include fire prevention and deterrence. Fires in lodging properties are quite common but so is the fact that most hotels, motels and resorts are equipped with state of the art equipment to suppress fires when they occur. Executive housekeepers can help prevent fires by fireproofing guestroom furnishing.

Curtains, carpets, pillows, blankets, and upholstery should be purchased labelled as fire-retardant or flameproof, as cigarette smoking in bed by guests is the typical cause of fires in guestrooms. Foam rubber products are particularly dangerous as they ignite easily and burn rapidly.

Excessive accumulation of lint in dryers, painter's supplies, and oily rags can also start fires by spontaneous combustion. Kitchen oily cloths should be kept in metal containers and washed or disposed of as soon as possible; painter's products such as linseed oil should be stored in tight containers. Frayed guestroom lamp cables and damaged cords, switches, or plugs may start smoldering fires, as is the case with overcrowded outlets that may overload fuses or circuits.

Safety programs should include fire protection instruction, including fire drills. Fire departments in most localities will participate in employee training by showing films on fire prevention, lecturing on the effects of smoke (generally smoke kills, not the fire itself), and demonstrating the use of fire equipment.

Fire safety programs should train employees in combating small, controllable fires, operating fire extinguishers, closing doors to contain large fires, keeping fire exits free of any materials, reporting immediately the smell of burning equipment or the presence of smoke, evacuating the building in an orderly manner if the fire alarm sounds, notifying guests of fire if asked to do so, and so on.

All housekeeping workers must be told, at orientation, where the nearest fire alarm, fire extinguisher, and fire exit are located. Above all, employees must be trained not to panic in case of a fire but remain calm in all cases. Panic emotion can cause people to feel disoriented, preventing them from acting rationally. The housekeeping department is also responsible for posting in each guestroom diagrams of evacuation routes and instructions explaining what to do in case of fire.

Security

One of the greatest concerns of the lodging industry today is the issue of security. Lodging properties in the past boasted one house detective to keep crime in check; today it is not uncommon for large properties to hire a team of officers to maintain security in the establishment. Besides security manpower, lodging properties must provide security training for employees and often are compelled to invest substantial resources in TV surveillance, in-room safes, and impenetrable room-entry systems.

As with safety, there are legal, ethical, and financial reasons to keep guests, employees, and the company's possessions secure. Innkeepers have the legal and moral obligation of providing reasonable care for guests and staff.

The costs of property stolen from guests and company, and from lawsuits resulting from criminal activity, can be very high. Security awareness for guests and training of employees must be ongoing concerns of management in order to prevent theft. Examples of guest security awareness are reminding travellers to keep valuables in the property's safe, asking them to use locks and chains, and recommending they look through the peephole before opening the door.

The main outcome of any security training program should be ensuring that a property's entire staff understands its security role. Some specific training goals can be to close every guestroorn door found open, to notify the security department of suspicious characters loitering in hallways, and to report anything unusual inside guestrooms, for example, weapons of any type, illegal drugs, blood stains on wall or carpets, etc.

Security-conscious properties should provide printed instructions on table cards for guests explaining how to deter crime and, in some cases, include a direct telephone number at which to contact the security department in case of emergency. Some lodging companies routinely assign single female travellers to rooms that are close to elevators so they don't have to walk down long hallways; others place female guests on their club floor, to which access requires a special key.

Employee theft

Estimates of employee theft in the workplace are very high. While accurate statistics are difficult to obtain, it is believed that half of all employees steal from their employers. This is particularly credible for the hospitality industry where wages are low and working conditions leave much to be desired.

Housekeeping employees have ample opportunities to steal and pilfer—they can steal from guests, as they have master keys to access the guests' rooms; and they can pilfer company property, particularly guest and cleaning supplies, linens, and tools.

Often, employees steal because of sheer need, as their minimum wages are not sufficient for them to make ends meet. Other times disgruntled workers, feeling frustrated by the way they are treated, decide to get even by taking away the company's possessions. In other cases, employees steal simply because security is lax and everybody else is doing it.

Minimizing theft

Employees who steal use several methods to get supplies out of the property. The most common is using bags, purses, or parcels. An effective way of controlling this type of theft is by implementing a parcel-pass system by which employees leaving the property must show security officers a signed authorization to remove any items from the premises. A designated entrance/exit for employees that is controlled by security can be very effective, deterring individuals from exiting the premises through unmonitored doors.

However, employees concealing items under their clothing are very difficult to detect and management does have to rely on observation by supervisors or on anonymous tips from loyal workers to pinpoint the culprits.

Management should also establish effective controls on linens and supplies, insisting on monthly physical inventories, strict issuance procedures, and on allowing admittance to storerooms and floor closets to authorized employees only.

Another method of stealing is by filling trash bags with linens and supplies and depositing them near the trash dumpster, to be picked up after work or by an outside accomplice. Any trash container left outside the garbage compactor or dumpster should be considered suspicious. Employees should also be asked to park away from the building so that no goods may be easily placed near vehicles.

Properties that use keys rather than cards must establish an effective way of limiting access to guestrooms, floor closets, and storerooms by establishing a key-control system. The loss of a floor master key or grandmaster key can be disastrous to the department. Keys must be accounted for at all times by logging them in and out at the beginning and end of shifts. To avoid misplacement, master keys should be attached to a cord or lanyard or placed in large metal rings. Guestroom keys should never be left unattended on the keyhole or on top of service carts.

An effective way of avoiding this problem is having a secured locked metal box with a slot on the cart where keys may be safely kept until they are returned to the front desk.

Housekeeping staff should be instructed to report any faulty lock on an emergency basis; in no case should a room be handed over to the front desk as ready if its access control device is inoperative.

Theft by employees can also be effectively curtailed by establishing theft-prevention measures in the department. The first step is to make sure that application forms are carefully scrutinized and that references of all employees hired are thoroughly checked.

Gaps in employment history, for example, may indicate attempt to hide a job from which the applicant was fired because of theft. References can be effectively checked by establishing an information network by telephone with other executive housekeepers in the area for mutual cooperation.

Once employees are hired, it must be clearly stated at orientation and on the employee handbook that theft will be an automatic cause for dismissal. Usually, the safety committee is also in charge of security matters, such as investigating patterns of theft, conducting security inspections around the property, and maintaining records of crime incidents.

Theft by guests and intruders

The proverbial filching of towels by guests is as common today as it has ever been. In some cases, cash-only guests take with them bathroom appliances, coffee makers, blankets, pillows, clock/radios, telephones, TV sets, and, in rare cases, the entire furniture of rooms by parking a van behind the room sliding door/window.

Guest theft can be minimized by the establishment's not admitting travellers who don't own a credit card. In any case, section housekeepers should be trained to report immediately any missing item from rooms or when observing a guest's suitcase loaded with linen or other items.

The detection of empty suitcases or trunks and the presence of suspicious characters loitering in hallways should also be reported. Section housekeepers should also be instructed to never open a guestroom door to anyone claiming to have forgotten the key in the room;

instead, room attendants should kindly request the person to obtain an extra key at the front desk. It is particularly important to train housekeeping employees to spot and report suspicious activities taking place on guest floors, hallways, public areas, and back of the house.

Security in guestrooms

TV sets and light appliances in guestrooms should be bolted down or secured to the wall, furniture, or electrical socket. Entry doors should close automatically and be fitted with latching bolts that lock the door when it is closed.

Besides the latching bolt, guestroom doors should have dead-bolts, chains, and peepholes. Sliding glass doors on balconies should be provided with "charley bars" which, when extended down, prevent prying the door open from the outside.

Special attention should be given to the connecting doors between rooms. Besides the primary lock on the connecting doors, an additional security chain or dead-bolt that can be activated by the guest from within each room should be installed.

Room keys, in use for decades, are not effective to deter crime from occurring; as a matter of fact, lodging properties using traditional guestroom keys are considered to be at a competitive disadvantage. That is the case because it is practically impossible to prevent crooks from keeping room keys if they rent a room, then keeping the key upon check-out, and coming back in the evening to enter the same room when the current guest has gone out. This problem can only be completely corrected by changing the locks each time keys are missing, which requires substantial labour costs and additional manpower.

Card entry systems, on the other hand, are designed so that every guest checking into the property receives a card with a combination different from that used the previous night. In fact, the computer terminal issuing cards at the front desk is capable of providing millions of combinations for entrance to the room.

Card entry systems can also register around the clock the time and what specific card was used to enter the room. That is to say, printed records can indicate the time guests and staff used the card at any time during the day or night. Besides, if a master card is lost, the entire floor or floors can be reset very quickly.

Some entry card systems are designed to encode two different tracks, enabling the property to control not only the guestrooms, but access to other designated areas such as pools, health clubs, elevators, and in-room safes.

Other cellular control systems allow guests to use personal credit cards as room keys. State-of-the-art cellular control systems can be programmed to issue cards that can limit employee access to rooms by name, time, and date. For example, a section housekeeper card can be programmed to access a group of rooms at certain times during the day and on specific days of the week only.

The guest's personal valuables can be effectively protected by providing a small safe in every guestroom. Most in-room thefts take place when guests leave jewellery, travel checks, cameras or cards unattended while they are swimming in the pool or having a meal in the dining room.

In-room safes can be operated with keys, cards, or touch-pads, on which guests can punch their own safe-opening codes. While the smallest in-room safes should be able to hold a 35-mm camera or camcorder, business properties need to install briefcase-size or larger units to accommodate portable computers. The housekeeping department is usually in charge of providing baby-sitting services to guests travelling with children. The job of baby-sitting should be offered as a voluntary service to trusted, reliable, long-tenured housekeeping employees. When outside baby-sitting is used, the executive housekeeper must make sure that the agency has an impeccable record and that it is bonded.

Environmental management

Since the end of World War II, the population of the world has more than doubled and industrialization has become a widespread phenomenon. This out-of-control growth is altering the earth where we live and the air we breathe to the point of threatening our own health and safety and those of thousands of other living species.

Some of the current global environmental problems include the accumulation of wastes and the pollution of air and water due to the dumping of toxic by-products. As a result, a substantial reduction (in the order of over 80%) in the generation of pollution per unit of economic output is necessary just to keep the current global unhealthy levels.

Most scientists today believe that humans must agree to adopt some strategies to begin recovering the sustainability of planet earth. Executive housekeepers in lodging operations are in a privileged position to help prevent the continuous decay of the global environment.

Recycling garbage

The amount of trash generated in North America alone stands at 200 million tons per year, with an average waste per person per day of about 3.5 pounds. This enormous amount of trash is deposited in landfills, where rain can wash toxic elements into the soil, and in some cases into the water table. Landfill space to bury waste is becoming scarce. The alternative to burying trash is burning it, but this solution is equally harmful to the environment because of toxic pollutant emissions.

To address the solid waste problem, the Environmental Protection Agency (EPA) has identified some possible solutions, such as reducing waste before it is originated, and recycling by-products as raw materials for making other products.

Specifically, executive housekeepers can minimize the cost associated with hauling garbage to be landfilled by strategically placing labelled bins around the property for the disposal of reusable products. This should include guests' areas, as many travellers appreciate the idea of recycling waste even when they are away from home. Common solid by-products that can be recycled are:

— aluminium cans

— tin cans

— glass bottles and jars

— newspapers polyethylene plastic grass clippings, leaves and twigs

Those that are not recyclable include mirror glass, crystal, light bulbs, and nonpolyethylene plastics. There are some potential savings from recycling. Corrugated cardboard, for instance, can be sold for over $ 100 a ton. Local recycling companies will also pay for newspapers and aluminium cans.

Savings can also be realized for every ton deferred from landfills as some close and tipping fees rise for transporting the waste to out of state dumps. In addition, executive housekeepers can cut the costs of cleaning supplies used to maintain the facilities by using source-reduced products.

Source reduction can be defined as pre-cycling, as it prevents waste from occurring before it starts. Source reduction involves considering the final destiny of products when making decisions on what to buy: for instance, products that are designed to last longer, and that require efficient dispensing methods and less packaging.

Hazardous waste disposal

American throw away over 4 million tons of hazardous waste per year, and part of this toxic waste is discarded by lodging establishments. Prolonged exposure of humans to toxic substances can increase the risk for degenerative diseases such as cancer, severe respiratory illnesses and, in some cases, death.

Products labelled as toxic, poisonous, corrosive, or dangerous should be stored carefully and disposed of safely. For instance, toxic products should not be poured into sanitary or storm drains because they can contaminate the water. If placed out with the regular trash, they contaminate the atmosphere if they are disposed of in incinerators.

Particularly noxious when burned are synthetic foams and some solvents and cleaning agents whose atoms destroy the ozone layer when they reach the stratosphere. For this reason, hazardous products should be disposed of following manufacturer instructions.

Some noxious products commonly found in housekeeping departments are paint and paint strippers, drain cleaners, wood finishes, and antifreeze and motor oil discarded by guests in general trash containers.

Executive housekeepers committed to saving the environment should follow some basic steps to implement a source-reduction program, such as analysing the purchasing of supplies that are recyclable and that minimize waste while maintaining high performance, controlling product usage where possible, and buying concentrated supplies which usually go farther and cost less than pre-prepared products.

Executive housekeepers should also remember that basic cleaning jobs could be performed with green cleaners such as vinegar, vegetable oil-based soaps, borax, and baking soda, although they are not as convenient as using ready-made cleaning products. Pump dispensers with hand triggers are much safer than aerosols whose gas propellants, when released into the air every time the product is used, affect the ozone layer.

Green lodging facilities

Some hotel companies are recognizing the fact that environmental improvement in their establishments may lead to economic benefits and competitive opportunities. By establishing programs aimed at minimizing waste and reducing energy consumption, operating costs are lowered; by advertising to guests the actions taken to help keep a clean environment, companies can gain customer loyalty and enhance public image.

The housekeeping department can help regain the sustainability of the planet by implementing recycling programs for employees and guests. Some examples include: reusing as many items as possible, for instance, making cleaning rags out of worn towels, giving partially used soaps to local charities, and using ceramic mugs rather than foam cups; purchasing recyclable and biodegradable products; and composting yard debris, such as twigs, dry leaves and grass clippings. Some of the waste generated in housekeeping can be hazardous to the environment if discarded inappropriately.

Hazardous waste includes substances that are poisonous or toxic, such as insecticides, drain cleaners, flammable liquids, and some cleaning products. In order to keep hazardous products from reaching sensitive environmental sources, their disposal should not be poured into the city sewer, where it could contaminate the city's water-treatment plant, nor into the storm-sewer system, for fear of it seeping into the ground and contaminating the water table.

Likewise, toxic waste should not be discarded with the regular trash as it may be incinerated, contaminating the atmosphere. Some common hazardous materials in the housekeeping department are paints, stains, thinners and strippers, wood finishes, and antifreeze and car fluids discarded by guests.

Some lodging companies have introduced the concept of environmentally friendly guestrooms, often called green rooms, which appeal to the over 40 million "green travellers" or environment-conscious guests the industry claims exist. These eco-friendly properties stock the rooms with amenities packaged in recycled containers that are themselves recyclable, with recycled paper supplies, and with soaps that are biodegradable; that is, made with vegetable fats and oils without chemical additives.

Some hotel chains, focusing on targeting travellers with respiratory ailments, have gone as far as installing special filters in the air-intake ducts in guestrooms and filtering the water in the sink and shower. The usual extra fee to guests for these niceties is $ 10 per room per night.

Another way to save energy and minimize the generation of waste is to place desktop signs in guestrooms asking travellers to request changing sheets and pillow cases if they are staying over, and giving them the option of reusing the bathroom towels. This reduces drastically the poundage of linen to be processed, with the consequent reduction in water, energy, and chemical product usage.

The American Hotel/Motel Association provides on request laminated notices endorsed by the U.S. Environmental Protection Agency for their use in lodging establishments to inform guests of this save-the environment program. Besides helping the environment, lodging properties can save around $2.00 per occupied room per day when they provide their guests with these choices.

Indoor air quality control

Indoor air pollution can have negative health effects on guests and employees. Lodging properties built as tightly sealed buildings, if polluted, can cause workers and guests to suffer headaches, dizziness, allergies and other problems associated with poor air quality. Indoor air pollution may be caused by the presence of dangerous substances, such as chemical cleaning compounds. The problem is accentuated if polluted indoor air is re-circulated.

Chemical analyses of air from sick buildings frequently show compounds known to be human irritants. In most cases, toxic levels are quite low and difficult to detect, but when several pollutants are present at the same time, even at below-toxicity levels, they can cause symptoms of irritation and discomfort in humans.

Some of the chemicals used in the housekeeping department may be air pollutants; for example, products containing formaldehyde, which is used as wood, linen, and carpet treatment, some cleaning products, and most pesticides and drain openers. Microbial contamination can also result in a potentially serious health condition known as hyper-sensitivity pneumonitis.

The contamination may be caused by bacteria or mold present in damp carpets, furnishings and ventilation systems, or simply by allergenic microorganisms such as mites suspended in dust. The most effective way to improve air quality is to control the sources of pollution by not using toxic chemicals in the building and by increasing ventilation and cleaning.

Housekeeping departments should have a policy in place to open windows whenever possible to circulate in fresh air from outdoors, although this may not always be practical, particularly if the air-conditioning or heating system is in operation at the time.

Regular vacuuming of carpets and furnishings can also be effective, as dust mites thrive in areas where moisture and skin scales deposit, such as carpets and sofas. Faulty vacuum bags, however, can spread more allergens than they remove. To prevent air contamination when vacuuming, high retention vacuum cleaners holding particles larger than 0. 1 microns should be used.

In the hospitality industry, great attention is generally accorded to fighting bacteria that can cause food-borne illnesses but not enough consideration is given to the fact that microorganisms are also present in guestrooms and public areas of lodging properties, where they may contaminate guests and employees.

Executive housekeepers need to have a basic knowledge of how microorganisms spread and about infection control so that they can be part of employee education programs and provide effective sanitation services. For example, although employees often have serious concerns about contracting a disease while at work, particularly the HIV/AIDS infection, they often don't know that the HIV virus can rarely be contracted by casual contact, from sharing bathrooms or utensils, and even by shaking hands with infected individuals. However, hospital and health-care workers who have intense exposure by direct contact with patients' body fluids and needles should be instructed about these potential dangers.

There are two kinds of microorganisms that may cause illnesses: viruses and bacteria. Viruses are infective agents, smaller than common microorganisms, which require living cells for multiplication. Viruses cause poliomyelitis, hepatitis, AIDS, and the common cold if they find their way into the human body, where they may multiply.

Most bacteria are the simplest group of vegetable organisms that are involved in fermentation and putrefaction of matter and, unfortunately, the production of disease. Bacteria cause illnesses such as cholera, dysentery, tuberculosis, enteritis, and typhoid. Given the right conditions, bacteria can grow in incredibly large numbers and at a very fast pace. For instance, under ideal conditions, one bacterium can reproduce over two million bacteria in 7 hours.

Luckily, most germs do not cause humans to become sick; as a matter of fact, only some, the pathogenic germs, can be deadly. Nevertheless, and just in case, lodging properties must provide employee training and effective cleaning services to prevent the spread of infection. There are three effective methods of reducing the spread of germs in the workplace.

The first, sanitation, consists of cleaning surfaces, articles, and material to reduce germ count to a safe level according to public health standards and codes. The second, disinfection, deals with using cleaning products to selectively kill specific types of germs. Sterilization requires steam to eliminate germs in a pressurized container. A variation of sterilization, although not 100 percent effective, consists of washing items at high water temperatures, usually 160-180°F. Several types of disinfectants are available in the cleaning supplies market. Most disinfectants belong to the following four categories.

Natural phenolic compounds are made from carbolic acid and are very effective in destroying germs but are poisonous to humans and corrosive to metal surfaces. Synthetic phenolic compounds are milder phenolic products that are effective in killing most germs but without causing corrosive effects. Halogens, noxious to human skin and corrosive to surfaces, are composed of the negative elements fluorine, chlorine, iodine, or bromine. Quaternary ammonium compounds are safe to use and have very high disinfecting power. Most cleaning jobs can be effectively performed with quaternary disinfectants; however, when cleaning blood stains or any other potentially infectious spills, a stronger disinfectant such as phenolic should be used.

[illegible]

[illegible]

In the meantime [illegible] bearing in mind the [illegible] of the participants, the [illegible] management and [illegible] and the [illegible] the industry generally.

To limit their price risks market makers [illegible] books that are broadly matched, for example by duration and currency. In the short run, however, there are some open positions that must be hedged, at least in part, and [illegible] within prudent bounds until matching positions can be established through new swaps or the [illegible] of existing ones.

In some cases, mainly in short maturities, market makers can best hedge their open swap position by off-balance-sheet forwards, futures or options transactions. In other cases, with balance sheet and capital requirement consequences, the cash markets can be tapped. For example, a market maker can hedge the fixed-rate payment side of a fixed/floating interest rate swap by purchasing treasury bonds of the same maturity financed by a repurchase agreement. In [illegible] but swap rates [illegible] the derivatives [illegible] markets.